Dreaming and Storytelling

"*How <u>dare</u> you come home in this condition!*"

Dreaming and Storytelling

Bert O. States

Cornell University Press

Ithaca and London

First published 1993 by Cornell University Press.

Library of Congress Cataloging-in-Publication Data

States, Bert O., 1929–
  Dreaming and storytelling / Bert O. States.
    p.   cm.
  Includes bibliographical references and index.
  ISBN 0-8014-2896-3
    1. Dreams. 2. Narration (Rhetoric)—Psychological aspects. 3. Storytelling—Psychological aspects. 4. Fiction—Psychological aspects. 5. Dreams in literature. I. Title.
  BF1078.S673   1993
  154.6'3   dc20   93-13099

Printed in the United States of America

⊗ The paper in this book meets the minimum requirements
of the American National Standard for Information Sciences—
Permanence of Paper for Printed Library Materials, ANSI Z39.48-1984.

for
Amanda, Jesse, and Michael

Contents

Acknowledgments

Parts of this book appeared first in essay form as the following: "The Persistence of the Archetype," *Critical Inquiry* 7 (Winter 1980): 333–44 (© 1980 by The University of Chicago and published by the University of Chicago Press. All rights reserved); "The Art of Dreaming," *Hudson Review* 31 (Winter 1978–79): 571–86; "Dreaming and Storytelling," *Hudson Review* 43 (Spring 1990): 21–37; "The Meaning of Dreams," *Dreaming* 2 (December 1992): 249–63; "Bizarreness in Dreams and Other Fictions," in *The Dream and The Text: Essays in Language and Literature*, ed. Carol S. Rupprecht (Albany: State University of New York Press, 1993): 13–31. I thank the editors of these journals, the Human Sciences Press, the SUNY Press, and the University of Chicago Press for permission to reprint them here, in greatly revised form. I also express my appreciation to New Directions for permission to reprint William Carlos Williams's "The Red Wheelbarrow" from *Collected Poems, 1909–1939*, vol. 1 (© 1938 New Directions Press Corp.), and to *The New Yorker* and Al Ross for permission to reprint the drawing (from *The New Yorker* of January 14, 1991) that serves as my frontispiece. Finally, I owe a special debt to two colleagues and close friends: Dan McCall at Cornell University for his careful reading of the manuscript and invaluable suggestions for improvement and Paul

Hernadi at the University of California, Santa Barbara, for his customary good advice and wisdom in literary, theoretical, and editorial matters. Thanks, too, to Milton Kramer, director of the Sleep Disorders Center at Bethesda Oak Hospital in Cincinnati, for his encouragement and generous commentary on my work.

B.O.S.

Dreaming and Storytelling

I think that one of the fields in which formal logic can give a false picture is aesthetics; and that the false picture is only avoided if we think about art in terms of its capacity for fusing, or con-fusing subject and object, seer and seen and then making a new division of these. By suffusing, through giving it form, the not-me objective material with the me—subjective psychic content, it makes the not-me 'real', realisable. Clearly the great difficulty in thinking logically about this problem is due to the fact that we are trying to talk about a process which stops being that process as soon as we talk about it, trying to talk about a state in which the me–not-me distinction is not important, but to do so at all we have to make the distinction. But it is only, I think, in this way of looking at it that the phrase 'art creates nature' can make sense. So what the artist, or perhaps one should say, the great innovator in art, is doing, fundamentally, is not recreating in the sense of making again what has been lost (although he is doing this), but creating what is, because he is creating the power to perceive it. By continually breaking up the established familiar patterns (familiar in his particular culture and time in history) of logical common sense divisions of me–not-me, he really is creating 'nature', including human nature.

—Joanna Field, *On Not Being Able to Paint*

Introduction

Once upon a time there was a clever fellow who worked in a factory that manufactured wheelbarrows. One day, it occurred to him that he might improve his lot if he could somehow smuggle wheelbarrows out of the factory and sell them privately on the open market. But—how to get them past the main gate? Then a plan struck him. Why not simply fill the wheelbarrow with debris from the plant and wheel it straight past the gatekeeper in broad daylight? And indeed, to make a short tale even shorter, he did this and it worked, and he went on to become a modestly successful retailer of stolen goods whose career need no longer detain us.

This tale has many variants, among them the episode of the Trojan horse. For me, its main interest lies in the complacency of the gatekeeper who perceives the wheelbarrow as a *vehicle* or *tool,* rather than as a *commodity,* much as the Trojans perceived the wooden horse as a beautiful gift rather than as a nest of deadly Greeks. Both tales suggest the sense in which we are all subject to what might be called perceptual bondage: we see what we are used to seeing—or rather, we *don't* see what we are used to seeing. The world goes past us inconspicuously at face value. We are tranquilized by the parade of recurrent contexts.

For my purposes, the wheelbarrow story serves as an allegory for two different ways of looking at dreaming and, by extension, storytelling at large. In the first—broadly the psychoanalytic—the gatekeeper might stand for the censor at the gate of the preconscious whose duty it is, in psychoanalytic theory, to protect the sleeper from disturbing thoughts rising from the unconscious. The worker-thief would be the id, which is trying to outwit the censor; the wheelbarrow would be the latent (or hidden) dream content obscured by its load of debris, and the debris itself would be the manifest content, or what we actually see and experience when we dream. In other words, in this reading the dream would be a meaning-laden event with a two-tier construction—a manifest and a latent tier, debris and wheelbarrow—that can be understood only if you look past the decoy of the first to the truth hidden in the second.

The other reading requires that you see the allegory from an entirely different perspective. The wheelbarrow, the debris, and the worker-thief would all constitute a single unity—that of the dream process itself: the brain working in the moonlight after the body has been shut down for the night, hauling its strange load of daytime and lifetime experience to and fro for purposes we do not yet understand, each night different in kind, yet each night much the same in certain ways that concern me here. Finally, the gatekeeper could be any of us: the waking person who has dreamed from childhood on, approximately 750 hours a year, who no more thinks about what dreaming is than the gatekeeper ponders the mystery of the wheelbarrow. Dreams are simply odd things that happen to us at night, sometimes pleasant, sometimes terrifying, not to be taken too seriously; or, if we think about them at all it is usually to ask a question like "Why should Aunt Sarah turn into a bird and invite us all to dinner in her sycamore tree?" In short, what do dreams mean? And here, as "gatekeepers," we are asking the same questions psychoanalysts ask, all of which are concerned with the "search for antecedents," or for meaning.

Much the same thing can be said about our reading of fiction: as gatekeepers most of us read for the plot, for the load of significance, suspense, and gratification that is borne on the vehicle of the text.

Of course, literary theorists think a great deal about the nature of the text these days. But we have not got around to thinking about the dream in quite this way, or at least we are not as far along with the poetics of dreaming as we are with the poetics of fiction. Our interest in the dream, from Joseph in the Bible to modern psychoanalysis, has been largely an interest in the cargo being transported by the dream. "What does my dream mean?" the pharaoh asks Joseph at the beginning of our history; and, as the Bible says, "Joseph interpreteth." In so doing he gave us (as Freud realized) the mode of psychoanalytic interpretation—the main difference being that Joseph used the dream to foretell the future, whereas Freud used it to retell the past.

Let me say that I have no quarrel with dream interpretation, psychoanalytic or otherwise. Nor do I doubt its validity in the treatment of neurosis and personality disorder, or simply in self-education. Here I simply offer a complementary approach that is, in certain respects, a continuation of themes I pursued in *The Rhetoric of Dreams* (1989). What became more and more apparent to me in writing that book was that dreaming is the ur-form of all fiction. This is not to claim that we write fictions because we dream or that dreaming teaches us how to write stories, only that the dream precedes the creation of written or oral fictions in both the historical life of the species and the personal life of the individual. We now know that most animals dream, and there is suggestive evidence that they dream in narrative form. This means, in a loose sense, that animals tell themselves stories, and the stories may well be about survival routines. If one can see a parallel, then, between human dreams and the dreams of animals, it would seem incumbent upon us to think of storytelling, in all its forms, in somewhat more biological terms than we are accustomed.[1] I hasten to say that this is not my project here. What does interest me, however, is the question of what dreams and stories have in common as *involuntary* activities; for it seems to me that Jean-Paul Richter's definition of

[1] On the possible relationship of dreams to evolution, see Ornstein, 1991: 192–200.

dreams as involuntary poetry might apply to all poetry (including stories) as well, given that we don't, as a species, seem to be capable of not telling stories. What, then, might be the relationship between these two involuntary activities beyond the obvious fact that both are narrative forms (to allow, for a moment, that something as insubstantial as a dream may be said to be a form)? How do their narratives differ? How are they alike? What influence, precisely, do the conditions of waking and sleeping exert on the shape they take and the coherence of their structures? What might a careful comparative examination of dreams and fictions tell us about our need to give experience a narrative order?

In my discussions here, I (again) put primary emphasis on the dream, principally because it is the narrative form in greatest need of examination. Indeed, the study of fictional narrative is perhaps the most flourishing enterprise in literary theory today. It is unfortunate that the few literary people who have been concerned with dreams have considered only their role as a thematic element within fiction or poetry, as a subgenre of literature (surrealism, the dream play), or as a form of symbolic language legitimated by Freud and useful mainly as a medium for deconstructing texts (including those of Freud's own dreams). To my knowledge, few (if any) literary theorists have been centrally interested in the dream as a phenomenon to be studied in its own right or in a serious poetic relation to fiction. Reasons are not hard to find. There are, after all, no texts of dreams, and dream reports are of negligible literary value (apart from the dreams of canonical writers such as Kafka). So in a very palpable sense there is really nothing there to study. Still, everyone dreams, and dreams are virtually pure instances of narrative creation unfettered by the demands of literary traditions or intelligibility. There is a naivete about dreams: they are marvelously aloof from the tendentious; they go about their business without advertisement or responsibility, as if they were a perfectly adequate equivalent of life in the waking world. Dreams, one might say, constitute a private literature of the self, and it seems that, if nothing else, they might tell us something about the nature of our "public" literature.

My approach is probably best described as phenomenological (inasmuch as I try to confront dream and poetic images, as Gaston Bachelard would say, at their point of origin), though I am considerably indebted to the work on dreams in cognitive psychology and what neurobiology is accessible to a lay scholar. Fortunately, much of the recent work on dreams and consciousness, both experimental and theoretical, is not beyond the reach of an interested humanist. What is everywhere apparent is that we are undergoing a radical revision in our thinking about dreams, which have become of increasing interest to scientists because, I suspect, they are so close to the lower border of consciousness. The dream, as it were, occurs just slightly above the point where electrochemistry turns into psychology. Hence, the dream is the site of an essential energy conversion where "ignorant" cells turn into smart (or creative) cell groups. In the dream, we can literally observe "the thinking of the body" and, with it, the birth of the literary process. Indeed, the subject of dreams and dreaming may constitute one of the few areas of mutual concern between humanists and scientists, and it is my belief that there is much to be gained by a cautious exchange of what humanists are saying about our creative productions and what cognitive scientists and neuroscientists are discovering about the synapses that produce them.

It is evident that a comparative poetics of two such different expressive forms presents methodological problems. First, there are many kinds of dream and fictional plot structures (not all dreams have plots), and it is impossible to say much that might account for all of them. Moreover, there are dream structures in fictional narratives and good evidence for assuming that fictional narratives have a structural influence on some dream narratives (for example, the adventure and detective story dreams) and that the advent of cinema and technology may have "revolutionized" dreaming: how realistic were dreams of flying or space travel before the movies and the airplane allowed us see what can only be seen from the air? So we are immediately faced with a variation of the dilemma posed by Elder Olson in his study of plotting techniques: should one approach the task as a Lumper, seeing "nothing but resemblance," or as a Splitter, seeing "nothing but difference" (1966: 31)? Another set of considerations involves possible differences among various kinds of dreamers. Children, for example, certainly dream differently from adults. In what way might the dreams of males or females, or (while we are splitting) Fiji Islanders, or Tibetan monks, or Japanese business men, or French deconstructionists, differ from (or resemble) one an other? What is a narrative or a plot? And another dilemma: will the procedure be inductive or deductive? Shall we start with a definition or arrive at one? Then there is the most subtle and ubiquitous dilemma of all: does one not tend to find only what one is looking for? In the present instance, there is a danger that in dealing with dreams in reported form we have already made them into waking narratives, which is what we were putting them against in the first place. Have we not altered the phenomenon, done something to the dream that is tantamount to what the dream does when it drags waking experience onto its premises, cuts it to dream-size bites, and consumes it for its own delectation?

Some of these problems I hope to avoid by being alert to them. As for the first, my inclination is to split the difference between lumping and splitting and try to arrive, not at categorical descriptions, but at a schema broad enough to describe tendencies, or some of the things that dreams and fictions do most of the time. As for the second, my "evidence" is based on my own dream experience and what confirmation I can find for it in the experience and commentary of other dreamers. I cannot speak for the dreams of the Fiji Islanders, and I have read only one essay on Fijian dream experience. Apparently, the beliefs of the Fijians respecting dreams differ from my own (for example, they believe dreams are real experiences of the wandering soul released by sleep; they do not make clear distinctions between dreams, waking fantasies, or hallucinations; and they tend to dream predominantly about fear and anxiety; Herr, 1981: 334–35). But I see nothing to suggest that Fijians, when they fall asleep, dream any differently from me with respect to how their brains conjure images and spin plots in which their dead (like my dead) live again and the animals and denizens of their forests (like those in mine) speak to the dreamer. In short, I assume there is something "dreamlike" about dreaming that is unaltered by cultural adaptation, era, age, or gender; otherwise we could scarcely talk about them cross-culturally. In any case, I am not concerned here with the sociology or anthropology of dreaming or fiction, much as these questions fascinate me. I would like to know what conclusions, if any, we may draw from the fact that the human brain finds it necessary to create narratives in both the waking and sleeping states; and I would like to know what these narratives *characteristically* have in common, how they may differ from one another, and—if possible—what uses narratives could conceivably have for the species.

Finally, a word or so about the problem of dream reports as evidence (a subject that tends, I have noticed, to raise eyebrows among scholars who work with real texts). In writing a comparative poetics of dreams and waking fictions we are forced, in a manner of speaking, to compare apples and oranges. On one hand, literary texts are complete and nonreferential in the sense that they do not depend on specific prior "texts" for their value and coherence. By this I mean only that one can easily refer to the text of, say, Shakespeare and be assured of sharing with the reader a sense of its rhythm, its mood, the quality of its experience, and whatever else one may look for in such texts. On the other hand, dream reports are an odd and impoverished sort of text. They have no merit (usually), none of the seductive power of literary texts, and they are the poorest of substitutes for the real—or should I say unreal—thing: the dream itself. The good news is that our situation is somewhat better than that of the cosmologist who is trying to evaluate the nature of the invisible dark matter whose presence in space is detectable only from the behavior of the matter surrounding it. Whereas the cosmologist must depend on inferences drawn from what science already knows, the analyst of dreamlife knows, at first hand, something of the laws that govern dream behavior. In short, we have all been inside the dark matter of the dreamworld and we carry a memory of how things *are* there—what it is *like* to dream. Thus, what is most valuable in a dream report is not its "literary" or textual quality, or its accuracy in describing someone else's mental experience, but its "exchange value," or its vehicular power to evoke a peculiar kind of experience shared by all dreamers. Indeed, one can use a fake dream to make a point about dreaming as well as a real one, as long as it is consistent with dream experience. Here, for example, is part of a fake dream by one of the world's most accomplished dream artists:

> As Gregor Samsa awoke one morning from a troubled-dream, he found himself changed in his bed to some monstrous kind of vermin.
>
> He lay on his back, which was as hard as armor plate, and, raising his head a little, he could see the arch of his great, brown belly, divided by bowed corrugations. The bedcover was slipping helplessly off the summit of the curve, and Gregor's legs, pitiably thin compared with their former size, fluttered helplessly before his eyes.
>
> "What has happened?" he thought. It was no dream.

In the technical sense, *The Metamorphosis* does not recount the dream of its protagonist. As the text plainly tells us, Gregor has just awakened from a troubled dream and is now presumably back in "reality." But no student of dreams would deny that from beginning to end *The Metamorphosis* itself evokes the quality of dream experience as perfectly as any waking fiction (short of another Kafka story) or any dream memory. And what is so evocative is precisely the story's imitation of the single-mindedness of the dream state (an issue I address in detail in Chapter 1), the condition of the dreamer's unquestioning belief that the dream and everything in it are utterly real. Thus "It was no dream" may, in a sense, represent Gregor's conclusion, but the narrative itself takes the reader vividly into the dreamworld, which is not, after all, a surreal world of fantastic shapes and distorted sliding walls but a world of such incredible clarity and intensity that it provokes in the dreamer a complete acceptance of the most bizarre happenings. In terms of the accuracy of its atmospherics, there is not much difference between Kafka's dream and this real dream report from Jean Piaget's case file on a six-year-old boy who "for several months in succession . . . had dreamt that there was a basin on a stand in his bedroom":

> In the basin I saw a bean that was so big that it quite filled it. It got bigger and bigger all the time. I was standing by the door. I was frightened. I wanted to scream and run away, but I couldn't. I got more and more frightened, and it went on until I woke up. (1951: 179)

I offer this dream because it seems to me so innocent of awe and other "adult" emotional embellishments ("It was all so strange") that attend reports of dreams on the waking side of life. We have here, then, a naive version of Kafka's highly sophisticated evocation of the dreamworld. Both carry the true imprint of the dream: the complete credulity of the dreamer, the seemingly self-generative and autonomous power of the dream image to appear without apparent volition on the part of the dreamer, the astonishing power of the simplest image to provoke an extreme emotional charge, and the helplessness of the dreamer in the face of his own creation. These, we might say, are the basic conditions of dream experience. The possible faulty memory of the dreamer ("I don't recall what happened next"), the absence of details about the room and the color and shape of the bean (in the boy's dream), the sketchiness of the report, and so on, are irrelevant factors for all purposes that dream reports might possibly serve. I can see the boy's room—the basin, the growing bean, the door—as well as I can envision the details of Gregor's room and the "great brown belly, divided by bowed corrugations." This is not to say I see what the boy saw or experienced, but I see my own dream room constituted of a thousand dream rooms in which I have been a "helpless" undoubting occupant. Unless we are are concerned with dream interpretation, then (and I am not), we do not study dream reports per se; we use them much as we use maps to find our way through the terrain of waking reality. Maps do not resemble the reality they refer to; but we are not surprised by this fact when we arrive at the place to which they have directed us. And so it is with the dream report. It is not a science, but then poetics never claimed to be a science.

The plan of the book is fairly simple. I begin with the problem of bizarreness in the dream and poetic image because it is the inevitable starting point for any phenomenological consideration of the behavior of mental images. Each of the following three chapters deals with a particular aspect of what we might broadly call the conditions of composition (beginnings and endings, character functions, causal relationships, generic forms, archetypes, scripts). The final chapter is concerned with meaning. What is meaning, as it may arise from dreams or stories? Do dreams, for example, have meanings or do we thrust meaning upon them? Finally, can dream integrity be explained without resort to the term *meaning*, if by meaning we are referring to something the dream is saying about the experience it depicts in the manner in which a poet is saying something in a poem about, say, the death of a toad or the sinking of the *Titanic*? Do dreams, in short, have titles?

Throughout the book, I now see (for introductions are always written last), I am continually concerned with the respect in which plots, however orderly in stories or chaotic in dreams, are based on the narrative forms offered by real-life experience. Fictions, dreamed or written, depend on waking life in subtle ways, not only for their content (stories of frustration, fear, guilt, revenge, and so on) but for their form as well. In his book *Time and Narrative*, Paul Ricoeur makes a strong case for fiction being as quasi-historical as history is quasi-fictive: "History and fiction each concretize their respective intentionalities only by borrowing from the intentionality of the other" (1988, 3:181).[2] Here I develop the notion that

[2] To be more specific: "History is quasi-fictive once the quasi-presence of events placed 'before the eyes of' the reader by a lively narrative supplements through its intuitiveness, its vividness, the elusive character of the pastness of the past, which is illustrated by the paradoxes of standing-for. Fictional narrative is quasi-historical to the extent that the unreal events that it relates are past events for the narrative voice that addresses itself to the reader. It is in this that they resemble past events and that fiction resembles history" (3:190).

both dream and fiction borrow from the empirical world its habit of unfolding its events in certain patterns of self-repetition. This has little to do with questions of probability and verisimilitude but only with the idea that real life, being what it is—a continuously self-emptying, self-filling parade of individual life cycles, institutional hierarchies, and social rituals and situations—tends to repeat itself (like history), and it is these repetitions that form the natural plot contours of the narratives of both poets and dreamers (however differently adapted they may be to the needs of dreaming and reading). Indeed, we may situate the dream midway between history and fiction in the sense that it borrows something—hardly intentionality—from each. The dream is like history in the sense that it based on the lived historical past of the dreaming individual. But the dream also borrows fiction's privilege of rewriting the past as imagination conceives it. It is not "what happened," as Aristotle says of history, but "the sort of thing that might happen." So the dream is quasi-historical and quasi-fictive. On one level, we can claim that it is completely fictive in that no dream ever copies events as they occurred in reality. Thanks to the dream's unique ability to unfold its narrative as a living present, however, it is experienced by the dreamer as having all the characteristics of reality, which fiction has not—or at least not so many. So there is another characteristic the dream shares with history: both have actually taken place in a present—history, before it was history, took place in the empirical world, the dream in the dreaming brain. Of course, we can never know history as a present, as it took place, but only as a past filtered through the quasi-fictional preterit. By definition, history is what has already taken place. But this is equally true of the dream that becomes a dream, also by definition, only when the dreamer awakens, at which point, as we say, the dream is history, of which we have only the memory, or in some cases the remembered report of what "actually" happened.

The difference, alas, is that the dream, unlike the waking life, has no awareness of a history beyond its own frontiers on which it is itself based. I am endlessly fascinated by the notion that I can vividly recall the world of dreams and my experiences in it while I am awake, but that the waking world disappears completely, as either memory or as possibility, during a dream. What to make of this one-way street? Perhaps the explanation is that the dreamworld is the land of pure consciousness that can conceive of nothing beyond or other than itself. It may be whimsically likened to the realm of Pointland, "the Abyss of No Dimensions" in Edwin A. Abbott's marvelous romance, *Flatland:* "It fills all Space . . . and what it fills, It is. What It thinks, that It utters; and what It utters, that It hears; and It itself is Thinker, Utterer, Hearer, Thought, Word, Audition; it is the One, and yet the All in All. Ah, the happiness, ah, the happiness of Being" (1983: 109–10). I hope that some of the implications of this analogy become clear in what follows.

I

The Problem of Bizarreness

It is often said that in a dream you are able to see what you are thinking as it occurs. This is a somewhat slippery notion because you can also think thoughts about what you are seeing in a dream (which is also what you are thinking). For example, if I am confronted by a dream image of my friend Simon, I may think, "Simon seems very cheerful today," which is a thought about an image but not an image in itself. If, however, it should occur to me that Simon looks like Alan Bates, the actor (and he does), I may well lose Simon and gain Alan Bates—or someone I do not know who remains Simon (and/or Alan Bates) even so. So there I am, caught in a kind of cognition sandwich: seeing what I'm thinking about what I'm seeing. The whole process certainly has something to do with Freud's "considerations of representability" whereby, in my example, Alan Bates is visually representable (if you know what he looks like) but cheerfulness is less so, unless it is attached to a person, which was the case to begin with. But let us simplify the point by saying that dreaming affords us an opportunity to inhabit thought processes that occur regularly in waking thinking but are beneath observation due to the pressing sensory demands of life in the waking world. Dreaming involves thought and perception in a world state in which it is difficult to distinguish one from the other, means from ends, or processes from products. This is all made possible, as we see later, by the principle we now refer to as single-mindedness (Rechtschaffen, 1978), which is the agency that takes the dreaming consciousness to the scene of thought itself, fixing it there in what one might call a metaphorical suspension in which the monads of reality are dissolved but maintain a deceptive similarity to their referents. My first project is to examine this behavioral condition behind the dream image, which I take to be the basic unit of dream construction, and to see what differences and similarities may exist between the images that compose dreams and those of waking fictional narratives. In short, I begin with the basic building material of narrative composition and then work gradually outward (in later chapters) to questions involving structure, narrative logic, thematics, intentionality, and meaning.

Perhaps the most universal point of agreement among people who study or think about dreams is the assumption that dreams are bizarre—that is, they contain extraordinary images that are inconsistent with realities in the waking world. Thus an examination of the principle of bizarreness is perhaps the best point of entry to the subject. My objective here is not to correct a mistake I think everybody has been making but to worry the problem of bizarreness from a perspective that might bring dreams and waking fictions closer together as variations of a common operation in which bizarreness, so-called, is the *modus operandi.* My leading question could be phrased, why is it that the bizarre becomes bizarre? In other words, the best way to understand the phenomenon might be to trace it to the preconditions of its appearance.

We should begin by noting the obvious: where dreams are concerned, we are attaching the words *bizarre* and *distorted* to a form of mental experience that strikes us as perfectly normal, however frightening, while we are having it. One might argue that reality is so obviously an objective fact and that dreaming is so palpably insubstantial and subjective that there is little doubt about which should serve as the standard of normalcy, especially since waking reality is the place in which we do all our measuring and theorizing.

But I am always struck by the paradox posed by Chuange-Tse's famous butterfly dream[1] and by a more recent variant of the same dilemma—let us call it the Two-Body Problem—offered by the German phenomenologist Medard Boss:

> While waking observers see him fast asleep in bed in Zurich, the dreamer may feel that he is skiing, with consummate physical grace and pleasure, down an Alpine slope. The question now is, which body is the "real" one, the body that others see lying in bed, though the dreamer is unaware of it, or the body that the dreamer himself feels so intensely but that no waking observer can perceive? We are at a loss for an answer, probably because the question is inadequately formulated. We may discover that both bodies, the recumbent and the active one, belong equally to the bodyhood of the sleeper's existence. In any case, however, physicality has shown itself to be no criterion for distinguishing between the human waking and dreaming states. (1977: 197)

So too it is possible that we have inadequately formulated the question of the dream's bizarreness. If we proceed from the standpoint of physicality (what is possible in waking reality) we arrive at one view of the matter; if we proceed from the standpoint of consciousness (the reality one *thinks* one occupies) we arrive at another. The word *bizarre* itself carries the implication that the bizarre image

---

[1] "I, Chuange-Tse, once dreamed that I was a butterfly, flitting to and fro with a butterfly's goals and motivations. I knew only that, like a butterfly, I was following my butterfly whims; there was no awareness of my human nature. Suddenly I awoke, and there I was, 'myself' again. Now I am left wondering: was I then a man who dreamed of being a butterfly, or am I now a butterfly dreaming that he is a man." Quoted in M. Boss, 1977: 175–76. Boss uses the Chuange-Tse experience as the motto for his earlier book (1958).

It may turn out that Chuange-Tse was closer to the truth than we tend to think. Recently, Rodolfo Llinás and D. Paré have conducted morphological and electrophysiological studies that suggest that "paradoxical [REM] sleep and wakefulness are . . . almost identical intrinsic functional states in which subjective awareness is generated" (1991: 522); "We may conclude that a possible approach to understanding the nature of wakefulness is to consider it as one element in a category of intrinsic brain functions, in which REM sleep is another element. The difference between

could have been presented realistically had the system been working differently. And indeed, most dreams are not noticeably bizarre
at all, most of the time, but consist of fairly normal events and
images. Suddenly, however, a dream will produce one of these
"bizarre intrusions" (Crick and Mitchison, 1986: 231) that may be
strong enough to awaken the dreamer or to provide a topic of
conversation at breakfast. But somehow this division of dream
images into normal and bizarre seems rather like a visitor reporting
from a foreign country that the people there behave in strange
ways. Would we say that water becomes bizarre at 32° F or unreal at
212°? To understand the behavior of water properly, we must consider what happens to *it* under a range of conditions—*it* being not
simply the liquid that runs from our faucets but a certain chemical
proportion of hydrogen to oxygen that also assumes the forms of
ice or steam, depending on temperature conditions. In short, steam
and ice are not variant forms of water but, along with water, variant forms of H^2O. H^2O is the genus; water, ice, and steam are the
differentia. If we apply this principle to imaging behavior, we must
surely say that in distinguishing bizarre dream images from normal
images we are treating differentia as genus, or at least implying that
bizarre images are an aberrant form of normal image, deformed
either by censorship at the preconscious level (Freud and most psychoanalytic theorists), by chemical processes in the brain (Hobson

---

these two states would be that in REM sleep, the sensory specification of the func-
tionalities carried out by the brain is fundamentally altered. That is, *REM sleep can be
considered as a modified attentive state in which attention is turned away from the sensory
input, toward memories. This hypothesis could, in principle, explain the total rejection of or,
otherwise, the alteration of sensory input into our dreaming* [thus accounting for the
phenomenon of bizarreness, or what Llinás and Paré refer to as the "irrational"
element of dreams]. Let us formally propose then *that wakefulness is nothing other than
a dreamlike state modulated by the constraints produced by specific sensory inputs"* (p. 525).

As for the argument that the waking world is physically real, and the dream world
simply fantasy, Llinás and Paré point out that "the degree to which our perception of
reality and 'actual' reality overlap is inconsequential as long as the predictive processes of the computational states generated by the brain meet the requirements of
successful interaction with the external world" (p. 531). Presumably, one might
continue the hypothesis by adding that the dream process is designed to meet the
requirements of successful interaction with the internal mnemonic world.

and McCarley), by the brain's attempt to "trash" unwanted memory (Crick and Mitchison), or by some other intentional or nonintentional influence (fever, drugs, psychosis).

Many researchers are well aware, as David Foulkes has said, that
"characterizing images, or image sequences, or image contents as
. . . 'bizarre' . . . almost inherently directs attention to [the
dream's] affect on us, rather than to its own constituents." Indeed,
Foulkes cites the need for further study of what bizarre features may
"reveal about peculiarities in the processes by which the dream
organiz[es] its mnemonic sources" (1985: 89, n. 34). In the end,
however, even Foulkes does not abandon the idea of bizarreness but
sees it, along with Hobson, Crick, Mitchison, Snyder, and many
others, as the characteristic that distinguishes the dream from other
cognitive processes and can be tabulated on a quantitative-
qualitative scale. Hobson, for example, conceives of the brain in the
dream state as somehow struggling to make sense of the bizarre
things it produces as a consequence of random chemical bombard-
ment. "How can a companion be a stranger?" he asks in connection
with the "Customs Building" dream. "He cannot. Therefore the
dreamer corrects the situation by turning him into a known person," the assumption being, I gather, that the dreamer is somehow
aware of the dream's inconsistencies and strives to change them
into regularities. Or, he asks, why are there confusions in the
dream? Might they not "reflect the undistorted efforts of the brain-
mind to perform one of its most essential functions: to establish
orientational stability"? Above all, in the REM stage of sleep, the
brain/mind suffers from "disorientation"; that is, "external orientational cues are absent (because the dreamer is asleep and cut off
from the world), and . . . his own brain compass is spinning (because the brain mechanism serving memory, attention, and insight
are disabled)" (1988: 222–75).

What Hobson refers to as disorientation leads us to the phenomenon Allan Rechtschaffen calls the dream's single-mindedness. To
review briefly, single-mindedness is "the strong tendency for a
single train of related thoughts and images to persist over extended
periods without disruption or competition from other simul-

taneous thoughts and images." Waking consciousness consists of "at least two prevalent streams" of thought: voluntary mental productions and sense impressions, on one hand, and, on the other, "a reflective or evaluative stream which seemingly monitors the first and places it in some perspective." In the dream state, however, this second, "reflective stream of consciousness is drastically attenuated"; that is, we are (normally) unaware that we are dreaming. Rechtschaffen expresses this idea still another way by saying that dreams "lack imagination"—meaning that the dream state, lacking "reflective awareness" (that is, being single-minded), has no "capacity to conjure up images and thoughts which may occupy consciousness simultaneously or near simultaneously with another stream of thoughts and images." Although he acknowledges that in another sense dreams may be "considered among the most imaginative of human productions," they are nonimaginative in that the dreamer cannot, as a waking person can, dream of one thing ("sitting at my desk") while "simultaneously imagining a tennis court" (Rechtschaffen, 1978: 97–101).

Though the general idea is plausible, this notion of imagination seems to me restrictive. For example, Arthur Koestler has independently used the same terminology, in reverse, to describe the difference between the mind in a routine state of waking thought, which he calls single-mindedness (or capable of thinking only on a single plane), and the mind in the creative state, or double-mindedness, which is a "transitory state of unstable equilibrium where the balance of both emotion and thought is disturbed" (might we say bizarre?) and the mind is capable of operating "on more than one plane" (1969: 35–36). Thus, where Hobson would find disorientation (disequilibrium) a somewhat crippling state as regards clarity of thought and insight, Koestler would find it ("unstable equilibrium") the special province of creativity. For Koestler, imagination implies a metaphorical operation of thought, or what he refers to as "bisociation," the fundamental mental process of all scientific discovery or artistic production. And one of its strongest manifestations occurs in the dream state, in which "*we constantly bisociate in a passive way*—by drift, as it were; but we are, of course, unaware of it because the coherence of the logical matrices is weakened, and the codes which govern them are dormant" (p.178).

Still, I think both Rechtschaffen's and Koestler's meanings of single-mindedness are valid in their own contexts; indeed, I should add that they are not talking about precisely the same processes of thought. At the same time, I also feel that Gordon Globus offers a useful critique of Rechtschaffen's thesis in reminding us that we fall into single-minded or nonreflective states in our waking life as well (1987: 80–84), and we also produce involuntary thought in this state. Moreover, Milton Kramer has argued that single-mindedness "is part of all fantasy, not unique to dreams, and inappropriately contrasted with waking goal-directed thinking" (1991a: 104).[2] Perhaps we can sum up the case by taking as a graphic model the Ross cartoon that appears as a frontispiece, which we might title "The Housewife's Nightmare." Here we have a comic demonstration of the difference between double- and single-mindedness. The humor of the cartoon springs from the tension between these two states of perception. You and I see the husband double-mindedly, or bisociatively; that is, he isn't really a modern work of art but a metaphor for how "getting smashed" can make you feel as if your body had been redesigned by Picasso; it probably wouldn't even occur to you to call the husband bizarre, so evocative is the metaphor. If anything, it is the wife's reaction that seems bizarre. She has no

[2] Henri Bergson, whose essay *The World of Dreams* remains fresh after almost a century, offers still another approach to the problem of mindedness in dreams in a hypothetical conversation between his waking self and his dreaming self: "Sleeping means becoming disinterested," the dreaming self says. "You sleep in proportion to your disinterest. . . . You [the waking self] take me, your dreaming self, me, the totality of your past, and you manage by making me smaller and smaller to fit me into the tiny circle which you draw around your present activity. That is what it means to be awake and to live a psychologically normal life. It means struggling. It means willing." As for dreaming, it is "the state into which you naturally fall back as soon as you give yourself up, as soon as you no longer have the strength to concentrate on a single point, as soon as you stop *willing*. . . . [The dream] is the wonderful mechanism through which your will instantaneously and almost unconsciously manages at a particular moment to concentrate everything that you are carrying around inside yourself on one and the same point, the point that interests you" (1958: 50–51).

such bisociative power, no imagination. To her, the husband's condition isn't metaphorical but a natural consequence of too much alcohol, and before she's done he'll probably feel more like a de Kooning. She is like a person in a dream who single-mindedly takes whatever appears as the only reality in town. In short, the dreaming brain is capable of imagining anything, but what it imagines loses the status of the imaginary. On one hand, the dream state is one of pure imagination (Koestler's double-mindedness or passive bisociation); on the other hand, paradoxically, though the dream is driven by imagination, it has no imagination (in Rechtschaffen's sense) with respect to its own productions, which is to say that it cannot, like the brain in the waking or the daydream states, willfully change its mind and follow a new course unlike the course it has set; nor can it keep two courses in mind simultaneously. And this limitation bears centrally on Rechtschaffen's conjecture that dream hallucinations may, after all, be "secondary to dream single-mindedness" rather than the other way around (1978: 101), as Hobson would apparently have it.

I doubt that we can so securely claim what the brain can and cannot do in the dream state, because there are so many different declensions of "mindedness" from lucid dreaming to hypnogogic imagery to the state of half-sleep in which one seems to be a creature of one world as much as the other. But let us at least grant the point that there is this gross difference in capability between the waking and dreaming states and see where it may lead. Let us apply the idea to a practical example that can enable us to compare literary and dream experience and to arrive at some notion of what bizarreness actually involves in the way of mental processing. Here is a passage from a hypothetical work of fiction I have written for this occasion:

> It was perhaps the way she was sitting, or the familiar blue dress she wore, but as I looked at Sarah crying there on the sofa I was reminded of Aunt Julia sitting in her kitchen on the afternoon that Edgar was killed in the car accident. I can still hear Julia say, "The last thing Edgar said when he left the house was 'I won't be back!'"

I have composed this passage in the most straightforward style possible in order to see what sorts of mental transactions are involved in the reading of normal fiction. The most elementary thing to be said, perhaps, is that the passage virtually disappears as an object (words on paper) and reappears as an experience in the mind's eye. Or, as Georges Poulet puts it in his phenomenology of reading, it becomes a mental object "in close *rapport* with my own consciousness" which "is modified in such a way that I no longer have the right, strictly speaking, to consider it as my *I*. I am on loan to another, and this other thinks, feels, suffers, and acts within me" (1980: 43–45). And indeed something of this kind happens in the typical daydream and even more profoundly in the REM dream state: I perceive the dreamworld not in the "weak" way I perceive a literary text, no matter how well it has been "internalized," but as a world I somehow inhabit which "thinks" itself in me, as Poulet says, even though I myself am responsible for all the thinking. Hence, the dream is a kind of Strange Loop, or a Tangled Hierarchy, in Douglas Hofstadter's terms—"something *in* the system jumps out and acts *on* the system, as if it were *outside* the system" (1980: 691)—in which the dream I have created seems to be taking place outside me, or around me, as an independent reality.

But to return to my fiction, notice what is asked of the brain in the process of inhabiting this "second self," this I—Not I. I begin with a mental image of Sarah sitting on the sofa in tears. (If I have not met her earlier in the story, I will simply supply a generic or facsimile Sarah from my memory of "Sarah" possibilities which I will amend as her character and appearance become established.) But immediately, I am *reminded*, through certain cues, of Aunt Julia, who recalls what Edgar said on the afternoon of his death. In other words, Aunt Julia in some sense momentarily replaces Sarah in my mind's eye, though Sarah remains, so to speak, on hold in my attention; but abruptly Edgar replaces Aunt Julia and there could even be a flash of a scene involving a car accident somewhere on a highway on my peripheral mental landscape.

All this is effortlessly negotiated by the brain. We are, however, still debating what sort of images the brain conjures in such a sequence; they are perhaps what Nelson Goodman calls "undrawn pictures" (1984: 23), or concept pictures, or what Edward Casey calls images of "pure possibility" (1979: 36–37). A particularly attractive approach to the mental image, with respect to bizarreness, is offered in Marvin Minsky's concept of the simulus, "a reproduction of only the higher-level effects of a stimulus":

> A simulus at the very highest levels could lead a person to recollect virtually no details about a remembered object or event, yet be able to apprehend and contemplate its most significant structures and relationships while experiencing a sense of its presence. A simulus may have many advantages over a picture-image. Not only can it work more swiftly while using less machinery, but we can combine the parts of several simuli to imagine things we have never seen before—and even to imagine things that couldn't possibly exist. (1988: 170)

Whatever the mind sees, however, it certainly amounts to a center of mental energy wherein an image, or simulus, of Sarah, or of Sarahness, gives way fleetingly to an image of Julia and Edgar and a wrecked car of some sort. A cinema version of the scene might achieve the effect through a dissolve in which the scene shifts to the kitchen and the quarrel(?) with Aunt Julia and Edgar, and then back to the scene between the narrator and Sarah, perhaps with some sort of ripple effect to suggest the pastness of it all.

In the space of two sentences, then, the brain has been caused, at some quasi-pictorial level, to replace one scene with another and to hold the sense of several scenes in a simultaneous or oscillating suspension, or what Rechtschaffen might call double-mindedness. What textually directs all this mental traffic are the two constructions, "I was *reminded*" and "I can *still* hear Julia say," which form an associational bridge, so to speak, into the past whereby the I of the narrative and the I–Not I of the reader are able to visualize and make sense of the sequence without bizarrely bunching everybody together on a sofa as a car comes crashing through the kitchen wall. They function like similes in poetic imagery in that they keep the hierarchy from *becoming* tangled: that is, "I was reminded" serves as a *like* or an *as* that says, in effect, "Sarah, here on the sofa, *resembles* Aunt Julia on that fatal afternoon in the kitchen." In any case, as Poulet says, we have "become the prey of language. . . . The universe of fiction is infinitely more elastic than the world of objective reality. It lends itself to any use: it yields with little resistance to the importunities of the mind. Moreover—and of all its benefits I find this the most appealing—this interior universe constituted by language does not seem radically opposed to the *me* who thinks it" (1981: 43).

I hope my example can be taken as an elementary instance of the elasticity of fiction and the capacity of human consciousness to shift scenes and focal points on linguistic cues, to convert a purely verbal world into a half-reality taking place in one's head. One would hardly call this transaction bizarre or distorted, because it involves a normal daytime mental operation (being reminded of something else) as common as seeing a face in a bush or remembering your high school prom while hearing a song. Yet—and this is my point—the mental process involved in such remindings is no different from the process by which dreams negotiate similar cross-associations and in so doing produce both so-called realistic and bizarre images. The only difference is that in dreams there is no text to mediate the experience or to preserve a conscious awareness that the association is *only* an association posited in a fictional universe rather than a part of dream reality as it appears to the dreamer in the dream state. In a dream based on our story, Sarah would suddenly *be* Aunt Julia; or, more likely, the essence of one would contaminate the image of the other; or Sarah-Julia might even turn into a familiar stranger, possessing inseparable attributes of both, somewhat as yellow and blue produce the color green when mixed.

Indeed, that is what often happens in a dream, and I suspect that the high frequency of strangers in dreams (four out of ten dream characters are strangers, according to Calvin Hall; 1966: 30), or the sudden confusion of a known person with a stranger, may have to do in part with the problem of representing in a single image a charge brought on by an overload of multiple associations. How, after all, is the dream able to move from Sarah to Aunt Julia without an equivalent of the literary device of the simile, a simile being nothing more than a verbal means of maintaining difference *in* the resemblance? In a dream such a transaction necessarily occurs as a metaphor rather than as a simile, meaning that the two (or more) images are not held apart by a *like* but are fused as one (thus becoming an elliptical simile), as in the case of the Picassoed husband in the cartoon or my double image of Simon and Alan Bates. There is simply no other way such a transaction can occur outside reflective consciousness. A person having this dream, on awaking and telling it to another person, might well say, "Suddenly, Sarah disappeared and I was with Aunt Julia in her kitchen and Edgar came in." And it would all seem bizarre. Yet the bizarreness (in this case, anyway) is a consequence of limitations—or, couldn't we say, if we were thoroughly rid of our normalcy bias, a consequence of imaginative enhancements—imposed by the condition of Rechtschaffen's single-mindedness or, if you prefer, Koestler's passive bisociation.

In any case, this is all somewhat beside the point, because it is unlikely that such a story would be possible in a dream, or that a dream could tell a story that required the deviation to another prior and as-yet-undreamed story element. A dream cannot deal in flashbacks in the sense that waking fictions almost require them in order to explore what goes on in the minds and prenarrative history of their characters.[3] This is one of the distinguishing features of dream stories: they are one-directional; a dream may *have* a flashback (to a scene from the dreamer's childhood), but thereafter the flashback becomes the center and focus of the narrative. It becomes the dream's present, though I suppose the dream could elect to return to its old present by flashing back to it. But that would require a

---

[3] There is a sense in which dreams rely heavily on the flashback principle. Every time a dream produces a character or scene from the dreamer's past, we have a kind of flashback, though a more appropriate term might be Gérard Genette's *anachrony*—any form of "discordance between the two temporal orders of story and narrative" [1980: 40]. The dream would not really be flashing back to an earlier time or place but converting all time and place into an impacted extratemporal now, a trick that would get a novelist into quick trouble.

reminder and a new operation. Moreover, just as dreams, like all imagined objects, are (as Casey says) "ineluctably front-sided" and have no "displaceability of standpoint" (1979: 92), they also have no agency comparable to the omniscient narrative voice of fiction which is capable of virtually infinite expansion or reduction of story perspective or temporal sequence. A dream might easily represent a fictional transaction like "John had never noticed how frail Mother had become" as long as John is the dreamer to whom the thought occurs. But I don't see how a dream could negotiate such hierarchical detours as those called for (for example) in a verbal construction like this: "Meanwhile, across town Sidney had left his apartment to buy Felicia a birthday present, having remembered while feeding her dog only that morning how he had disappointed her last year, how she had cried on the veranda, and how Mother had admonished him for forgetting something that had always been so important to his sister." That would be some bizarre dream.

This is simply to say that in the dream state the mind lacks "literary competence." When we read, thanks (among other things) to an acquired familiarity with literary conventions, we don't quite *see* what we read. We are able to keep the image at an "aesthetic distance," to see on through it. We involuntarily insert into our cognitive-visual circuitry a kind of resistance—a *like* or an *as* —a filter that strains out the literality of the image and allows only an edited version of its pictorial mass to appear in the mind's eye. Thus in Macbeth's contemplation of the murder of Duncan, when we encounter an image such as "his virtues/Will plead like angels trumpet-tongued against/The deep damnation of his taking-off," the most naive of readers is double-mindedly able to deliteralize it, or to accept *trumpet* and *tongue* not as images of things—tongue + trumpet, or a tongue shaped like a trumpet—but as a metaphor for a heavenly speech act whereby the murder is "blown" in every eye. The poetic context tames or anesthetizes the visual reality of the passage and we think of it, in our state of reflective double-mindedness, as being beautiful and densely meaningful rather than bizarre or grotesque. Playing about the edges of this affect, perhaps, we may see a vague representation of a trumpet and a tongue, but the images are almost instantly eclipsed by the attributes relevant to the context.[4]

If, however, Macbeth were dreaming the content of this passage rather than thinking out loud (for our benefit), it seems unlikely that he could conjure an image series capable of carrying the spatial and metaphysical complexity of this vision. It is certainly possible that guilt and fear of this magnitude could inspire and attend a dream; but the dream would necessarily have to compromise, that is, it would have *to choose* from among psychic associations that are possibly contradictory or nonrepresentable, in which case it would, in all likelihood, cross the line between the realistic and the bizarre. From the waking standpoint the result might even be considered a failed image in the sense that there is a point where thought of such subtlety has no possible visual equivalent. Happily, this is not a problem for the dream, which is not in the business of satisfying readers or communicating information or emotion to the dreamer. Indeed, one may say that in the dream the emotion precedes the formation of the image and requires only a fitting host for its embodiment; the visible portion of a dream is nothing more than a foundation on which memory, desire, and fear ride, like Macbeth's cherubim on the invisible horse-winds. Over against double-minded literary competence, then, we might speak of the dream as possessing a personal "mythic competence" wherein the image is always adapted from what is at hand in the memory and charged with a fresh significance. Thus the dreamer has something in common with Claude Lévi-Strauss's mythic poet-bricoleur, who "derives his poetry from the fact that he does not confine himself to accomplishment and execution: he 'speaks' not only *with* things . . . but also through the medium of things: giving an account of

[4] It may be argued that the bizarre imagery of poetry and fiction, being primarily linguistic, is of a different order from bizarre dream imagery, which is primarily visual. In terms of manifest appearance, this may be true. But I do not see how a poet could write a line like "the porches of my ears" or "your thighs are appletrees whose blossoms touch the sky" without at least some trace image of the metaphor, even in the waking state.

his personality and life by the choices he makes between the limited possibilities" (1966: 21).[5]

One of the consequences of this rigidity, this absence of a hierarchical "stacking" principle, is the occasional production of "bizarre" images that are no different in kind from other images (all dream images being, at bottom, condensations or composites) but whose associational logic does not survive the dream state. Bizarreness, in one of its aspects, may indeed mark the site of a transition, that is, a place where the dream is reminding itself of a related content, much as fiction might shift to a subplot. All a fiction has to do to accomplish this is to offer some variation of the "Meanwhile . . ." idea, and we are smoothly transported to another part of the forest. Moreover, a fiction always knows its way back to the point of origin. But the dream has no such locution and consequently shifts in scene are considered to be violations of probability, even though the dream may be reacting to associational urgencies every bit as natural as those of fiction.

As another case in point, Frederick Snyder cites as an example of a bizarre dream event ("the craziness of the dream") a cat suddenly turning into a rabbit (1970: 146). But let us put this crazy event where it properly belongs, that is, in the compositional stage. Let us say a waking writer is composing a story about animals. Suppose she decides on a cat but then it somehow occurs to her that a rabbit might be more interesting or better for all around story purposes. It is not clear to her, however, why she suddenly settles on rabbit. Would we describe this as bizarre? Certainly it is a quite common procedure in fiction writing and poetry, especially in poetry where the narrative is usually less important than the quality of

[5] Adam Kuper applies Lévi-Strauss's methodology to a dream sequence and develops the hypothesis that "dreams, like myths, are based on systematic transformations of simple structures [often] represented as a set of oppositions" (1983: 174). My interest here is not diagnostic, but I am concerned with the possible similarity between dream and myth formations. I am not sure the point should be carried beyond a loose metaphorical stage, but there is a sense in which dreams seem, like the myth poet (and unlike the literary poet), to make do with what is available, building up a meaningful structure "by using the remains and debris of [past] events" (Lévi-Strauss, 1966: 21–22).

the image. In the case of the dreamer, aren't the same procedures involved? Couldn't the dreamer suddenly change cat to rabbit without the slightest implication that it was one of those bizarre metamorphoses typical of horror movies. The cat suddenly becomes a rabbit and that's that, very much as mother might suddenly become father in appearance while remaining mother in essence. What probability has really been violated—assuming we consider the dream as a composition continually in progress?

Let us say, however, that we are reading a story featuring a cat and we encounter a sentence of this sort: "Emily was petting the cat but all of a sudden it began to change before her eyes. First it grew long white ears, then its tail became a round ball of fur; and lo and behold it was suddenly a—rabbit! Emily was beside herself with shock." This is a bona fide bizarre event, "outside the conceivable expectations of waking life," as Snyder says, though hardly outside the expectations of certain kinds of fiction. The point to be made about this example of bizarreness, however, is that it is designed (by the absent author) to be taken as a bizarre event; but in the compositional stage, when it first occurred to the author that it might be an interesting development to change Emily's cat into a rabbit, we can hardly say that the author's thinking was bizarre. Likewise, in a dream—which has the unique quality of being composed and experienced simultaneously—unusual changes are not necessarily bizarre.

I am hardly arguing that there are no bizarre events in dreams, though, as Snyder's study suggests, they are more the exception than the rule. It is quite possible in a dream that a cat will undergo a metamorphosis and become a rabbit before the dreamer's eyes, arousing any number of strong (or weak) emotions from fear to astonishment to curiosity. But I wonder whether the emotion would be caused by the transformation itself or by the affective tenor of the dream in progress. The state of normalcy in the dreamworld is, by its very nature as simultaneous thought and experience, quite different from normalcy in the real world, and it seems to me that is what we must try to understand if we are to determine the similarities and differences in the compositional processes that go into the production of dreams and art. The whole concern with bizarreness in dreams seems to me misplaced. Indeed, as far as mental processes go, we experience bizarreness on a regular basis: every time something reminds us of something it is not, the brain makes a bizarre move in the form of a metaphor. When you see a face in a shrub, are you not, in effect, producing a sort of Arcimboldo painting?

No one can be sure what brings on a noticeably bizarre image, but outside cases of drug-induced hallucination, sleep deprivation, fatigue, psychosis, high body fever, such an image must occur as a kind of blending or collision of associational priorities that are simply beneath determination. This is not, however, a collision from the dreamer's point of view: no matter how bizarre the image may be, it is experienced as normal and the dreamer has no choice but to believe it, like the wife in the cartoon. Indeed, in this respect dreams approximate living conditions in the waking world: they are authorless, unmediated by language, and they unfold intrepidly in a world no different from the waking world with respect to the authenticity of the experience. As Boss (1977: 175–83) and Globus (1987: 91–109) have said, the dreamer is thrown into the dream as Dasein is thrown into the everyday world. But as dreamers we have lost a crucial capacity of waking thought—reflective awareness, the capacity to stand back and assess our experience as we have it. In its place, however, we have gained a capacity to rearrange the contents of the real world according to a nonhistorical, extratemporal, and subjective directive and at the same time to perceive this new content as being in every sense a reality in its own right.

Consequently, the reliability or recognizability of dream shapes according to a waking standard of coherence is not a relevant consideration in dream imagery, any more than it is in nonrealistic fiction and art in which we freely enter any world offered to our suspended disbelief.[6] The dream state is not reflective with respect

---

[6] For example, in the world of Expressionist art, as described by Walter H. Sokel: "The Expressionist dramatist, like the dreamer, concentrates entirely on the purpose of expressing an inner world and refuses to let conformity to external reality divert him from this purpose . . . . The scenery of the Expressionist stage changes with the

to a waking reality, it is reflective with respect to its own created reality. If you wish, it is self-reflexive, meaning that it is in constant reaction to its own productions, continually self-departing, continually creating representations that "slide smoothly from like idea to like idea," as Mary Warnock puts it in *Imagination*, "and . . . continue in any course once set, producing more and more similar ideas according to the principles of association" (1978: 133). The one restriction on the dream's inventive power is that it is bound by the rule of metaphoric advancement, or what Montague Ullman calls "metaphor in motion" (1969). It cannot get out of its topic any more than Dasein can get out of the world, unless by waking or by death, two forms of "story" termination that paradoxically amount to the same thing—exile from a reality in which one has been utterly absorbed.

Still, one thing must be said about the absence of the reflective capacity in dreams. If I have lost the power to assess my experience during the dream as being "only a story," as Rechtschaffen puts it (1978: 99), I have not lost the power to reflect on what happens *within* the dream and to bring to bear on my dream experience the same forms of awareness—or what we might call dream double-mindedness—available to me in the waking state. I can perfectly assess my dream experience just as well as I can assess my waking experience. In short, I can see that Simon is cheerful and I can even go on and reflect philosophically on why everyone in the world can't be as cheerful as he. It may be that I will later regard my assessment as gibberish, or I may develop an intimate conversation with an animal or a deep fear of shrubbery, or a faith in the power of a bathtub to get me across an ocean; but who is to say that these

---

psychic forces whirling about in it, just as in the universe of relativity space is modified by the matter it contains. . . . Landscapes reflect the emotional situation of the characters." And finally, "By the functional use of lighting, the Expressionist reproduces the dream process. The sudden darkening or illumination of a particular corner of the stage indicates the leaps of the dreaming mind. The lighting apparatus behaves like the mind. It drowns in darkness what it wishes to forget and bathes in light what it wishes to recall. Thus the entire stage becomes a universe of mind, and the individual scenes are not replicas of three-dimensional physical reality, but visualized stages of thought" (1959: 38, 41).

bizarre things don't have their own validity and logic in the dreamworld, had we but the means to trace the clash and fusion of graphic priorities to their source in the neuronal memory banks? Furthermore, I am not sure how my accepting them as natural in the dream
is any different from my acceptance of stationary bathtubs and
speechless animals in reality, or, for that matter, from talking animals, menacing trees, and such things in the world of fantastic
fiction and Disney movies. The so-called willing suspension of
disbelief we undergo in the waking aesthetic mode of thought differs from *involuntary* suspension of disbelief in the dream state only
in degree rather than in kind. In reading fiction we do not suspend
disbelief entirely but only to the degree that we can "believe" in the
story as a virtual experience. The famous country rube who leapt
onto the stage to prevent Othello's murder of Desdemona is a
classic illustration of how the principle might conceivably get carried too far.

Another way to state the problem is offered in J. T. Fraser's
concept of the *Umwelt* (developed first by Jacob von Uexkull early
in the century). An *Umwelt* is a "species-specific universe" in which
an organism's capacity ("receptors and effectors") to receive and act
on the things of its environment determines "its world of possible
stimuli and actions. . . . What is not in [a species'] *Umwelt* must be
taken as nonexistent for the members of that species. For instance,
ultraviolet patterns on certain butterflies exist for other butterflies
but not for vertebrates: vertebrates have no sense organs through
which they could read those patterns. What an earthworm cannot
know might kill it but it won't know what hit it" (1980: 148).
Applying the notion of *Umwelt* to dreams, we may say that the
dreaming brain has certain receptors and effectors through which it
performs its unique process of converting mental stimuli from the
memory into a sequence of narrative images. Why or how it does
this we don't know, as we don't know why or how ultraviolet
patterns are necessary to certain butterflies and not to others or to
other species. But the process is, in a manner of speaking, a species-
specific operation, at least to the extent that the dream process can
not only create a world of images (as the waking brain can) but

make the creator one of that world's inhabitants. This process can be assessed in retrospect by the (same) waking brain, but the dreaming brain cannot, in its turn, know that it is in any way contained within the larger *Umwelt* of its waking host any more than the earthworm can know of the existence of the fisherman's hook. What is not in the *Umwelt* of the dream "must be taken as nonexistent," which is simply to say that the dream knows only the dream *Umwelt,* and all its unique operations, however foreign to the *Umwelt* of the waking brain, must be conceived as being necessary and natural to its livelihood.[7]

Defining bizarreness as discrete monstrosity or, as Allan Hobson does, according to *Webster's New Collegiate Dictionary* ("strikingly out of the ordinary"; Hobson, 1988: 259) effectively ignores a fundamental point of dream bizarreness: it is a bottom-to-top condition beginning in the composition of the image; monstrosities are simply extreme variations of the dream image's peculiar normalcy. The dream is just as distorted when it is being realistic and sensible as it is when it is producing outrageous aberrations of nature. In

---

[7] I am in trouble on this count with lucid dreamers, and so a word or so by way of qualification seems in order. Lucid dreaming seems to me an oxymoronic term, at least conceived as the state of being fully aware in the dream state. Any reflective or lucid act performed during sleep—such as awareness that "this is only a dream"—is necessarily carried out within the condition of dreaming. Otherwise, one would be awake within the dream, a patent impossibility. "The lucid dreamer," Globus says, "does whatever he or she decides to do, and wherever he or she decides to do it, *within that dream horizon,* and that horizon is clearly not the horizon for [waking] phenomenological reflection" (1987: 88). In brief, there is only one *Umwelt* to a customer. Lucid dream theorists can certainly challenge this assumption by maintaining that lucid dreams are similar to waking meditation and the out-of-body experience. As Hunt says, "they share with out-of-body experience, and especially with meditation, the special sense of clarity and exhilaration (reminiscent of Maslow on 'peak experience') that comes with the emergence of a detached receptive attitude in the midst of our more narrow everyday involvements, whether dreamt or real. . . . [Lucid dreams] *transform* dreams in the same way that meditation transforms wakefulness" (1986: 218).

My problem is that, outside of certain tantalizing experiences on the hypnopompic fringe, I have never experienced what I could seriously call a lucid dream; and since my approach here is substantially phenomenological—that is, based on my own perception of dreaming—it is difficult to know how to deal with something I haven't experienced at first hand. I add hastily that my reservations are unexamined

other words, should a dream image suddenly break out into an impossibility—a double-headed man, a giant, a talking plant—that is simply one of the *probabilities* of dream transformation, like anger or fear suddenly breaking out of temperate human behavior. To the dreamer, any truly impossible image might, at best, produce the sort of shock that news of a four-car accident or a volcanic eruption might produce in the waking world.

Let us come at this problem of the ubiquity of bizarreness from a literary perspective. Here I am primarily interested in seeing how waking fictions imitate the single-mindedness of dreams. How does a genuine dream artist succeed in putting a conscious double-minded reader into something *like* a dream state? Surely not by producing bizarre images one after another, as the surrealists might, for this amounts simply to producing literature of the grotesque, or literature, as Selma Fraiberg says, whose "distortions of language have already stamped the experience as unreal" (1956: 55);[8] and surely not by imitating the seemingly arbitrary and incoherent current of the dream narrative wherein, as Strindberg says,

---

and based on a pronounced degree of ignorance about lucid dream research. Therefore, rather than deny the possibility that lucid dreamers experience genuine and full "reflective awareness" (double-mindedness) within the "dream horizon"—as I am defining these things here—I simply withhold judgment in the hope that my position on bizarreness may contribute to the debate on dream consciousness. From what I gather, most discussions of lucid dreaming do not imply the paradox of a waking state within the dream state but something more like a state of self-enhancement in which "the representational capacity is still dominant even though there seems to be a de-embedding from the normal orientation of the dream ego. Although we know it is a dream, the dreamt representation remains and in fact the awareness of dreaming does not hinder the 'felt reality' or 'otherness' of the dream experience" (Gackenback, 1991: 118). This is an encouraging distinction and, on this basis, I might on occasion have experienced a lucid dream myself. Certainly, there are many different levels of dream awareness. Here I am really trying to isolate certain differences between waking consciousness and dream consciousness as they relate to the phenomenon of bizarreness. If lucid dreaming falls somewhere between the two states it would be extremely interesting to know, among other things, precisely how bizarre dream events are perceived by a lucid dreamer: single-mindedly or double-mindedly?

[8] The basic idea is that the uncanniness (or bizarreness) of the dream "is not a property of the dream itself or of unconscious experience" but belongs rather to "the ego, the representative of consciousness and reality." Thus, "a narrative which

"the characters split, double, multiply, dissolve, condense, float apart, coalesce" (1986: 646), so that you can finally count on nothing because you can count on everything. However interesting Strindberg's dream plays may be from other standpoints, they succeed only in imitating the unreal or supernatural aspect of dreams as opposed to the condition of dreaming itself. What is missing from most so-called dream literature is precisely the reality of the dream experience, that is, the dreamer's complete conviction in the exclusivity of the dream *Umwelt*.

I take as my window on the problem (and it could as easily have been a Kafka work) Poe's "Fall of the House of Usher," a story that would certainly qualify as containing bizarre or uncanny events. The opening sentences offer a sufficient sample of the text:

> During the whole of a dull, dark and soundless day in the autumn of the year, when the clouds hung oppressively low in the heavens, I had been passing alone on horseback through a singularly dreary tract of country. At length I found myself, as the shades of evening drew on, within view of the melancholy House of Usher.

This passage has nothing to do directly with impossible events or distortions of the laws of nature as we know them in waking life. In

---

attempts to simulate the experience of dreaming or to evoke the 'uncanniness' of the dream must deceive the critical and judging faculties of the ego through a prose which apparently sustains logic and belief at the same time that it affirms the delusion. The ideal prose for this treatment is everyday speech, a factual narration in simple declarative sentences. The narration of events and visions from a night-world in the ordinary, accustomed prose of waking life produces exactly the sense of dissolving reason which makes reality a dream and the dream a reality, in essence the quality of uncanniness" (Fraiberg, 1956: 54). I would only add to this that, though the general perception seems to me accurate, I am not sure that everyday speech is as central as Fraiberg suggests. In what follows here, I argue that Poe achieves the same sense of the uncanny, and Poe's language is scarcely of the everyday variety and he does not write in simple declarative sentences. I think the key is rather in the factual tone of the narrative voice, or in its refusal to see distortion *as* distortion in the uncanny environment or in the creatures it may throw up. It simply "sustains logic and belief at the same time that it affirms the delusion."

what respect, then, does it belong to the bizarre? Certainly the bizarreness is not to be found in the images themselves in the sense that a reader, having read this far in the story, would be apt to say, "How bizarre!" It is rather present as a potentiality and an expectation. Kenneth Burke might say that the passage establishes the tale's scene/act ratio, the sense in which the quality of the scene implicitly contains "the quality of the action that is to take place within it" (1962: 7). In this case, the bizarreness inheres in a certain monochromatic quality that is the hallmark of the Poe world. Altogether it may be described as a condition of morbidity (*dull, dark, soundless, oppressive, melancholy*). More important, however, is the narrator's passive acceptance of this mood, as if nature on this particular day, even though singularly dreary, were nothing generically out of the ordinary; indeed, *singularly* dreary suggests that days are always dreary, though not quite *this* dreary. To change the whole quality of the passage, imagine the addition of a sentence such as "How I longed for the sunlight and cheerfulness of my native city!" or "So foul a day I'd never seen." Such sentiments would effectively drive a qualitative wedge between the I describing the scene and the scene itself, suggesting that the narrator had come from, or at least knew, a world in which such morbidity was strikingly out of the ordinary, as Hobson might put it. It would be, in short, a product of double-minded thinking in that it would demonstrate "a reflective or evaluative stream" of thought (Rechtschaffen) through which the narrator was placing the scene in some normative perspective.

Tzvetan Todorov would call such a moment one of "hesitation." In his view, hesitation is the distinctive feature separating the literature of the fantastic from overlapping genres such as the uncanny and the marvelous, a point we need not debate here. Hesitation is marked by the character's inability to explain an extraordinary event as obeying the laws of our normal world, on one hand, or as an "illusion of the senses, . . . a product of the imagination," on the other. It is the reaction of "a person who knows only the laws of [waking] nature, confronting an apparently supernatural [or bizarre] event" (1980: 25). Hesitation is a state-specific reaction and for our purposes may be considered as another form of double-mindedness, in Rechtschaffen's sense of the term: to hesitate involves the power of reflection in which one says, "Whoa! Hold it! This can't be real!"

But there is no such moment of hesitation in the Poe passage, as there is no such moment in a dream. The Poe narrator creates and then inhabits a Poesque world where only Poesque things can happen. Even though the sentence directly following reads, "I know not how it was, but with the first glimpse of the building a sense of insufferable gloom pervaded my spirit," we have not so much a change to a new emotional state as an atmospheric intensification of the monochromatic state. Overall, there is a collusion between world and the self encountering it. Thus the passage is a virtually perfect example of *literary* single-mindedness and the best word to describe it is *dreamlike*. Here at the very opening of Poe's tale the atmospheric conditions necessary for the advent of the uncanny events to follow are metonymically established through a kind of stylistic greenhouse effect. And the sense of impenetrable gloom that pervades the narrator's spirit pervades the reader's as well; the reader, as Poulet says, is "on loan to" this gloom which graphically exposes the world preconditions in which (in due course) a sister will naturally rise from her tomb, die (again) simultaneously with her brother, and the great "melancholy house of Usher" will topple from the precipice and disappear, as though in sympathetic remorse, into the "deep and dank tarn" naturally (and conveniently) situated below it.[9]

Bizarreness, then, does not simply erupt in uncanny or fantastic fictions but is conditioned and prepared by the possibilities of the

[9] George Poulet has written an excellent treatment of the dream quality of the Poe world in *The Metamorphoses of the Circle* (1966: 182–202). Of particular relevance to my argument I cite the following passage: "In the dream as in the awakening, in stupor as in full consciousness, the mind always finds itself encircled. It is in a sphere whose walls recede or draw together, but never cease to enclose the spectator. Pleasure and terror, extreme passivity and extreme watchfulness, hyperacuity of the senses and of the intellect, are the means by which the mind recognizes the insuperable continuity of its limits. No one before Poe has shown with as much precision the essentially circumscribed character of thought" (p. 198); and this: "This atmos-

scene. And this is the case in dreams as well, though for *scene* and *style* we must substitute terms like *mode* and *medium;* for the dream, unlike fiction, has only one available style and that, as we have seen, is the single-minded style in which bizarreness is the constant behavioral norm and all images, as Poulet says, are "the habitual inmates of an identical thought" (1966: 184). We see this everywhere in dreams in subtle textural ways: natural and architectural proportions, even when realistic, are somehow unreliable, stairways rise and descend differently, rooms are furnished differently, bathrooms (when you can find them) are either nonfunctional or crowded with people drinking cocktails; we approach and depart from objects differently in dreams; car doors open differently, inside the car seating arrangements are always inadequate, and heaven help you if you decide to drive in traffic or shift into reverse and then try to find the brake. Even bodily motion is different in dreams: everything is either more difficult (try getting back to your hotel room in a busy city) or much easier to do (flying, skiing, running), as the theme of the dream dictates. Finally, the peculiar *presentness* of dream temporality is unlike anything in the normal waking state. The dream present, as J. T. Fraser says, is "informed of past and future. We may see in a dream something motionless, yet we know that it is going to crawl, or grow, or shrink—and it does; or, we see someone move and we know where he came from and where he is going . . . . The situation rather resembles the second reading of a story, or the assumed omnipotence of a divinity: we are simultaneously surprised, and not surprised, by knowing the future" (1990: 291).

I can sum up the point best by applying it to a personal dream used by Harry Hunt to demonstrate how "unexpected visual-spatial transformations do not so much disrupt narrative continuity, . . . as provide the dramatic sense that fulfills and completes it":

------

phere is a sphere. Without affinity to the air of heaven, reflected in the waters of its own tarn, the House of Usher exists only in the dense vapor issued from its ground. It has, so to speak, created its own space. It has also created its own particular duration. Not only does it exist in the spherical continuity of its own surroundings, but also in the linear continuity of the family it shelters" (p. 201).

I am traveling with my wife and children, looking for a parking place in order to visit the Tibetan National Museum. The only parking areas I can find are in highway rest areas and I realize that unless I hurry the museum will close. Accordingly, I now drive directly to the museum (a huge building with multiple wings and four or five floors). Leaving my car and family in front, I run inside. I enter a massive foyer and find to my intense disappointment that the museum has just closed.

Looking about, I notice an open door to a small room off to one side. Entering, I find myself in the private apartment of an older, very thin women [sic], who is apparently the museum caretaker. The room is primitive and archaic. The women [sic] is in one corner steadily stirring a very large pot of boiling water. As I approach more closely I see in the pot a carved wooden manikin about two feet tall. As the woman stirs, ignoring me, the room is filled with an eerie, high-pitched wailing sound. I realize with growing horror that the sound emanates from the wooden manikin, which is becoming progressively more lifelike as she stirs—its scream of pain becomes more and more shrill and frenzied and then begins to turn into an uncanny and strangely beautiful song. I realize that the price of the vivification of the manikin is the terrible agony that produces this song, and I awaken in a cold sweat (1989: 166).

I could not agree more with Hunt that the manikin scene "dramatically fulfills" the dream and that "such departures" are not "merely a randomized process of disruption" but "the very fabric of dream semantics" (p. 167). I would simply go a step farther and claim that the manikin episode is not a departure at all but a visual intensification of the bizarreness that underlies the whole dream— indeed, all dreams. What else is occurring in the opening sequence—"unless I hurry the museum will close"—but the dream's bizarre assurance (as Fraser says) that just that will happen—"the museum has just closed"? It was not, after all, the lateness of the hour that caused the closing of the museum but Hunt's "teleprojection" of the fear that it would close. Ergo, close it does. Moreover, why are there no parking places? And is it not strange that Hunt would abandon his family in a (probably) illegal zone in order to get inside the museum to find—what? However possible that such things could occur in the waking world, in a dream the absence of parking places and the urgency to do something at all costs are ordained by the emotional logic of the dream, just as the day in Poe's story is dull, dark, and soundless in keeping with the emotional logic of the story. In short, I do not see much difference between the visual bizarre and the cognitive/semantic bizarre, in terms of dream fabric or semantics; nor do I understand why they should be separated, one of them studied and the other virtually ignored. One is perhaps more noticeable and shocking than the other, but both are aspects of a single process whereby everything in the dream, unlike the real world, is governed by the law of resemblance. "Resemblances," Maurice Blanchot tells us, "abound in dreams, for everyone in them tends to be extremely, wondrously similar: in fact, this is their only identity, they resemble, they belong to a domain that scintillates with pure resemblance: a resemblance that is sometimes steady and fixed, sometimes unstable and adrift (though always certain), fascinating and stirring each and every time" (Leiris, 1987: xxv).

Bizarreness in dreams, then, is everywhere and in everything, unquantifiable and pandemic; it is the enzyme that causes the dream image to shimmer with instability and otherness. And this level of bizarreness is precisely what does not survive in dream reports, however fresh and detailed (except perhaps in statements like "Everything was so strange"), and encourages us to make a categorical distinction between realistic and bizarre imagery. That this distinction can be more or less accurately made in the light of day is not at issue here; nor am I implying that quantitative studies of bizarreness are not useful in such projects as identifying classes of dreamers who, for one reason or another (superior creative abilities, good spatial balance[10]), manifest a higher order of bizarreness in their

---

[10] See Harry T. Hunt, 1990: 9–11, a discussion of the relation of bizarreness to spatial balance. For a review of work on the correlation of bizarreness and creativity in general, too numerous to list here, see also Hunt's *Multiplicity of Dreams* (1989), esp. pp. 8–14. Like Globus's *Sleep Life, Wake Life,* Hunt's book is indispensable to

dreams. I am simply suggesting that bizarreness should not be regarded only as obvious visual deformation but as a continuous and ever dynamic process that is virtually synonymous with imagination itself—at least in the sense that imagination is the power of the mind to decompose received conceptions and experiences and to recombine their elements according to a creative association. It is helpful that cognitive psychologists have discovered a connection between bizarreness and creativity. Like many such discoveries, however, it becomes almost tautological after the fact, rather like saying that imaginative people tend to be more imaginative.

Looked at from the standpoint of the microdynamics of the dream image, then, bizarreness is the means by which the dream represents objects, persons, or experiences that cannot—in the single-mindedness of the dream state—be isolated from the dreamer's history in time and space. In the dream state we recreate the diachronic world from the standpoint of its synchronic coherence as established in a unique memory.[11] I have no idea whether the function of dreams is to correlate new and old experience or to process new information with old, as John Antrobus (1977) and

---

an understanding of the whole question of dreaming and imagination and the peculiar freedoms and limitations in mentation that arise from the dream state. Some of my own ideas here, though substantially developed before I read their work, are prolongations of theirs, aimed at a closer examination of similarities in the poetic and dream processes. For further research on the relationship of bizarreness to creativity, see also Richard A. Bonato et al., 1991, and Ross Levin, Jodi Galin, and Bill Zywiak, 1991. Finally, there is Lawrence S. Kubie's *Neurotic Distortion of the Creative Process* (1970), which approaches the problem of distortion and creativity from a very different perspective.

[11] Another explanation of the cause and role of bizarreness in dreams is offered by Ignacio Matte Blanco's concept of multidimensional space in his study of the unconscious as infinite sets: "If we take any solid object as perceived by our senses, it is easy to apply to it the Cartesian system of (three) [spatial] co-ordinates." But certain mental happenings (metaphor, Matte Blanco suggests) entail more than three variables if we are to envision it as mental space in any sense of the word: "If we represent thoughts or feelings in terms of images, these images must show that each thought or feeling occupies the whole of the ego while being at the same time only a part of the ego. This is what in fact the dream-thought does in the work of condensation, in which exactly the same image may serve in its totality to express various thoughts. *These two requisites of 'partness' and wholeness cannot coexist if three-dimensional material images are employed for a representation. Hence the peculiar impression that dreams*

others (e.g., Palombo, 1978; Evans, 1983) have suggested. But it seems an unavoidable conclusion that the dream state somehow enhances the correlational powers of the brain by means of a relaxed cooperation of discrete and qualitative expressiveness—or between a more or less realistic representation of a specific subject (say, one's sister) and its membership in a thematic history. We do not know why the dream does this, but we do know that one of the brain's primary activities is to categorize knowledge around part-whole divisions;[12] therefore, shouldn't the law of parsimony suggest—until we have proof to the contrary—that the distortion of real experience in dreams should be approached as a useful brain function designed to recover a certain field of congruity that lies beneath awareness (like the butterfly's ultraviolet patterns) to which the experience itself stands in a synecdochic (or part-whole) relationship? One of the most compelling arguments I have read in support of this idea occurs in Mikkel Borch-Jacobsen's brilliant revision of Freudian dream mimesis in relation to dream consciousness. Borch-Jacobsen's discussion is exceedingly dense, and quotations cannot do justice to the interdependency of its points. Still, I offer the following passage on resemblance and its relation to dream distortion:

> Between desire and resemblance there may well be a more essential, more fundamental complicity, for the following reason: by selecting from among all the logical relations included in the material of the dream those that express similarity and identification,

---

produce when they behave as though this were possible" (1975: 449). "In contrast, this representation is no problem if we are dealing with a space of more than three dimensions which is being represented in terms of three dimensions. As we saw, in such a case a volume may appear several times. Therefore, each element which represents a condensation of various others could be metaphorically compared to a volume which is present several times. In this way, what appeared chaotic becomes perfectly well-ordered. The apparently absurd way of dealing with space which we observe in dreams becomes, therefore, perfectly reasonable if we assume that *the dreamer 'sees' a multiple-dimensional world with eyes which are made to see only a three-dimensional world"* (p. 418).

[12] George Lakoff discusses part-whole relations in *Women, Fire, and Dangerous Things* (1987), esp. p. 47.

the dream-work specifically chooses to retain those very relations that serve to fulfill the wish in the fantasy that inhabits the dream-thoughts ("I am like this or that person"). The result is that between the dream-thoughts and the manifest content, the dream-work is not solely the distorting (and therefore censoring) grid that Freud often seems to see: on the contrary, if only because of its enigmatic preference for resemblance, the dream-like representation rediscovers a fundamental feature of fantasy that is ensconced in the heart of the dream.

Thus we shall doubtless have to challenge the overly simple schema of a "translation" (which would be at the same time a betrayal) of the straightforward utterance of the dream-thoughts into the foreign, opaque, and at first glance undecipherable medium of dream language. There is, instead, a fundamental continuity in the order of the wish-fantasy, which is always already dissimulatory, because it is always "worked" by resemblance. (1988: 22)

Hobson would place dream bizarreness at the whim of a chemical substance called acetylcholine and claim that it "is not only gratuitous but even possibly hazardous" (1988: 258). I have no expertise in neuroscientific matters and I have no doubt that acetylcholine figures in the dream process; but it is difficult to see why the brain should routinely produce useless and harmful images, especially since these images seem to bear so relevantly on our psychic life. Moreover, if acetylcholine is responsible for bizarre dream images, then it must play a similar role in the formation of bizarre images that occur to us in the waking state. Or, if not, why not? (Was Poe's or Kafka's acetylcholine discharge especially copious?) As Gerald Edelman has cautioned, "It is a long way from acetylcholine to the incest taboo, and great care must be exercised in relating physiological states to the contents of conscious states in language-bearing animals" (1989: 212).[13] Finally, should we not consider that the dream may be as focused, for its own purposes, as most forms

[13] Gordon G. Globus addresses the question of the meaningfulness of dreams in a refutation of Hobson's theory, among others, in "Dream Content: Random or Meaningful?" (1991).

of waking thought?—that it is making the best of an impossible situation (instantaneous fiction!) by pitching its narrative on the frequency of resemblance, jumping, as Shakespeare's Chorus puts it, "o'er times [and] turning the accomplishment of many years" into a single image that (for the time being) represents the accomplishment "cubistically"—that is, not only the frontality (or appearance) of the experience but its spatial and temporal depth as well? The consequence may be an ostensible deformation in the image, but the image was not, after all, formed for our understanding any more than the heart beats so that we may hear it. The image is simply (and complexly) an act of thought that draws two (or more) different things together in an atmosphere where semantic accountability means nothing.

In saying all this, I am hardly denying that dreams are capable of representing real-life situations in more or less faithful terms. My concern is not to delimit the behavior of dreams but to determine why they so persistently produce images and narratives that fly in the face of waking reality. I am suggesting, in sum, that a key parallel may be found in the images of poetry and fiction which routinely thrive on the bizarre to the point that it becomes the norm of poetic discourse. "It is in the study of image distortion," Bachelard says in his book on Lautréamont, "that we find the full extent of poetic imagination. We see that metaphors are naturally tied to metamorphoses" (1986: 30). "Metamorphosis thus becomes the specific function of imagination [which] cannot comprehend a form except by transforming it, by dynamizing its becoming, by seizing on it like a sectioning of the flux of formal causality, precisely as a physicist cannot understand a phenomenon except by grasping it in a sectioning of the flux of efficient causality" (p. 89). Indeed, the bizarre is ubiquitous in the world of expressiveness. It is a form of what Victor Shklovsky calls defamiliarization, or estrangement, which "is found almost everywhere form is found" (1965: 18).[14]

---

[14] See also R. H. Stacy, 1977. More specifically, Don Kuiken and David Miall have examined the relevance of Shklovsky's principle of defamiliarization and Mukarovsky's concept of foregrounding to dream expressiveness. They suggest that dreams, like literary texts, "foreground" certain events, thus producing feelings of "surprise and attention" in the dreamer. Such "striking moments" may also "involve

Among other things, it is the way form captures the attention of the auditor. In the world of advertising, for example, the bizarre has become a kind of genre expectation. Thus, a recent TV commercial features a sports car "hanging" on the wall of an art gallery. A young man walks up to it, opens the door, and in defiance of gravity gets in and drives away. An elderly woman comes by, sees the tracks on the wall, and is astonished.

Here the impossible has become probable, reminding us of what Freud said about the uncanny: "In the realm of fiction many things are not uncanny which would be so if they happened in real life" (1973 [1919]: 250); fiction retains the quality of the uncanny "so long as the setting is one of physical reality; but as soon as it is given an arbitrary and unrealistic setting . . , it is apt to lose its quality of the uncanny " (p. 160). To the man in the car, a citizen of the "dreamworld" of the superior product (where technology "makes things happen!"), the event is perfectly natural; to the unbelieving woman it is a bizarre event taking place in her very real reality (where such things don't happen); to the TV viewer the bizarreness virtually disappears or is reduced to an amused curiosity about technical execution (How did they do that?). We accept improbabilities, in short, under the conditions of the imitation. Bizarreness is all about us, the means, as Shklovsky puts it, by which we remove objects and information "from the automatism of perception" (1965: 13). Yet it goes without saying that no one would be moved to tabulate or quantify these products of waking human imagination as we do the images of our dreamworld. They simply speak for themselves as strategies of communication. Not bizarre for bizarre's sake, but bizarre as thematized metaphor: bizarre as consumer incentive.

As we all know, most dream narratives are mundane, rather like life: Paul and I are playing tennis; Paul wins or I win, or the dream, having something else up its sleeve, takes us both to lunch. But now and then a dream becomes extraordinary: Paul and I are play-

---

temporary suspension of movement" (muscular inhibition, "weakness or inability to move") and "narrative discontinuity" in the dream itself (1991: 7–8).

ing tennis and we are interrupted by the dancing bears I saw on the TV two nights ago. In the perfect vacuum of the dream's metaphor chamber there is nothing to keep dancing bears and dancing tennis players apart once the association has occurred. As we say, bizarre. But would it be bizarre if during a real tennis game, being played on a real court at mid-morning, Paul should suddenly do something bearlike that reminded me for an instant of the same dancing bears? Obviously not. Unless of course real dancing bears should thereupon suddenly appear on the court, or Paul should turn into a dancing bear. Now that would be bizarre, cause for a radical *hesitation*, something happening in one *Umwelt* according to the natural laws of another—which is simply to say, a dream come true.

❦

2

Beginnings, Middles, and Endings

So far I have tried to show that dream images are no more bizarre or distorted than poetic images if you consider them in their proper perceptual environment. If, as philosophers have argued, we can know the world only as a construction of our consciousness, who is to say that the world constructed during dream consciousness is more irregular than our constructions of the so-called real world which are specific to the needs of locomotion, survival, pleasure, and all other waking activities? Dreams, we might assume, offer something like a complementary definition of the world, one (among other things) that rescues the "real" world from certain limitations of linear and spatial probability. One of the increasingly more prevalent assumptions underlying this idea is that dreams, in some way, play a role in the imprinting and storage of experience. I suspect this is such an attractive proposition because it explains dream "distortion" as a form of classification whose logic is simply too reliant on personal experience to be understood. For example, from one standpoint the dictionary, as an efficient instrument of classification, could be said to use distortion when it puts words next to each other according to the logic of alphabetization. Thus close neighbors like *garb* and *garbage* or *badge* and *badger* form bizarre teams that otherwise have nothing to do with each other.

46

I consider the question of bizarreness a central one because it carries a tacit dialectical assumption that dreams *could* have been more direct, open, or realistic in representing the dreamer's experience and that they *would* have been so were it not for some underlying factor, either psychic or physiological in nature. And this idea is reenforced by the habit dreams have of representing their scenes and characters realistically most of the time and falling into noticeable bizarreness only occasionally, like a TV set when the picture gets scrambled. All the more reason, then, to think of realism as the norm and bizarreness the exception. There is (or used to be) an analogous situation in aesthetics whereby we unconsciously evaluated a style in terms of its departure from a more or less strict realism. It is not that we preferred realism, or even knew exactly what that was, but that it was the style that was maximally mimetic of the world as it currently appeared to the perceiving eye. Realism is the starting point of all representational measurement, something like the zero in the world of numbers.[1] Thus, naively regarded, nonrealistic works (abstraction, impressionism, surrealism) come to possess a quality of mediation and authorship, as if something had been *done* to reality. In the same vein, distortion in dreams implies a tampering with the image; this might imply, in the case of the new dream science, a randomness brought on by purely physiological "motives" that have little to do with, or perhaps interfere with, a function of representation. Or, in the psychoanalytic tradition, distortion might imply evidence of censorship and disguise.

But on the same evidence one might erect a very different theory: for example, one can think of cubism as a departure from realism, or one can take it as a realistic way of looking simultaneously at the same object from several different perspectives. In short, form follows function. And similarly, we might assume that the principle applies to the dream as well: distortion is the only means by which the dreaming brain makes sense of things—or, more specifically,

---

[1] E. H. Gombrich engagingly takes up this issue in the Introduction to *Art and Illusion* (1965), pp. 1–30. Richard A. Bonato et al. suggest that the term *bizarreness* be replaced with *impossible/improbable*, which more accurately "denotes reality, the universal measuring-stick" (1991: 60).

the means by which it deals with properties of things belonging to different categories; to come back to my earlier analogy, imagine a dictionary whose words were ordered according to attributes of meaning, like a thesaurus. As Paul Armstrong has put it, "We can understand the unfamiliar only by grafting it onto the familiar" (1990: 28), which is one definition of the grotesque. We need not posit the notion that this is the purpose of dreams, simply that correlation of diverse psychic materials figures in the dreamwork, and whatever the function of dreaming may turn out to be it must bear centrally on this principle of image composition. There is no reason, then, to assume that the dream would not have the same visual and combinatorial character whether it was censored or not. The point can be easily illustrated by turning to Freud's dream of the botanical monograph, which I choose only because it has the advantage of being brief: "*I had written a monograph on a certain plant. The book lay before me and I was at the moment turning over a folded coloured plate. Bound up in each copy there was a dried specimen of the plant, as though it had been taken from a herbarium*" (1973 [1900]: 169). it is impossible here, without extensive quotation, to summarize clearly the things in Freud's personal experience that lie behind this image; but by my count there are at least fifteen major determinants of this dream. Whether all them did, in fact, figure in the dream we cannot know, but it would be difficult to find a better example of how a single point of thought might arise from such a dense archae- ological base. Moreover, this veritable "factory of thoughts" touches on even more remote memories belonging to an "infinite combination" of such associations (1973 [1900]: 317), and they pro- duce the single image of the monograph which, we can assume was simply the most attractive nodal point for a visual intersection of all the dream thoughts.

Yet one must ask, what is being repressed here but everything that could not be got in? How could any dream image, censored or not, possibly have contained even a fraction of all these referents, not to mention the emotions that attended them? Censored or un- censored, wouldn't the dream be forced to condense such a plenum of psychic energy into a compromise image or image series, leaving much unsaid or, as Lacan would put it, "below the bar"? The dream was not really *about* a repressed content; it was about a group of complex emotional vectors that require a representative image to stand in for the group. Indeed, evidence of censorship can be determined only by what arises in the analysis itself, and Freud is at no loss to see how the dream becomes, as Meredith Skura has put it, "a quietly symbolic image of [his] lifelong conflict" (1980: 362).[2] But this does not constitute evidence that it is the dream that has done the repressing. So we are back with the point that there is no internal way to tell a censored dream from a noncensored one.[3] Why assume, then, that the dream has censored anything? It has simply done what dreams do or, for that matter, what artists do when they concentrate a great deal of energy on a single symbolic point of focus.[4]

Without "distortion," then, which literary people refer to as metaphor and brain scientists as feature detection, the brain would have no way of recombining the things of the world for various purposes

[2] Skura finds opposing meanings in the dream which pertain to Freud's work, leading him away from "flowers" and life and love and also preserving "flowers" (dreams) in his great book ("he pulls them apart to treasure them"). She concludes: "The dream's indirections do not always disguise but sometimes express something otherwise inexpressible. The dream is not about a single wish (which it has failed to represent), but about a whole network of associations, thoughts, and images related to each other and represented in the dream in the strangest, most diverse ways" (pp. 362–63).

[3] Freud might respond to this by saying that the presence of overdetermined elements in the dream—that is, elements that are represented in the dream thoughts many times over (1973 [1900], 4:284)—would constitute internal evidence of censorship; but that would in turn raise the further question of what the function of overdetermination was and whether it might not occur in an uncensored dream as well.

[4] My intention here is not to suggest that Freud's concept of censorship is naive or one-sided. Skura, who makes somewhat the same point about the mechanism as I am making, suggests that Freud himself treats censorship with ambivalence and even "waffles at times and wonders whether some of the dream's distortions are not attributable to other constraints on representation besides censorship and independent of its operations" (1980: 354–55). Freud, she goes on, "looked for the reproduction of a single, explanatory wish—and saw only censorship if he failed to find that wish. We, however, can see that the dream's indirections do not always disguise but sometimes express something otherwise inexpressible" (p. 363). I return to Skura's treatment of censorship in Chapter 5.

of invention and imaginative retrieval. I think, therefore I distort; or, I think, therefore I make metaphors. In any event, I am unable to find anything in Freud's own dream interpretations, or anybody else's, that necessitates the intervention of a censor. The same interpretation could have been arrived at without the presumption that the dream is a rebus or a disguise. Indeed, what made Freud such a brilliant dream analyst was his poetic ability to classify the dream images of his patients into patterns of meaning by means of the same technique the dream used to produce them—metaphorical association or feature detection. On the part of the patient, this technique was called censorship; on Freud's part it was called diagnostic science.

This argument against censorship in dreams should be qualified further. I am not implying that there is no such operation as censorship in the brain. As Marvin Minsky points out in *The Society of Mind,* much of our thought process involves one form of censorship or another: "The surer you are that you like what you are doing," he says, "the more completely your other ambitions are being suppressed" (1988: 94). The censor, or "negative recognizer" (p. 276), is an early deflector mechanism based on the individual's history of certain states of mind or actions leading to undesirable ends. Accordingly, the censor, recognizing the signals that might emanate in such a consequence, intercedes before it occurs; but instead of *"blocking* the course of thought, the censor can merely *deflect* it into an acceptable direction" (p. 276). This is very close to the Freudian notion, as Minsky himself notes. Why then might not such a device of thought be operating in dreams?

I am not sure we can ever say that it isn't, especially in cases of serious mental instability. In any event, my problem is not with the principle of censorship as an activity of mind. My belief is simply that censorship does not operate normally in dreams in the manner Freud and much psychoanalysis insists. This belief rests on several considerations. First, as I suggested above, there is no way to prove that censorship has been involved, since the selected image carries no trace of deflection: you can never prove that an image wasn't the one the dream wanted for its own expressivity in the first place.

Even if you can find, through analysis, what seems to be a more volatile determinant behind an image, there is no guarantee that the image selected isn't the best equivalent, or compromise, for a set of thoughts (perhaps even contradictory thoughts) that go endlessly back in the dreamer's history. Second, in Freud's theory censorship is virtually identical with distortion: "The fact that the phenomenon of censorship and of dream-distortion correspond down to their smallest details justifies us in presuming that they are similarly determined" (1973 [1900] 4:143). As I have argued here, distortion is the basic condition of dreaming without which the dream would be radically limited in its powers of association; therefore, to prove that an image is censored *because* distorted is tantamount to saying that censorship is identical with dreaming itself. And Freud would agree, since in his view nothing "can reach consciousness from the first system [the construction of the wish] without passing the second [the censor] . . . [which] allows nothing to pass without exercising its rights and making such modifications as it thinks fit in the thought which is seeking admission to consciousness" (4:144). Among many other things, however, this does not explain why so many volatile images get past the censor (assuming there is one) in dreams. The disturbing content of dreams, as reported the world over, would scarcely make a case for the intervention of a censor. Indeed, as the recent reinterpretation of Freud's own dreams has repeatedly shown, Freud's analysis of his dreams appears to be the source of any censorship rather than the dreams themselves—which is to say that Freud's dream reports (the botanical monograph, the Irma dream, and others) contain elements of Freud's life that the waking Freud apparently suppressed, or was unable to see or preferred not to publish, but which are visible to others who can read the dreams more objectively. In any case, the analyses are based on the assumption not of censorship but of similarity between the dream image and other elements of Freud's psychic history. Along this line, George Mandler has suggested that "the accessibility of . . . 'repressed' structures [may be] changed during dreams" since sleep itself cancels the possibility of "feared action. Thus it is possible that repression only operates when the

action becomes potentially possible. . . . In dreams, such 'emergence' [of repressed thoughts] may be possible because no action is
possible and real-world conflict can be avoided" (1975: 215). I am
not in a position to advocate this theory. I bring it up only to
suggest that there are many ways of looking at the problem. Finally, like many others working with dreams today, I have precisely
Piaget's difficulties with the concept of censorship: "[Freud's] idea
of censorship, linked with his conception of passive consciousness,
is obscure. Consciousness censors, we are told, when it wishes to
remain unaware of a repression. But how can consciousness be the
cause of ignorance, *i.e.,* of unconsciousness? Such a state of affairs
is only comprehensible if consciousness is compared to a
searchlight, lighting up certain points and avoiding others at the
will of its manipulator. . . . It is, of course, true that consciousness
frequently wishes to remain unaware of what it dislikes, but there is
no question of it being duped" (1951:191).

One more comment: once we make such a sweeping assumption
that the dream is a censorship mechanism, what is to prevent our
saying that all image making, in and out of art, is based on the
same principle? Personally, I find this idea acceptable—indeed unavoidable—if we are referring to Minsky's conception of censorship: any choice involves the suppression of other choices. The
rightness of a metaphor, for both the metaphor maker and the
auditor, depends as much on the cancellation of certain features of
the comparison as on the admittance of others (see Cohen, 1986). Is
it not, after all, a "negative recognizer" that tells us to suppress
green, oblong, and *spiny* when someone says "She is cool as a cucum-
ber"? Even Michelangelo was, in a manner of speaking, censoring
certain parts of the marble in order to release the statue within.
Without censorship we would be putting our fingers into light
sockets long beyond childhood. But of course this is not at all what
Freud had in mind.

I move now from the problem of distortion to the relationship
between fictional and dream narratives. This is an immense subject
that leads us into all the dimensions of dreaming and storytelling.
Before we examine possible similarities and differences between

dreams and literary texts, however, I should say a word or so about the similarities between dreaming and reading. A literary text in itself is nothing but words committed to paper in a certain arrangement; it may be used to provoke an experience in a reader, it may become the food supply for library worms, and it may be used to fuel a fire or stop a door. In any case, we read these words one by one and the text is constituted as an experience only by the interplay of text and reader. This interplay, Paul Ricoeur says, allows us "to speak of the work of reading in the same way we speak of the dream-work." What he means by this, I assume (he says nothing further on the subject), is simply that reading and dreaming involve the "play of retentions and protentions" that creates the expectations of a reader (or a dreamer). Dreaming is like reading in that it "consists in traveling the length of the [dream/text], in allowing all the modifications performed to 'sink' into memory, while compacting them, and in opening ourselves up to new expectations entailing new modifications" (1988, 3: 168). What in the dream, then, is comparable to the text? Certainly not the dream report, which is a text of sorts, but it is more like a second-hand summary of a fiction one hasn't read. In the dialectic of reading there is, as Ricoeur says, an implied author who is "a disguise of the real author, who disappears by making himself the narrator immanent in the work—the narrative voice," and an implied reader, "the receiver to whom the sender of the work addresses himself . . . [who] remains virtual as long as this role has not been actualized" (p. 3: 170). It appears that in a dream the implied author function and the implied reader function of the fictional text are, so to speak, conflated in the consciousness of the real dreamer. The dreamer is both author and reader. He tells the story to himself, in a manner of speaking, like the identical reader and listener in Samuel Beckett's dream play *Ohio Impromptu* who "grew to be as one."

Let us look more carefully, however, at certain differences between dreams and fictions with respect to authoring and experiencing. Let us compare fictions and dreams as perceptual experiences. But on what basis? What would be the best unit of comparison? Should we compare the perceptual experience of the author of fiction to that of the dreamer, on the ground that the dreamer too is an author? This might be interesting except that the dreamer, unlike a waking author, has no perceptual experience of the act of authoring. Therefore, a better basis would be the parallel between reader and dreamer, since both experience the contents of an imagined world. This is not a perfect fit either because the dreamer is (usually) the protagonist of the dream in a way that the reader is not the protagonist of a fiction. But at least the reader is, as Poulet says, surrounded by "fictitious beings" (1981: 43) who in a sense cease to be fictitious and constitute a virtual real world; moreover, in Poulet's terms it is equally valid to say that the protagonist is inside the reader's head and that the reader is inside the protagonist's. Let us refine the perspective further, however, and take as our object of study the perception of characters, since characters are (in one respect) common to both dreams and fictions and seem to be the best carriers of the salient features of both.

I begin with the perception of characters in fiction. Without attempting to say all that might be said on the subject, I suggest that we perceive fictional characters on at least four levels, though these obviously form a unified impression. For convenience, I call them the personal, the dialogic, the thematic, and the stylistic. On the personal level, the character is seen as a single person (Hamlet, Ophelia, Brutus, Cassius) or an individual (I, he, she) consisting of a bundle of traits that form a disposition distinct from that of any other character in (or outside) the fiction. Brutus is Brutus and Cassius is Cassius. On the dialogic level, characters may be said to create each other. In a dialogue speaker and listener merge and are dependent on each other for life and identity; when Cassius and Brutus argue over what to do about Caesar, they coresponsively create each other's characters before our eyes through the dialogical principle of stimulus and response, one provoking the display of emotions, traits, and attitudes of the other. At this level, in other words, character has begun to distribute itself beyond the personal phase of the discrete human entity, and we begin to see that character is a reactionary formation, not a self-starting autonomous entity. Brutus is now Cassius—and Caesar and Portia and Marc Antony as well—or at least Brutus owes his liveliness to these people. On the thematic level, characters begin to manifest a super-psychological cast in that their individual subjective positions, or interpositions, are perceived as part of a larger harmony. For one thing, Brutus and Cassius, unlike us, always talk on the same sub-ject that other characters talk about when they aren't around (Rome, Caesar, conspiracy, assassination), and it never occurs to them that there are other topics in the world, like love, revenge, or ambition, such as obsess Romeo, Hamlet, and Macbeth, who don't care in the least what happened in Rome. Finally, at the stylistic level, as Eliot said of Shakespeare, character and author "speak in unison." If characters are each different in their own way, there is the imprint of another individuality in them—that of their author, who endows all their speech and actions with the characteristics of an single individual style. And style, as Mikel Dufrenne has put it, is "the locus in which the artist appears" (1973: 105). At this level of perception we may say that Hamlet is Brutus, Romeo, Cassius, Macbeth, and all were fathered by the same creator.

I have greatly simplified this spectrum in order to suit it more comparatively to a discussion of dreams.[5] In the dream, obviously, something happens to this nested relationship of perceptual planes. Perhaps the main thing is that, whereas the characters of the dream (and its world) are created by the dreamer, the dreamer is now inside the world as a participant and the activity of creation, of imagining the world, no longer takes place from a superior stand-point. Indeed, from a purely phenomenal perspective, creativity does not take place at all; it is reality that unfolds before the dream-er's eyes. For the dreamer, for instance, there is no consciousness of theme any more than Brutus and Cassius are conscious of being bound by the theme of conspiracy or by an awareness that they are creatures in a play by William Shakespeare. As a consequence, any anticipations the dreamer may have about how things will turn out have only to do with personal expectations and nothing to do with

---

[5] I discuss this and other aspects of character more completely in *"Hamlet" and the Concept of Character* (Baltimore: Johns Hopkins University Press, 1992).

aesthetic pleasure. Moreover, the dreamer does not perceive other characters in the dream in any such perceptual depth—or even a gestalt of this depth—as I have outlined for the reader: characters are simply others in the same world and it is a world without theme or style.

Still, there are echoes of something akin to an authorial function in the dream, though it can be perceived only in retrospect (apart from cases of lucid dreaming). Just as Brutus is, in part, made of Cassius—caused by Cassius—so the people conjured in the dream have what we may call fluid identities. They do not appear to the dreamer as composites, but they are subject to revision, or change (facial structure, gender). To put it another way, if *Julius Caesar* were a dream dreamed by Brutus, Cassius might well become Casca or Trebonius or Cinna on the ground that all are conspirators and thus to a degree interchangeable as actional functions. Moreover, though the dreamer is not aware of a thematic dimension in the dream, there is one there in the sense that all elements of the dream cooperate in sticking to the subject (my endangerment, my defeat of the villain, my unsuccessful love affair). Here we arrive at a level at which the function we call authoring in the waking world asserts itself as a subtle condition of existence in the dreamworld. It is not that I, as dreamer, can change things as I want them, making enemies kindly toward me when I am in danger. Precisely like tragedies, comedies, and romances, dreams follow certain genre expectations (a topic I take up in the following chapter). We know at the beginning of *Hamlet* that only tragic things will happen, just as we know that causality will be more benevolent in a comedy and somehow bring the lovers together. Dreams too seem perfectly capable of maintaining an emotional consistency. If it is my wish, as author/protagonist of my dream, that strangers behave kindly toward me, the dream must be motivated, in advance, by a theme of kindliness, which is to say that the emotional tenor of the dream must be one conducive to kindliness rather than fear. For example, in a recent dream in which I was visiting a family of brothers in Greece (complete strangers to me) with a friend (also a complete stranger), I thought, "These are nice people," and I began to work alongside them as if I were a member of their family. And I thought to myself, "They approve of me," and the expression on the face of the eldest brother, the leader, immediately indicated this approval. As unknowing author, I had willed the approving expression on his face, or at least his behavior toward me coincided with my hope. In the dream, it did not surprise me at all that the world was so obedient to my desire; for what is canceled out in the single-mindedness of the dream is exactly one's consciousness of being an originating creative force. If, in contrast, I carry a theme of apprehension and endangerment into a dream, the dream obliges by providing such events as bear out that theme. Thus the authorial act of the waking writer alternately putting herself into the minds of her characters, virtually thinking their thoughts and undergoing their fate, is repeated in the dream, in the cooperation between the author/dreamer and the dreamed characters. One cannot even claim that the dreamer knows more than the characters do, since in the end all are aspects of the same creative energy. This is what we might call dispersed authorship: there is a psychic bond between dreamer and dreamed character (and dreamworld at large) through which the dreamer unconsciously instructs the characters to do or to think certain things (even terrorizing the dreamer) in keeping with the emotion underlying the dream, and they oblige, having in a sense no mind of their own. This is, as we say in literary studies, the only evidence of authorship in the dreamworld: a qualitative compatibility in all images or, if you will, a commanding emotional key, as in a musical composition, that controls possibilities of development and harmony. This has nothing to do with conscious intelligent planning on the part of the dreamer; it occurs more like a sequence of sympathetic vibrations.

Given these different conditions of composition, then, along what line of logic would the dream obey the narrative standards for fiction Ricoeur sets forth elsewhere in *Time and Narrative*? Since the dreamer is telling the story to himself, the telling is exempt from all the criteria of waking fictions that arise from the division between teller and hearer. This is not to say that the dream obeys none of the criteria we expect in fiction (for instance, it is well known that dreams foreshorten and expand their stories along the lines of waking narratives[6]), only that it disregards those that pertain strictly to the demands of communicability, the salient (however obvious) point of distinction between dream and fiction.

Perhaps the most fundamental consequence of this distinction is that dreams do not have beginnings and endings but seem rather to be all middle with occasional crises. It is reasonable to think of dreams as having beginnings and endings for locational purposes, and it is likely that they do begin and end at some subsensory level of thought (otherwise, how could they come into existence?); but as far as our awareness goes, we join them "in progress" and leave them (so to speak) when we "fall asleep" within them or when they wake us up. We might erect a whole contrast of dreams and fiction on just this fulcrum. In poetics, we define a beginning of a plot—and here, for convenience, I am following O. B. Hardison's commentary on Aristotle's *Poetics*—as "the incident that initiates the process of change" and the ending as "the completion of the action represented" (Aristotle, 1981: 140–41). The beginning has no antecedents, the ending no consequences, and the middle, as Aristotle says, is "that which is itself after something else and which has something else after it" (p. 14). This is the basic respect in which fictional plots differ from life histories, in which "every incident

---

[6] For example, consider how dreams skip over "boring" parts of their narrative. If I am entering a building in a dream, the dream automatically foreshortens my trip to a dream office on the fifth floor, just as a movie does. Moreover, when a critical event takes place—say, a confrontation between me and the manager of the office—the dream develops it in a much more sustained manner. Obviously, dreams aren't always as obliging as good fictions in these regards, but they do show a high level of competence in getting from point to point, and we should not take this for granted simply because fictions have taught us to expect such abbreviations. Rather, one might assume that there is something like a density gauge in the dreaming brain that allows action (or attention to detail) to move at the speed of the atmospheric (emotional) pressure offered by the dreamworld. A reasonable explanation for this faculty—understood equally well by fiction writers—is that waking experience teaches us from infancy to be more attentive to certain zones of reality than others. For example, we would expend less interest on flat uninterrupted countryside than on an interesting tree or rock formation that might come into view. So it is with dream sights, events, and conversation (which are remarkably condensed into emotional highpoints).

leads on to something else—to a new action" (p. 140), or, as Tom
Stoppard's character puts it, "every exit here is an entrance someplace else"; and it is also the line we may draw between fictions and
dreams. So right off, on at least this basis, we can align life experience and dreams against all narratives, insofar as narratives have
beginnings and endings separated by middles. One can better appreciate the significance of this difference by trying to imagine what
the beginning of a dream might be like if it were abiding by Aristotelian logic. How would it be possible for the dreamer *to appear*
on the scene, like a protagonist, or to wait within a blank holo-
graphic screen, like a cinema audience, for the dream to begin?
Much less how could the dreamer say something like Viola, in
Shakespeare's *Twelfth Night,* "What country, friends, is this?" and
another dream character respond, "This is Illyria, lady"? How
would it be possible for the dream to bootstrap its own "Once upon
a time," the "incident that initiates the process of change," without
the forethought of an author who—or which—has already authored the dream or at least knows in advance what is to be
changed?[7] For all plots, as Frank Kermode has put it, "have something in common with prophecy, for they must appear to educe
from *the prime matter* of the situation *the forms of a future*" (1970: 83,
emphasis added). In sum: no future, no beginning.

Of course, one might cite Jean-Luc Godard's remark, "All my
films have a beginning, a middle, and an end . . . but not necessarily in that order," as proof that certain kinds of narratives are like
dreams in not abiding by Aristotelian principles.[8] An even more
thorough illustration would be Harold Pinter's play *Betrayal,* which
traces an adultery from its conclusion to its beginning, causing one
of my colleagues (at the intermission of a performance) to say, "I
can hardly wait to see how it begins." Such examples of modern
freedom do not, however, really violate Aristotelian rules (at least
as I think Aristotle himself would interpret them were he con-

[7] Hence the cassette theory of dreams, which holds that "all dream narratives are
composed directly into memory banks" and are thus recorded for later use (see
Dennett, 1976: 237).
[8] Godard's remark was brought to my attention by John C. Marshall (1983: 604).

fronted by such works). From the functional point of view, beginnings and endings have little to do with story chronology (indeed,
many fictions and films are all flashback). The true beginning of a
narrative is not the first event in a chronological series but the event
that offers the most appropriate way into the story to be told or the
event required for maximal comprehensibility. It is one of the characteristics of narrative that it can begin anywhere in a series of
events and go virtually anywhere as long as it continues to arouse
the "protentions and retentions" that constitute our interest and
comprehension. Thus, the only relevant ending of *Betrayal* would
be the beginning of the relationship it chronicles in reverse, somewhat as *Oedipus Rex* begins at the "ending" of a long series of
events and uncovers the true beginning. *Betrayal* is devoted, then,
to what we might call the teleology of origins by offering a literal
enactment of how things come about. "By reading the end into the
beginning and the beginning into the end," Ricoeur says, "we learn
to read time backward, as the recapitulation of the initial conditions
of a course of action in its terminal consequences" (1980: 183). In
short, the concept of a narrative whole and its subsidiary parts—
beginning, middle, and end—is probably infinitely adjustable in
terms of affective structuration. But all stories, insofar as they are
wholes, either have beginnings, middles, and endings—in that
order—or they raise problems in comprehensibility.

But dreams heed a different kind of poetics. Because dreams
collapse the compositional and the affective stages into one—as it
were, creating and devouring the "text" simultaneously—it is hard
to say what may be poetically going on in a dream outside of the
affective sphere. For instance, is anything going on *under* the
dream? Or is the dream itself all there is of thinking? This is one of
the reasons the homunculus image is so hard to keep out of dream
study, even creeping into arguments maintaining there is no such
thing. It is difficult to see how a dream could occur without a
thought process that is, to some degree, prior to and independent of
the thinking that is represented by the dream itself, or by the thinking the dreamer consciously carries on within the dream in reaction
to the events created by the dream thought. As Blanchot asks:

"Who dreams in dreams? Who is the 'I' of dreams? Who is the person to whom this 'I' is attributed, admitting that there is one?" (Leiris, 1987: xxi). And the complementary question: who, or what, is dreaming up the dream that this "I" is simply dreaming? But then one might ask the same questions of the waking poet, since it is clear that when the poet says "Ha! I have it!" and writes down a brilliant figure, something—a poet inside the poet—has *provided* the figure. It did not simply occur in the way that one might decide that it is time to water the tomato plants. Or did it?

Thus we awaken within the dream, as opposed to entering it as one enters the world of a book. In this sense, one might say that dreams do have beginnings (or onsets) and endings (or stopping points), but they are not of the same deliberate species as beginnings and endings in waking fictions, which, as Kermode says, have something in common with prophesy in knowing how one is inevitably produced by the other. Indeed, one can only call dreams fictions ex post facto by virtue of their being (now) seen as *having been* imaginary constructions of the mind, and that gets us back to the problem of what is real. (The very thematics and meaning of fiction rest on this principle of "prophesy.") Beyond this, dreams have no artifactuality; they are probably best approached as a state of being, albeit, as Harry Hunt says, one that "frames itself for inspection in a way that waking consciousness does not" (1986: 222). Still, apart from such factors as the ubiquitous bizarreness of dreams, events in dreams occur like events in life: dreams imitate— or should we say carry on—the process of living within the living process itself, much as ontogeny is said to recapitulate phylogeny. The dream offers "a second life," in Nerval's phrase, into which the dreamer, like Dasein, is "thrown." Properly speaking, the dreamer does not even awaken in the dream but was simply always already there. And since there is no consciousness of origin, there is no expectation of conclusion, at least in the fictional sense of denoue- ment, since conclusions, as we have seen, become such only by virtue of having sprung from known beginnings that contain them in embryo. One might casually speak of an evening as beginning and ending, or of a chapter of one's life closing, but these are metaphorical conveniences for demarcating time. True beginnings and endings, as Ricoeur has put it, "are not features of some real action but the effects of the ordering of the poem" (1984, I:39).

Hunt's dream of the Tibetan museum (see Chapter 1) is as good a vehicle as any to illustrate this idea. It is obviously of the dramatic type inasmuch as the manikin scene, as Hunt says, "dramatically fulfills the dream and confirms its semantic significance, casting back on and reorganizing the dream's initial events. . . . Ostensible narrative discontinuity or bizarreness thus actually served to weld this dream together as a single dramatic whole. . . . Without it the dream would have been more action sequence than story" (1989: 167). Here the concept of whole (hence, implicitly, beginning and ending) is invoked by Hunt metaphorically. From the poetic stand- point, Hunt's dream is a fragment rather than a whole. It lacks what Aristotle calls magnitude, that prophetic principle that shapes the fiction according to the expectations of its readers. The incidents of the dream are certainly arranged in a mounting and comprehensive order and may be said to have a certain closure; but there aren't enough of them to satisfy a reader who may be reading it as a story as opposed to experiencing it in a dream. And what is lacking is precisely a beginning and an ending—or, to put it another way, the beginning and ending are buried in the mnemonic museum of Hunt's brain, unformulated in semantic terms and unnecessary for oneiric purposes. A version for readers would require an exposition (Who is Hunt? Why is it so urgent that he get to the museum? What does he expect to find there and what is its relevance to the present tension in his life?) and a denouement (What is the import of the boiling manikin? How does it resolve the tension in Hunt's life?). Fiction, then, is framed by altogether different expectations: not simply by the frame of "the real world," to which one returns at "The End," but by an Aristotelian understanding that what one is reading (or in the case of cinema, seeing and hearing) has already occurred—or, as Peter Brooks puts it, that what is occurring actu- ally composes a past "in relation to a future we know to be already in place, already in wait for us to reach it" (1985: 23). Beside the dream a fictional imitation can only be a virtual experience, in Susanne Langer's term, though the paradox here is that fiction can carry a powerful aesthetic charge (whereas the dream normally doesn't) only because it is ontologically weak—which is to say that fiction is not dominated, as the dream is, by the consideration that what is happening is actually happening. Fiction may imitate life but it can only weakly imitate living; it cannot be a form of being in the sense that it confines the reader to the *Umwelt* of the fiction. The simple fact that I will probably answer the telephone, should it ring while I am reading, separates the dream from fiction ontologically and structurally. In a dream, I am more likely to absorb the ringing into the dream in the form of a sound event belonging to it, as in the famous case of Maury's falling bedpost.

Thus dreams are immune to all expository and developmental necessities of waking fiction. This doesn't mean that the dream is aimless or random, or that it doesn't move toward something. But, as in life, the something it moves toward may or may not transpire, and if it does it can be said to be conclusive only in the sense that an incident in life is concluded, as in a divorce, a dinner, or a course in music appreciation. Indeed, this beginninglessness and endlessness of the dream is pervasively carried into the structural character of the middle (the dream proper) in the form of a peculiar openness in the dream's developmental logic. And we must try to see how, or if, this openness is any different from the openness that obtains, for example, when in the waking world I decide to go for a walk and then change my mind and have a nap instead.

A convenient point of departure is offered by Jonathan Culler's notion that "every narrative operates according to a double logic, presenting its plot as a sequence of events which is prior to and independent of the given perspective on these events, and, at the same time, suggesting by its implicit claims to significance that these events are justified by their appropriateness to a thematic structure." These two logics, Culler argues, "are in contradiction but they are essential to the way in which the narrative functions" (1981: 178).[9] It is easy to see how fictional narratives embody such

---

[9] There are other terms for these logics: for example, Paul Ricoeur's causal explanation vs. teleological explanation (1984: 132–43); the Russian Formalists' *fabula/sjuzet;* Roland Barthes's proairetic vs. hermeneutic codes (1974: 203–4, 209–10). The latter two are discussed, along with Culler's terms, by Peter Brooks (1985: 3–36).

double logic: the events appear to have happened of their own deterministic accord (Prince Andrey dies of a wound in battle); yet every event has been thematically conceived toward an ending that is already set (Natasha must be left free to marry Pierre, who is to be the chief carrier of most of Tolstoy's ideas). Understandably, since Freud we have always viewed dreams as a product of these two logics: at least, we see the events of dream structure, as they unfold for the first and only time within the sleep of the dreamer, as being controlled by an underlying thematic principle, planned—or anyway supervised—at some level by the dream and available to diligent interpretation. But it is not really clear that dreams do this sort of thing, or how they do it if they do. Could dreams be dominated by a logic of sequence with only a negligible thematic input? Or, to put it another way, could this thematic input possibly have a different character from the one we have given it from literary interpretation and psychoanalysis? Finally, how could one tell if a dream was *not* thematically organized? For instance, take this dream of a young man from the collection of Calvin Hall:

> I remember being at a train ticket window. I guess I was buying a ticket. A girl at the ticket window kissed me in a way that seemed to give promise of better things when I returned from wherever I was going. I got on the train and it looked like the inside of a boxcar. I knew I was on the wrong train and I believe I tried to get somebody to pull the cord of the air brake. (1966: 164)

What can one say about the logic of this sequence of dream events? Here we see just how indispensable the associations of the dreamer are to any possible interpretation. How could one possibly know that, in this particular dreamer's case, "getting on the wrong train [was] the emblem of misconduct and putting on the brakes [was] the symbol of moral pressure" (p. 164), unless, like Hall, we had studied several of the young man's dreams and were privy to his thoughts about them, his self-estimation, and so forth? In fact, how could one tell whether this was a dream report or an excerpt from a letter the young man had written to a friend about his attempt to

board a train after a drinking party? Surely if the latter were the case
the incident could not be said to have a theme or to contain meaning, except perhaps in the sense that one of the themes of the young
man's life was, through "misconduct" of this sort, to find himself
repeatedly in situations like this one. In other words, on this occasion, as always, he was behaving like himself and reality obliged
him by behaving like reality. In this sense, even reality is thematic
in being characteristic of what reality is and does. If this is theme,
everything in the world is full of it.

But let us take the passage as a bona fide dream report. If Hall is
right in saying that the dream was based on "conflicting conceptions of impulse and conscience" (p. 163), hasn't the dream been
thematically structured to represent this dilemma? This is possible.
The point is that one cannot derive it from the dream alone any
more than one could by treating the text as the fragment of a letter
pertaining to a post-party experience. This introduces the possibility that in giving a dream an interpretation one may inadvertently become involved in a hermeneutic circle whereby one finds
that the dream supports a certain semantic sense and can then claim
that this sense explains and is the cause of the dream's structure. A
deconstructionist may well insist that such interpretations are based
on a paradox of origin. Again, Culler: "If the effect is what causes
the cause to become a cause, then the effect, not the cause, should
be treated as the origin. . . . If either cause or effect can occupy the
position of origin, then origin is no longer originary; it loses its
metaphysical privilege" (1985: 88). This opens the question of
whether dreams are any more thematically organized than life itself
(a question I deal with more thoroughly in subsequent chapters). In
short, dreams—or at least some dreams—might unfold according
to a strictly *"proairetic"* sequence of actions, in Roland Barthes's
term—that is, according to the logic of events as opposed to a logic
of hermeneutics. Or, put in the terms used by Wilensky, an "action
sequence" is confused with a "story," the former being a simple or
complex causal sequence without "a point to it," the latter implying
a thematically controlled sequence (1983: 583).

I am not trying here to do away with theme or meaning or

structure in dreams but only to see how these things can occur without the notion of a dream author, or agency—an unconscious, or even, in Hunt's term, "an imaginative narrative intelligence" (1989: 103)—that does not appear in the dream, is separate from the dreamer, yet like a poet has the capacity to guide it along an appropriate path of development and conclusion. For example, let us come back to Hunt's Tibetan museum dream and ask a simple question: did the dream know in advance that the old woman would show up later as the final event of the dream? To answer this question affirmatively one must posit something like an author/homunculus who has, among other things, the *restraint* to delay an image's appearance for artistic purposes or in order to surprise or in some way affect the dreamer. Here we directly confront the conditions that obtain in the waking author-reader relationship, not to mention the two-mind system. Moreover, there is every reason to assume that if the dreamwork knows the destination of the dream it probably knows the route it will take to get to it as well. Thus it has an editorial capacity to avoid gaps, cul de sacs, false starts, and so on, in view of which dreams should be perfectly structured as narratives. They would be teleologically controlled action sequences. But such is far from the case.

Plainly, answering our question positively would involve us in some very elegant postulates. It seems more reasonable, and parsimonious, to argue that the dream is blind to all such matters and that the appearance of the old woman, though in all respects appropriate to the dream, simply *occurs* to the dreamwork at the moment it occurs in the dream plot proper. But how can something appropriate occur without the intervention of an author that (1) *knows* what is appropriate and what is inappropriate and (2) is distinct from the dreamer who is experiencing the dream as an altogether surprising reality? Surely determining whether something is or is not appropriate involves us, again, in some form of conscious thematics. Let us try a middle course.

Reading Hunt's dream from rear to front, it seems to me it has at least three initial features that prepare the way for the appearance of the old woman and the manikin. These hardly predict her appearance, but they do narrow the range of appropriate possibilities without the assistance of an author or the assumption of a teleological purpose. First off, Hunt is looking for a museum, not a grocery store or a medical office; we need not ask why that is the case, but having chosen a museum—or the museum having chosen Hunt—there is an implication, as he himself notes, of a place that is full of "dead" things from the past (1989: 167); to this we may safely add such normal museum artifacts as statues, dolls, manikins of representative citizens in costume, and the like, which might indirectly explain the manikin. In any case, we can probably assume that if Hunt had been looking for the Museum of Modern Art the dream would have unfolded along very different lines, perhaps producing a bizarre character more like our Picasso inebriant in the cartoon. Then too, he is looking for a specifically *Tibetan* museum. I can scarcely speak for Hunt's personal associations with Tibet, but I am not seeking the determinants of his dream as much as trying to understand how determinants and associative bundles may motivate the plots of dreams without the foresight of a waking author. My own associations would include such things as monasteries and temples, high places, exotic remoteness, mystery, priests (and priestesses?), Eastern spirituality, ritual, ceremony, high thin music, and extraordinary longevity. Finally, the museum is closed, it is therefore vacant of patrons, and there is a suggestion of the forbidden in entering it at this hour. Only the caretaker is about the place, and she occupies a "primitive and archaic" room "off to one side." In short, things are increasingly coming to a boil in the dream: the strain of possibilities is getting narrower and narrower. There must have been other things as well, either in Hunt's personal memory of Tibet and museums or in the dream itself, that may not have survived the report.[10]

---

[10] For what it is worth in the way of illustrating the depth of associative imagery, I note that there is an apparent typographical error in Hunt's dream as printed. Twice the dream report refers to women rather than to a woman. I wonder about the origin of this error. What offers itself to my mind is the scene in *Macbeth* in which the three sisters are stirring their fateful brew and conjuring a procession of dead children. I am not claiming that Hunt may have subliminally had this in mind; but such a

The point is that it is possible to explain dream plots, or some dream plots, as rising from a principle of development that does not presume an omniscient author. Let us call this the principle of metonymic accretion, by which I mean simply that a dream usually supplies the next incident as a response to what is already there. As Douglas Hofstadter has put it, "As fragments start to fit together coherently, the system continues to turn down its randomness knob" (1986: 655). It is rather like the structures that children build out of blocks of various shapes and sizes. The child establishes a foundation and builds upward, instinctively observing elementary laws of balance, tension, centralization, and support. Each new block advances, changes, and *limits* the dynamics of the structure, inevitably to a point of collapse. Hence there is a kind of self-determination in the process: it is a "What now?" situation, a way of getting from here to the next point by established means, which in the case of a dream would be a metonymic evolution. It is even possible that discontinuities and radical shifts in dreams may occur as a result of "overbuilding" or "deadending."[11]

---

gestalt—old woman, stirring vat, dead-live child—is suggestive of how we reinvest old structures with new images. It is even possible that Hunt didn't catch the error in proofreading (assuming he was the proofreader) because, in the context, women was quite natural; that is, *women* fits into an established literary gestalt.

[11] Metonymic evolution and accretion are purely personal affairs. My set of associations for a particular image or experience is quite different from yours, which means, in effect, that your dream will advance along very different lines from mine. Still another model of this view of plotting occurs in actor training: two actors (typically) improvise a situation that begins with an event provoked by one actor (a gesture, a projected attitude, a movement) to which the other responds naturally. And so it progresses in a series of stimulus-response stages, maintaining through it all a tit-for-tat coherence that is a little like the "coherence" of water seeking the lowest level: things that have been established in the dynamic tend to persist or to adjust themselves "in character" to changes that occur. By this means actors are taught the intricacies of interaction that at once frees them to discover things about themselves, to take chances with material, and to maintain an honesty of reactivity when they graduate to the planned coherences of written scripts. The point is that such improvisations have the character of a created empirical reality and illustrate (though perhaps too dramatically) that reality itself, by this very means, follows a plot more closely than we may think in which the persistent and the accidental interpenetrate each other. Like Feigenbaum's mathematics, "even though systems become chaotic, they do so in predictable or *regulated* ways" (Hayles, 1990:

The process has some metaphorical affinities with the Darwinian notion of natural selection. In the dream, as in the species, the law of conditions of existence, according to Darwin, is higher than the law of unity of type. This suggests that the dream environment, having established certain local conditions, tends to encourage certain "species" and possibilities of life and that modifications, mutations, and adaptations that favor the continuance of a species transform the species itself. In short, the fittest variations (even those occurring by chance) are retained and the poorest discontinued. Thus Aunt Sarah, getting on some pretext into a dream in which fright is a strong atmospheric element, would be frightful as opposed to her usual gentle self. Or, if not, she would be modified or replaced by another appropriate fright carrier. Indeed, one might explain the frequent identity changes and composite identities of dreams as resulting from a principle we might call instant natural selection. Other features of this analogy seem appropriate as well: some such principle in dreams would account for waste, cul de sacs, and sudden shifts, or for "species discontinuance" (that is, the disappearance of a dream character who becomes redundant in the

---

183). Suppose, for instance, that Hunt's dream had produced an ancient king with the dead body of his son draped over his lap. Could this not as easily be seen as an appropriate image on which to round out the sequence?

Finally, in this same vein, I must mention Daniel Dennett's *Consciousness Explained,* which offers a similar discussion of how stories may be composed without authors and how various forms of hallucination, including dreams, even perception itself, may be based (partially at least) on the principle of "expectation-driven" confirmations and disconfirmations. In other words, if, as I have suggested here, the dream offers one image—say, a burning house—the following sequence will be to a great extent derived from the dreamer's expectations of burning houses. If one of these happens to be a concern for any people who may be inside, the dream will (probably) confirm that expectation by providing people waving frantically from upstairs windows. If the dreamer should then think, "They can surely jump from that height," that is very likely what will happen. It is, as Dennett suggests, "a process that weaves back and forth between centrally generated expectations, on the one hand, and confirmations (and disconformations) arising from the periphery on the other hand." It depends on the "emotional state of the hallucinator" (dreamer, in this instance). In any case, "hallucinations are usually related in their content to the current concerns of the hallucinator, and this model of hallucination provides for that feature without the intervention of an implausibly knowledgeable internal storyteller" (Dennett, 1991: 12–13).

dream); it would imply no master plan behind (or above) the dream evolution, no divine author who has created the dream world for teleological purposes. And finally, the evolution of the dream need not have occurred according to a consistent meaning; the dream may be given meaning retrospectively (as evolution may be said to have produced the steady advance of the species culminating in the "triumph of Man"), but along the way it was really only coping with its own empirical situation. At any stage it could have developed differently had a stronger image presented itself. To whom? To the dreamer or to the dreamwork? The question is incorrectly put, for there is no distinction to be made between the two. It is a relatively common phenomenon, as Mary Warnock and others have pointed out, for an image to occur involuntarily even in the waking state which allows us to inspect it, experience it, and "feel in ourselves some of the emotions which [the image] would produce in us if it were there in reality" (Warnock, 1978: 169). This condition is perhaps seen most clearly in the hypnogogic and hypnopompic states in which images mutate before our eyes as if they had been independently formed. If you concentrate on the nose of a face you have conjured in Hypnogogia you may soon find yourself skiing in the Swiss Alps. Dreaming is simply the mental state that opens us most intensively to this possibility.[12]

---

[12] Wilson Van Dusen offers an unusually sympathetic discussion of the hypnogogic and hypnopompic states in *The Natural Depth in Man*: "It is clearest," he says, "in the state between sleeping and waking. Both sides must be present. One is totally relaxed and approaching sleep so inner processes can become more conscious. But one is awake enough to observe them. It occurs on the way into or out of sleep. If one awakens part way, it is quite easy to observe hypnogogic phenomena until one becomes so awake as to knock them out. *The main advantage of this difficult balancing act between sleeping and waking is that the conscious person can observe an* [sic] *indeed even talk to and experiment with inner process"* (1972: 89).
  Van Dusen seems to be capable of carrying on a verbal dialogue with the hypnogogic (as he calls it) and is convinced that the "eigenlichts" (entoptic light images) produced by the state "seem to be the bare beginning of inward self-representation" (p. 88). I regret to say that I have had no such luck, though I have frequently been able to control the course of hypnogogic and hypnopompic imagery by simply willing a certain kind of development ("Make a face. Now make a mountain range") or asking the hypnogogic to clarify an image. I have frequently been able to create oil paintings that would put the masters to shame. I am never able to survey the entire painting as one might in a gallery, but passages appear very distinctly and hold

In essence, I am suggesting that there is another form of logic that may govern the conduct of the dream. One might call it the logic of situational dynamics, and it can be illustrated by a common practice of looking up words in the dictionary: if word B is a synonym of word A and word C a synonym of word B, word C is not necessarily a synonym of word A (as, for example, we can move from *brave* to *daring* to *bold* to *rude* to *vulgar* along a strictly synonymic path, but *vulgar* is not listed as a synonym for *brave* (indeed, in conventional value systems *bravery* and *vulgarity* are more like antonyms). Yet there might be a progressive relationship among the stages that seems to be formed by a hidden dialectical principle that prepares the next event according to the dramatic principle of difference, or change. A certain degree of similarity would be maintained, but along a pathway of reversal, or what Aristotle calls "metabasis." Or, as David Lodge puts it in *The Modes of Modern Writing,* a contrast is "a kind of negative similarity," meaning that there is a logic of development that carries a plot from one extreme to the other while maintaining a principle of similarity or resemblance (1977: 81). Thus, there is a drama in the "plot" and one can imagine a brave character who, in the course of certain

---

still long enough for me to investigate sequences of color and shape with my eye. One of my chief regrets is that I am never able to reproduce these effects when I am awake—otherwise, the world would surely have a new master on its hands.

I am suggesting no such thing as a dialogue between two mental entities. Whatever the physiological origins of the hypnogogic, I am convinced, like others, that it is the threshold to the dreamworld proper—a kind of preview of coming attractions, or at least of coming compositional procedures. On many occasions I have taken note of the time before abandoning myself to sleep and have passed through Hypnogogia into and out of a dream into wakefulness within a quarter-hour; see also, along this line, Jerome L. Singer's "The Transition to Dreaming," in Singer, 1966. I have no idea whether REM activity would have been detectable during this time, but there is obviously a close generic relationship between the hypnogogic and the dream states. This suggests that the hypnogogic phase of sleep offers the best evidence for a phenomenological understanding of the liaison between the dream image and the dreamer who autosuggestively authors it. One might describe the hypnogogic as something of a lucid dream state in which one is already dreaming—not yet narratively—but is still capable of limited control over the proceedings. At any rate, one can consciously *observe* the process of image formation from a fringe perspective. For a comprehensive discussion and review of work done on the hypnogogic and related states, see Hunt, 1989: esp. 180–84; as on most topics related to dreaming, Hunt offers one of the most thorough and level-headed approaches.

events, becomes a vulgarian. The dream state may indeed be a
replica of waking experience in that it arises from certain cares—
fear, tension, desire carried from waking life into the dream—but
thereafter it is governed by a logic that is half thematic and half
happenstantial. And one may add, parenthetically, that this is also
the case in the formative stage of fictional composition: the writer
may stumble on images or cast off images, go up blind alleys, just
as dreams do, but waking writers also have the privilege of revision. (If you could somehow project a novelist's first draft thought
process onto a dream screen, you would find as much bizarreness as
we typically get in dreams.) For each imagistic leap the dream
makes by way of finding appropriate associations brings into it new
possibilities of association, and the theme is thereby subject to contamination (as *boldness* is open to the contamination of *rudeness*).
These are only analogies taken from the universe of language, but I
assume the reader can see how images might be thus affected. Each
new association carries with it uninvited relatives, hence new paths
of suggestivity and plot development. Presumably the dream
would continue along the path of strongest cathexis, though that
may be still another example of waking logic much like the concept
of the bizarre.

But even this is putting it poorly, for one might claim that the
dream is not concerned with coherence of theme as much as with
"living with" what it has produced. In this, dream consciousness is
like that of waking life: it must deal with each situation as it arises.
Thematically, you may want to spend your day in productive work,
or at the beach, and you would manifest a kind of self-consistency
in whatever you do, but a day is subject to interruption and revision
(Mother may arrive at the door and change your plans). There may
indeed be a coherent theme in the dream, but to piece it out one
would have to be privy to a chain of associational determinism of
Laplacian complexity. In contrast, some dreams might be quite
uncomplicated and thematically pure; it all depends on the conditions of existence within the dream itself.

It might be appropriate to think of the dream in terms of Chaos
theory. All systems, we now believe, contain some degree of disor-

der; indeed, their continual adaptation to disorder is what prevents them from collapsing into total chaos. The dream too is an unstable system; it is the mental and cognitive equivalent of a meteorological system whose "weather" cannot be predicted beyond a short time range, owing to the inevitable intrusion of an infinity of uncertainties that influence major patterns of development. Thus, the dream, like the weather, is a chaotic and complex system: it is both deterministic and unpredictable, at least in the sense that it tends to develop in a more or less coherent direction and yet one cannot tell where it will go next. Moreover, like other complex systems it is further characterized by feedback mechanisms that "create loops in which output feeds back into the system as input. In certain chemical reactions, for example, a product may also serve as a catalyst for the reaction, driving it to generate more product, which in turn becomes more catalyst. The resulting dynamics are instrumental in explaining why organized structures can spontaneously emerge from initially small perturbations in the solution. . . . they are magnified through a cascading series of bifurcations" (Hayles, 1990: 14–15).

For instance, in a dream, an image, person, or object may come into accidental prominence. Though it got into the dream in the first place by virtue of being only an incidental part of the scenery, it somehow attracts the attention of the dreamer, at which point it might suddenly summon its own evocations, blending into the narrative as it does, and yet it also alters the narrative's course, like the famous seagull that alters the weather in Chaos theory. One could not say precisely *how* it has done this because one never knows what the dream would have done otherwise. But we must surely consider the possibility that "innocent" objects, to use Freud's word, might have a radical effect on the dream once they are combined with other objects in a highly dynamic system. Perhaps the clearest instances might be the intrusion of external reality into the dream in the form of, say, a clattering screen door or my ringing telephone in the example above. Such things are always tolerated by the dream, which in effect says, "Now that you're here, you can help out." Having thought something into existence, or having something thrust into it from the outside, the dream cannot elude its presence any more than the oyster can elude an uninvited grain of sand. Owing, however, to the blank check offered by the "bizarre" principle—itself a form of feedback mechanism—the dream can assign a new function and identity to the thing by grafting it onto an established image. And surely the same thing may be said of images that arise internally in the dream-work. For example, the feedback mechanism may explain why the dream so often duplicates people or combines several people in one image. I have noted on many occasions how I may be talking about someone who is not in the dream—sometimes derogatorily—and the person suddenly appears and participates in the discussion without the slightest awareness that he or she is being referred to. I take it that, in simply bringing up the name of the person, the dream is on some occasions at least driven "to generate more product" which in turn influences the course of the dream. How could imagination know in advance the potential influence of any image that it might conjure until that image actually appears?

Let us come back to the structural relationship of dreams and waking fictions. Hunt has addressed this question at some length, using certain of Ricoeur's criteria for "genuine stories." Briefly, these stories (1) "are structured in terms of a beginning, middle, and end;" (2) "expand and foreshorten in a way that reorganizes the lived time of action sequences in terms of the temporal requirements of the narrative;" and (3) "reflect, and potentially vary, a distinct narrative voice or point of view" (Hunt, 1989: 176). Dreams, in contrast, are "protostories or *quasi-plots*," though some dreams come "closer and closer to Ricoeur's sense of story as an ur-organizational principle of the human mind. It is as though dreams (like lives?) are *trying* to become stories." "Dreaming shows a natural tendency to approximate the criteria of a dramatic story but also characteristically falls short. It is the way we spontaneously handle dreams on awakening that finishes the operation by turning the dream into a story in Ricoeur's meaning." Hunt goes on to say that dreams are more like historical narratives than fictions in the sense that their meaning is outside the narrative, as the events of history are outside the narrative written by historians: "We must go in search of the background context against which specific actions [of the dream] can be evaluated" (pp. 177–78).

One can only agree that dreams do not usually qualify as stories, in Ricoeur's or in most other definitions. Though Hunt's discussion is useful in bringing out certain differences between stories and dreams, it does not address the underlying question of the very different destinations of dreams and stories. To determine how dreams and stories are similar, or different, it seems to me one must go beyond structural comparisons that treat the recalled dream on the same level as a literary text. First, there is no text for the dream, and I doubt that converting the memory of the dream into a dream report brings it much on line with Ricoeur's criteria for the story. Indeed, I think the report only serves to accentuate the difference, with the consequence that the dream seems, on recall or report, a poor attempt at storytelling; or, as Hunt puts it, it is as though dreams are trying to become stories but inevitably failing. None of the dream reports we have dealt with here, or anywhere else, read like stories; on the contrary, most dream reports preserve the main structural features of dream narrative, including the in medias res beginning, the unexplained gaps and shifts in scene, and the inconclusive ending. And this is precisely why dream reports are so boring to other people: they do not arouse or fulfill a reliable set of anticipations. So we must ask not simply what is different about dream structure but why it is that dreams work as narratives *in dreamland,* if not in the light of day. Here reader-response theory offers a useful caution. For example, Stanley Fish puts the problem succinctly:

A criticism that regards "the poem itself as an object of specifically critical judgment" . . . is a criticism that takes as its (self-restricted) area the physical dimensions of the artifact and within these dimensions it marks out beginnings, middles, and ends, discovers frequency distributions, traces out patterns of imagery, diagrams strata of complexity (vertical of course), all without ever taking into account the relationship (if any) between its data and their affective force. Its question is what goes into the work rather than what does the work go into. It is "objective" in exactly the wrong way, because it determinedly ignores what is objectively true about the *activity* of reading (1980: 83).

I cite this not as a critique of Hunt but as a way of adjusting our critical perspective to account for the peculiar conditions of dreaming. Dream study might adapt the reader-response approach by putting more emphasis on the experience within dreaming rather than on the artifact itself, either as a dream report or as the dreamer's personal memory of the dream. What this would tell us is something about the inseparable collusion between the dreamer self, normally (but not always) the protagonist of the dream, and the dream as a set of events that happens to the dreamer. An affective approach would treat the dream not simply as a structure of events, reproducible by dream report and comparable—or not comparable—to the structure of a story; it would include the feelings that attend the structure, the structure being something of a support system in which, as Bergson would say, memory and sensation are united (Bergson 1958, 39). One might say that the dream leaves out precisely what a fiction demands for its affective success, and it does so because what is left out is already the cathectic basis of the dream. For example, if the reader of a fiction could miraculously be drawn into the fiction and become a character—dreaming the story, as it were—a great deal of the matter of the text would become supererogatory because it would be reconstituted as direct emotional experience. The story would now have the structure and aspect of a reality without the least literary apparatus. In short, a dream is fundamentally unlike a fiction, structurally and affectively, in that it is a lived experience as well as a narrative; it belongs both to art and to reality; it is, one might say, an empirical illusion.

Hunt cites a dream that illustrates how this reconstitution might work. It occurred on a night he had been "pondering the possible implications of Ricoeur's books for dreaming, specifically whether dreams could handle time and point of view like narrative fiction, and especially whether dreams had genuine endings" (1989: 177). Ricoeur had, so to speak, put Hunt to sleep (book in lap) and the dream that ensued concerned the solving of a nameless mystery by an interlocutor in an old house. As the interlocutor reveals the solution to the mystery, Hunt experiences a complete "clarification" and a "sense of total resolution" when in fact the mystery had not even been defined by the dream. The dream ends with a photograph of the (mystery) house that appears on the last page of the book (Ricoeur's "ostensibly") he had been reading. Thus the dream provides an ironic ending that answers one of Hunt's own questions about the narrative structure of dreams by using the book that inspired the question as its answer.

Having had such detective story dreams, I know exactly what Hunt means in experiencing a "total resolution" to an absolutely unknown, unposited situation. Hunt's comment on the dream is that without "the background circumstances in which [the dream] was dreamed" we could not possibly know that the dream had "a narrative point" and a "genuine" ending. "Without them . . , it is not a story in Ricoeur's sense" (p.178). And indisputably, this is true: without these exterior details, *we* could not possibly know what was going on. From a reader-response perspective, however, the point would be that in the dream Hunt *knew*, without benefit of these details, and that the dream had provided a structure of resolution according to what is objectively true about the *activity* of dreaming, as Fish might say. It *is* a story in Ricoeur's sense if we disregard the standards for coherence and resolution in the double-minded waking world and include the dreamer's reactions in the structure of the dream. Hunt's reaction—"Ah! I see!"—to the interlocutor's disclosure ("She wanted these abstract designs [carved into the patio wall] to point toward the grave") is a genuine instance of understanding, even though there is nothing to understand. Indeed, here is the pure algebra of understanding, just as the concluding photograph provides the algebra of story resolution.[13] It is

---

[13] Following Foulkes (who is in turn following Neisser), we might say that such algebraic understanding is an instance of "how to" rather than "what" cognition. That is, "action sequences are more directly elicitable than any particular products of such sequences. We remember 'how to' use an automobile jack, but also 'how to' recreate a picture of an old friend's face and 'how to' recite a childhood poem" (Foulkes, 1978: 161). In the present case, we remember how to experience resolution or clarification, irrespective of local content—or even the absence of content.

really beside the point that anyone hearing the dream report would be thoroughly mystified by it. Hunt wasn't mystified because he was inside the dream experiencing it, his affective reactions constituting an irreducible part of the dream structure. To appreciate how strange and unsatisfying dream reports are from the logical standpoint, try systematically deleting everything in, say, Kafka's *Metamorphosis* that pertains to Gregor's emotional or cognitive reaction to his situation. We can accept the bizarre happenings of the story— Gregor's and the family's incredible reaction to his metamorphosis, for example—only because Kafka is able to approximate the conditions of dream consciousness.

Ricoeur's criteria, however, are generally valid only in the world of waking stories, and to use them as a measure of the story quality of dreams can only demonstrate the difference between the conditions of understanding and conclusiveness in sleep and in wakefulness.[14] We can assess the similarities of dreams and stories only if we consider the dream's conflation of teller and hearer (to speak figuratively) as part of the artifactuality of the dream. If the dreamer is, so to speak, a character in the dream, he or she is part of the structure. As for beginnings, middles, and endings, who can say at what level of mentation a dream begins and ends, that point at which "I was somehow in this room" becomes the "Once upon a time" of the dream, or how it has prepared its beginning in still another form in preimagistic mentation, somewhat as the conventions of literary genre prepare the reader's anticipations in advance

[14] Even so, I do not find Ricoeur's criteria descriptive of the "ur-organizational principle" of storytelling itself. If there is such an ur-principle, then one must surely look for it not in the world of waking narrative, with all its public refinements based on cultural demands, restrictions, conventions, and communicational necessities, but in the first place stories were ever told—in the dreamwork, the primal storyteller preceding all fiction, the one story mechanism that produces a narrative structure that consciousness not only invents but inhabits at first hand. This seems to be the ur-principle of storytelling, at least insofar as storytelling arises from the fact that life experience itself unfolds as a narrative form consisting of events and human interactions. This is not to privilege the dream and make the same mistake in reverse but to suggest the good possibility that the first waking narratives were dream reports and that the instinct for storytelling arises from the same imagination that produces the dream.

of the "Once upon a time" that appears at the top of the first page. To come at the problem from still another direction, in the realm of fiction beginnings and endings may be said to serve two purposes. The first is cognitive-comprehensive: they enclose the narrative in a structure that is self-sustaining and complete, thus enabling an understanding of the story on its own terms in a (more or less) non-referential way. It does not, like a historian's narrative of history (which has neither beginning nor ending), refer to anything beyond it in the empirical world except the reader's familiarity with world experience itself. (Imagine, as a perfect confusion of these two realms, seeing a group photograph in the middle of Tolstoy's *War and Peace* captioned "The Bolkonsky family, ca. 1800. Prince Andrey lower right.") The second purpose of beginnings and endings is affective-cathartic: they are designed to evoke and purge the feelings, emotions, and interests relevant to the narrative. Obviously, these functions are not distinct or separable: they are only the two faces of narrative fulfillment, or what is usually called the *utile-dulce* function of art.

Now we see immediately how this criterion of beginnings and endings becomes irrelevant when applied to dream narrative. For one thing, it seems obvious that the dream is not intended to satisfy the dreamer's or anyone else's concerns with comprehensibility. Dreams may be interpretable, but that has nothing to do with the way they are organized, and indeed Freud insists that the dream could be understood only if it were structurally dismantled. Moreover, we can hardly claim that the function of dreams is to arouse emotion or feeling; it is rather nearer the opposite—that is, it is the dream that seems to be aroused by a seed emotion. This is, however, a speculative claim for which we have no evidence. But there is some reason to believe that dreams are the product of what Ignacio Matte Blanco calls emotional thinking (as distinguished from logical or analytical thinking). To be more specific, emotional thinking, according to Matte Blanco, has three aspects:

generalisation of the characteristics or features attributed to the object so that all features of this type come to be contained in it;

maximisation of the magnitude of these characteristics ["there are no half-measures, . . . everything which is good or bad is so in an extreme degree"]; and, as a consequence of both, irradiation from the concrete object to all others, which in this way come to be represented in it [that is, "a confusion of the individual with the class"]. (1975: 245 [p. 243]).[15]

Matte Blanco is not concerned with dreams, but his premises are adaptable to the production of dreams inasmuch as he associates emotional thinking with the unconscious. Dreams are a relatively straight form of emotional thinking (thus defined): they tend to "carry to their extreme and utmost potentialities the characteristics of a given situation or person." Thus the loved one or the hated one (to use his examples) is always maximized, or "idealized," and contains all possible attributes of the "type." "Fear of the dark, however much reason may tell us that it is fantastic, populates darkness with the most terrifying monsters with unlimited potentialities for evil and capable of rendering the subject completely helpless" (p. 242). Emotion, Matte Blanco says, is symmetrical thinking, as opposed to analytical or asymmetrical thinking: it "does not know individuals but only classes or propositional functions and, therefore, when confronted with an individual, tends to identify this individual with the class to which it belongs (or the propositional function applied to it)" (p. 244).[16] This is virtually a definition of condensation or symbolization; the dream's way of demonstrating this premise is to perform bizarre transformations wherein the image shuffles between the individual object and the

[15] I am greatly simplifying Matte Blanco's discussion of emotional thinking, choosing only what might be instructive to a study of dreams. I should mention, too, that he does acknowledge the existence of what he refers to as "tamed emotions," which have an aspect of "mildness [or] lack of intensity" (p. 241). Boredom would be a good example. As far as I can determine, dreams do not traffic much in such emotions.

[16] Symmetrical thinking implies infinite likeness, or a "spaceless-timeless reality" (p. 103) and is associated with the unconscious (in Matte Blanco's revised conception of Freud's Ucs), which is what he calls "a sea of symmetry" (p. 104): in such thinking "it is not possible to establish a difference between individual things; hence,

class of emotional associations to which it belongs in the dreamer's history. Thus the interchangeability of people or locales is in perfect keeping with dream logic—indeed, is indispensable to dream logic—since all dream individuals are representatives of an associational class, subject to replacement without qualitative (emotional) loss.[17] Whereas in the waking world of asymmetrical thought we would say of a dream image, "It was either this or that, I don't recall," the dream has actually said, "It is this *and* that, and much much more" (p. 420). Finally, it is the principle of irradiation that endows the dream with its peculiar monochromatic atmosphere, its single-minded quality. Just as in the empirical world when you are depressed the world takes on the characteristics of your depression, and when you are smiling the "whole world smiles with you," so in the dream the prevailing emotion radiates to all parts of the dream world: there are no half-measures in the dream, or, as Wilson Van Dusen nicely puts it, "everything in the dream is the dreamer" (1972: 103)—that is, the dreamer's emotion.

Suffice to say, this is only one possible set of terminologies we might invoke, and for my present purposes we could probably substitute resemblance and difference (or nonlinear and linear; intuitive and rational) for emotional/symmetrical and analytical/asymmetrical without much harm. The main idea is that in the dream emotion and event are inseparable: a dream event is simply a grounded emotion. It would be simplistic to claim that the dream begins with, or is based on, a particular emotion which the dream goes on to elaborate in visual images—as though the emotion were the discrete cause of the dream. This would suggest that emotion could exist without having an object (a belovedless love). What

---

the individual is . . . identical to the class" (p. 97). Asymmetrical thinking, in contrast, is logical and "takes one thing after another" (p. 98); it is associated strictly with the conscious. The concept of symmetrical thought is actually very Bergsonian. In his essay on dreams, Bergson speaks of memory as a pyramid whose "peak is wedged into our present activity." Below it are "thousands of [resemblances], stored away in the depths of the memory, down beneath the stage lighted by consciousness" (1958: 37).

[17] Mikkel Borch-Jacobsen (1988) offers a variation of this point in his discussion of wish fulfillment, already quoted in Chapter 1.

brings on a particular dream we do not know (and may never know), but the dream is the process of emotional, or symmetrical, thinking. How unnecessary, then, is the enclosure of a structure that initiates and concludes the dream narrative as if it were a grammatical sentence or a story to be understood. Unlike a fiction, a dream does not reach conclusions; rather, it worries relations among emotion-laden objects, maximizing the potentialities as it does so. A dream, one may say, plays out the emotion emotionally. On Matte Blanco's principle of emotion as an infinite set (or being infinitely extensible in terms of its possible objects and associations), we may say that a dream is potentially an endless story, and it is really impossible to determine how or why it stops except in those dramatic cases when a dream event shocks us into wakefulness. In any event, to apply the principles of waking narrative to dream structure amounts to translating symmetrical being into asymmetrical being—associational thinking into analytical thinking, an extratemporal-extraspatial structure into a temporal-spatial one. This is clearly a valid pursuit for anyone who wants to understand the phenomenon of narrative thought in all its manifestations, but the importation of criteria from one field to the other, as I have been suggesting, carries with it certain dangers of waking bias. All this being said, however, it is obvious that dreams possess a certain degree of narrative order that is common—to a different degree— to that of waking fictions. Emotional thinking is not simply a sequence of resemblances—"a sea of symmetry," in Matte Blanco's phrase—but a genuine development of plot. And having separated the procedures of dreams and fictions, we must now see what they might have in common, trying as we do to keep in mind that they are narratives of entirely different orders, designed for entirely different receptors—though perhaps, in the end, not for such different purposes.

3

The Master Forms

There is adequate evidence for assuming that dreams manifest a kind of order: the maintainence of certain themes (the search, the escape, the task); the continuance of characters or locale over several scenes; the tendency in some dreams to build to a "big event." The most important thing seems to be that we don't take order for granted where dreams are concerned, or think of order in strictly waking terms, but try to understand what orderliness may imply in the dream state and what relation that form of order might have to the kinds we find in fictions—or, for that matter, in "random" daily life. If we are thinking of dreams and stories (under different conditions) as having a common genesis in the human need to make narratives of our experience, perhaps we should ask what they may share in the way of generic characteristics. My personal dreamlife is singularly lacking in comedy, satire, and farce, and I can't really recall reading a funny dream dreamed by somebody else (apart from those we laugh at because they are so absurd or involve people we know in odd doings). This suggests that there is something about the comic that is generically uncongenial to dreams, and it may have to do with the nature and function of laughter itself. Freud has written an essay on the relation of jokes to dreams in which he finds technical common denominators in condensation, displacement, indirect representation, and the cathectic release of suppressed energy (1973 [1905]: 165); but he also points out that a dream is "a completely asocial mental product, [whereas] a joke . . . is the most social of all the mental functions that aim at a yield of pleasure" (p. 179) and requires two to three people to this end. In any case, it would be hard to imagine anything more ludicrously self-contradictory than a sleeping person in the throes of laughter. Terror, sexual arousal, certainly; but laughter—or even a smile—implies a lucidity or, as Freud might say, a feeling of self-superiority·that seems to be incompatible with the dream· state. This may also be the reason that we have few if any dreams that are tendentious or polemical. Why would one try to convince oneself of a preferred course of social or political action?

I think a case can be made, however, for dreams sharing certain organizational tendencies of the literary forms we refer to as dramatic, epic, and lyric. I am thinking of genre in something more than its literary definition. A more expansive view is offered by Ralf Remshardt in his study of the grotesque:

> Genre, which can be described as a conventionalized way of dealing with actuality, is a manner of 'framing' events such that we are clearly aware of what is included in and excluded from our 'horizon of expectations. . . .' Genre is a type of representational insurance; the security it provides lies in its tacit elimination of chaos. . . . As an instrument of literary economy, or expressive shorthand, genre can count on a set of assumptions it need not expressly manifest, and one of its salient feats is the *exclusion* of certain combinatorial, symbolic, or narrative possibilities. As in the eidetic operation of phenomenology, every genre 'brackets' certain elements of actuality to arrive at its own verity (1991: 243–44)

Technically speaking, epic, dramatic, and lyric may better be referred to as modes than genres, though they are classed in either category. The point is the same in either case: it is not a matter of the dream following the rules of poetry, for these primary modes of poetic discourse do not persist through human history out of obedience to poetic laws or tradition. They imply certain essential combinational strategies, or ways of bracketing the world. They are ways of thinking, natural tendencies by which imagination either formally (in poems and fictions) or informally (as in dream, reverie, or the improvisational bedtime story) perceives and expresses the basic rhythms of experience. So it would hardly be surprising to find the dream adapting epic, lyric, and dramatic strategies even before there were such literary forms, which are simply high refinements produced for a waking audience. Presumably, with the dubious exceptions of comedy and "thesis" literature, we might expect to find as many forms and purposes in dream experience as there are in waking art, if only because the dream, as the primary process, is the ur-form of all imaginative thought. I would willingly grant that much of this borders on tautology were it not that so much effort has been spent proving that the dream is guided exclusively by an urgent need to express the disturbed self, as opposed to the self's urgent need to express the possible structures of experience in imaginative terms. Fundamentally, then, we are talking about the available ways of structuring experience, an operation common to both dreams and waking narratives.

"Dramatic" dream structure almost speaks for itself, as in our common use of the term to describe dramatic events. The best example we have seen here is Hunt's dream of the Tibetan museum, which could scarcely have been better designed, considering what we have of it, by Alfred Hitchcock (recall the shock of Mrs. Bates's skeleton in the rocking chair in *Psycho*). Dramatic structure in dreams would offer a high degree of tension and endangerment and would probably be marked by strong contingency, surprise, reversal of fortune (as Aristotle would say), and crisis. We might say that a dramatic dream is a particular instance of a reaction formation. Let us look at one extreme example. Foulkes cites the case of a woman who dreams she kills her mother. He suggests that the most reasonable explanation, "from the evidence of just one such dream," is not that she really wanted to kill her mother. "The dream more likely reflects the fact that, given the dream narrative as it had developed up until the point of the murder, and given the mnemonic elements active at that point, the simplest path for the dream-production system to take at that point, given *its* requirements, was to have the dreamer kill her mother" (1985: 206).

What Foulkes seems to imply by "the simplest path" is that the dream had got itself into a plot bind and needed a way out of the fix, rather like a novelist who kills off a character because she has outlived her usefulness to the story. Perhaps Foulkes didn't have this in mind, but let us try to carry his idea in a more specific direction. I suggest that killing one's mother falls into the category of the dramatic and belongs, generically, with dreams in which a loved one is killed or dies or a husband betrays a wife or vice versa. By dramatic I do not simply mean violent or shocking or a plot that involves a cliff-hanger crisis. Dramatic dreams are what we might call "What if?" dreams in the sense that they carry the dream situation to its furthest possible extreme, an instance of Matte Blanco's concept of maximization. Of course, it is one thing to dream that one's mother falls off a cliff into the raging sea and quite another thing to push her. The point of overlap, however, is that "the dream-production system" is not (and Foulkes would agree; 1978: 32) necessarily consistent with one's standards of waking morality. To say the least, the dream is the servant of two masters—the moral system and the poetic (or form-making) system. And Foulkes seems correct in claiming that the dream's development may have *required* the murder—not, however, so much as the simplest path but as what might even be termed the most complex (in Aristotle's sense of the term), or most painful and radical path, given all the circumstances that may have been in play at that point in the dream. (Mortal situations "involving strong ties of affection," as Aristotle said, "are the ones to be sought" because they are the most productive of pity and terror; 1981: 24.) We tend to think that the instinct to make a story as good as possible—"good" meaning thorough—is a strategy of the waking author; but where does this strategy originate if not in the instincts of those for whom the story is intended? And where might this demand for thoroughness originate but in the same logic that drives the dream (now and then) to such terminal conclusions? We see the principle of thoroughness at work in all products of human thought: it is the form-making principle and form is sometimes achieved at the sacrifice of moral behavior (as we see in the brutal deaths of Astyanax and Cordelia). This is also the case in those dreams in which the dreamer is killed by an opponent of her own making. The last thing one desires in a dream is one's own death, but dreams do devise such scripts and the likely reason is not that we are suicidal but that dreams have a way of making realities out of possibilities. The problem of being confronted by an enemy in a dream is that one is likely to conceive unpleasant consequences; and in dreams, more often than not, to conceive something—one's own death or one's mother's murder—is to enact it. In sum, dreaming that you kill your mother is not very different from dreaming she is killing you. One of the things to be remembered about dreams is that they are instantaneous creations occurring at the threshold of thought: dreams think first and raise moral questions later, and it goes without saying that a good share of our waking morality depends on the constraints afforded by second thoughts. The best way to approximate the speed of dreams might be to imagine what life would be like if reality, in some Borgesian way, would instantly begin "imitating" whatever thought came into your mind respecting it.

Before leaving the dramatic I should mention one variation of the principle discussed by Adam Kuper, who has applied Lévi-Strauss's concept of structural oppositions in myths to dreams in a sleep laboratory situation. The idea is that dreams, like myths, "are based on systematic transformations of simple structures" that develop through oppositional pairings (inside/outside, male/female, inferior/superior) relevant in each case to the dreamer's particular conflict. There is little doubt that many dreams are based on such oppositions, but Kuper's sampling seems to me too narrow (one subject, two nights of dream recall) to enable the "strong presumption that we have [in oppositions located] the structure of dreams themselves." Moreover, the data seem somewhat biased by the fact that the dreamer, a psychology graduate student, was burdened by a strong identity crisis involving the very environment (his supervisor's laboratory) in which the dreaming took place (1983: 174).

What, then, about the dreams of people who carry less immediate burdens, or people who dream without interruption at home? Finally, there is the lingering problem that has been cited by Lévi-Strauss's critics: if one goes looking for oppositions in a dialectical frame of mind one is sure to find them in any system in which there are differences and transformations taking place. Any variation can be stretched into an opposition by simply altering the context. This very argument, however, has its recursive side: if the human brain tends to think oppositionally about unstable or differentiated contents, wouldn't the dialectical principle extend to dreams as well? My own point of view (equally based on dialectical thinking) is that dramatic dreams simply form one extreme of a spectrum that ends, on the other extreme, in the lyric. In any case, dramatic dreams would be those guided by a psychology of extremity, or what has been called catastrophic expectancy. They are, in a terrestrial sense of the word, apocalyptic, or they head in that direction if not ameliorated by other priorities—and we can be thankful that they usually are.

A lyric dream might assume many forms, but the essential point is that lyric is a nonnarrative mode that expresses a state of mind or feeling in an orderly way. The lyric poet, as Northrop Frye (quoting James Joyce) puts it, "present[s] the image in relation to himself," a statement that might, in a broader sense, be valid for all dreaming. "The radical of presentation in the lyric," Frye goes on, "is the hypothetical form of what in religion is called the 'I-Thou' relationship" (1957: 249–50). So one might say that the frequent appearance of the word *dream* in lyric poetry—for example, Theodore Roethke's "The Dream"—

> I met her as a blossom on a stem
> Before she ever breathed, and in that dream
> The mind remembers from a deeper sleep

suggests the sense in which the lyric is fundamentally a dreamlike form in its "radical of presentation" (the self speaking to itself); or, conversely, we might as easily say that dreaming is fundamentally lyric in *its* radical of presentation, irrespective of what it represents

as its content, be it epic, dramatic, or lyric in form. In a dream, that
is, the self always speaks to and of itself, though it might do so by
converting itself into other dream creatures. But, on the organizational level, the lyric principle would dominate those dreams, or
parts of dreams, in which some emotion, feeling, or thought asserts
itself in comparative isolation from the contingencies of interpersonal life. The dream of flight might be a typical example, insofar
as it is an exhilarating one; Freud's dream of the botanical monograph could be considered a lyric fragment in that it seems to be a
brief, intense, and free-standing condensation of a complex emotional field into a single image. Moreover, it seems to require nothing before or after it to achieve its intensity for the dreamer: it
speaks, so to speak, for itself, though an outsider could not understand it, or feel it, any more than one might understand or feel the
emotion of another person's lyric poem to the beloved. Another
type might be the dream in which the dreamer stands before a
sublime or impossible landscape and experiences intense awe or
pleasure. The dreamer momentarily comes to rest in an emotion
made graphic by an astounding image. An excellent example is
Gordon Globus's dream of the ocean grotto:

> I am swimming out of the ocean into a rocky grotto. I gaze up, and
> against the dark vaulted ceiling I perceive a starry display of luxu-
> riant, green, luminous growth, which I experience with a feeling
> of pleasurable awe. (1987: 93)

Of this dream Globus says, "My deep wish to experience life fully
is gratified as I perceive this green luminosity" (p. 96), a statement
that has much in common, generically, with Wordsworth's

> My heart leaps up when I behold
> A rainbow in the sky:
> So was it when my life began;
> So is it now I am a man;

An epic dream would accommodate what Goethe called "circumscribed activity" (as opposed to dramatic crisis or lyric rest and

intensity); that is, if the dreamer had several diverse things in mind, none of which was particularly pressing or troublesome, or was in an expansive mood, the dream might take the path of the episodic or picaresque—travel, picnicing, wandering through a strange or familiar city, and so on—whereby he or she could pass successively from adventure to adventure bound only by the loosest of themes or common denominators. My most intrepidly epic dream, far too long to report in detail, was a direct outgrowth of the appearance of the movie *Edward Scissorhands*, or so I assume. It began with a scene in which a colleague is feeding a small lobster perched on his shoulder as a kind of bio-ornament, similar to the scabbard pins that were becoming popular. In the dream I found this behavior disgustingly ostentatious and wondered how he could carry vanity so far. There follows a succession of scenes in which the lobster turns up in various social situations, with or without my colleague, ominously waving its claws and disturbing the peace. In the end my colleague leaves for England, abandoning the lobster which now becomes *my* responsibility. In the last episode it appears on a restaurant table next to my own and outrages the diners, to my great embarrassment.

This is hardly Homer's *Odyssey* but it remains one of the most perfect dreams I have ever had in terms of sticking so avariciously to its original motif. Indeed, it falls into the structural tradition of Labiche's *The Italian Straw Hat* or Gogol's "The Nose": an object serves as a binding principle, or clothesline, for a series of episodes that have very little otherwise to do with each other. Some of the scenes were, in themselves, quite dramatic, as when I am rescuing the lobster, at some personal risk, from falling off the Brooklyn Bridge (a residue of the TV production "The Civil War" I saw that week). And there was certainly a sense of dramatic irony operating in the theme of the dream which punishes me for my disgust at my colleague by uniting my own fate with that of his lobster. But in overall form I would have to classify it as an epic dream and conclude that such dreams, like epics, are a response to the continuity of life, which tends to outlast its own moments of dramatic tension or lyric arrest. In any event, there is no need to decide where it

belongs. My purpose is simply to distinguish various kinds of organizing tendencies, or "instruments of literary economy," as Remshardt calls them, and it goes without saying that these modes
rarely occur in pure form. We might speak of lyric moments within
epic or dramatic structures, or of confusions of form such as a
dramatic lyric (as in Browning's poetry).

All in all, however, the epic, in some variation, seems to be the
most versatile form for representing the episodic quality of life as it
is lived, in either the dream or the empirical worlds. Dreams seem
to be the brain's response to the continuous condition of life that is
best described by Sartre's phrase "being in situation," that is, being
in a world filled with demands, projects, and dangers that never
seem to end. Dreams are concerned primarily with the fact, or
facticity of our situation rather than with the situation's possible
origins or outcome. Of all the fictional forms that might be said to
fall into the epic class, dreams are probably closest to the soap
opera, which is to say that your dreams are the continuing saga of
your imaginary life. Obviously the soap opera is a voraciously
contemporary form. It ingests into its endless plot all sorts of cultural usage and debris: burning social issues, hair (or jewelry)
styles, new occupational hazards; a character has a fatal car accident
because the actor wants out of the role; an actress who becomes
pregnant in real life becomes fictionally pregnant as well. In short,
in the soaps there is a high incidence of "day residue," the absorp-
tion of immediate reality into the fantasy of sexual desire. So the
saga goes on, endlessly resilient, endlessly attentive to the integration of the *new* day into the *old* ongoing life "as the world turns."[1]

---

[1] The idea is perfectly illustrated by this quote from a summary of the week's
events on "All My Children" from the *Los Angeles Times,* November 18, 1991, F12:
"At the anti-landfill coalition ball, Natalie was surprised when Trevor arrived with
Erica. Dimitri, who came with Natalie, almost had a fist-fight with Trevor."
There is an even subtler resemblance between dreams and soap operas, which
brings us back to the integration of the dramatic and epic styles of organization. As a
consequence of this addiction to daily life, both the soap opera and the dream tend to
specialize in the tension between the mundane and the explosive. Harold Pinter once
said that his plays are about the weasel under the cocktail cabinet. And, indeed, a
Pinter play (which is sometimes likened to the dream) might be described as a soap

Like soap operas, dreams are drawn to the underlying psychic
significance of daily life, though on the whole dreams are noto-
riously casual about the important crises we face. As Calvin Hall
nicely puts it, we are likely to dream about the people who are at
home dreaming about us (1966: 29). Moreover, dreams gravitate
toward base-level emotions: fear, anger, desire, embarrassment,
sadness, guilt, or, simply, frustration—trying to do something
that, for some unspecified reason, has to be done against a resistant
world. One might say that dreams worry or ramify the emotion by
giving it a representational structure made of things that are personally associated with the emotion. When Stanislavsky urged his actors to consult their emotional memory he was, in effect, asking
them to dream—to find the antecedents of their character's emotion in their own emotional history. This history, of course, has no
temporal logic or sequential organization; it is rather synchronic
and extratemporal. Thus something from the day residue—like the
movie *Edward Scissorhands*—may activate a series of dream images
that, in some forgotten way, belong to the same emotional category
or in some way replicate an emotional structure.

---

opera written by Dostoyevski. A weasel, in any case, is not so much a violent secret
(though these are common in soaps) as a subtext, a speech beneath speech. In the
soap, for instance, everyone has the Pinter look, the look that says, "I *know* you're
lying to me about Edgar and you *know* that I know; but I'll pretend I don't in such a
way that *you'll* suspect I'm having an affair with Susan." Or, there is the casual
triviality that brings down the mountain of deceit: "I thought you said Ellen came
back to the apartment after jazzercize." This is pure dream stuff. In your dreams,
people *know*; they see through your self-deceits because they are simply yourself
perceived as others. Consequently, dream conversation, like soap opera conversation, is heavily subtextual with emotion, however nonsensical it may seem when
you awake. In a dream, a line like "Have you heard that Bill's BMW had a heart
attack?" can throw you into real grief. Just as the dream image is simply the visual
apex of a pyramid of dream thoughts, so its vocal images—its speech—always carry
more load than the sound or sense will bear. I am reminded of Freud's joke about the
paranoiac whose friend tells him he is going to Cracow. "What a liar you are," the
paranoic says. "If you say you're going to Cracow, you want me to believe you're
going to Lemberg. But I know that in fact you're going to Cracow. So why are you
lying to me?" (1973 [1905]: 115). This is perfect dream paranoia. This doesn't mean
that all dreamers are paranoiacs, only that the dream state itself is paranoid in its
capacity to project onto its characters, animals, and objects the motive that belongs
only to the dreamer.

Assuming these interactional structural strategies, then, how can we approach the dream as a narrative? Beyond them, what do dreams and narratives have in common? One approach may be to examine dreams along the lines of Vladimir Propp's famous study of 1925, *Morphology of the Folktale,* which analyzes some hundred fairytales in terms of their common components. Of primary interest to us might be Propp's concept of the *character function.* There are, in his view, seven character functions that remain stable in all folktales: the villain, the helper, the donor, the princess (and her father), the dispatcher, the hero, and the false hero (1970: 79–80). In Propp's definition, a function *"is understood as an act of a character, defined from the point of view of its significance for the course of the action. . . . Functions of characters serve as stable, constant elements in a tale, independent of how and by whom they are fulfilled. They constitute the fundamental components of a tale"* (p. 21). One might think of a character function, then, as being like the positions on a basketball team: there are two guards, two forwards, and a center. These positions can be occupied by any reserve player from the bench, but the function of the position in the game's "narrative" remains the same: guards always do this, forwards always do that, and so on. So a function is neither a character nor an action but something at the interface of the two. A function is an energy potential one needs in order to make a plot, any plot.[2]

Such an approach might allow us to find a narrative coherence in

[2] I am sure it is purely accidental that in David Foulkes's scoring system for latent dream structures in *A Grammar of Dreams* there are seven forms of human relatedness into which any dream unit (or association) can be classified: moving toward, moving from, moving against, creating, equivalence, means, and with. Like Propp's seven functions these "are exhaustive and mutually exclusive" (1978: 206). Clearly there is an overlap with Propp, especially along the oppositional axis of helping and hindering or, in Foulkes's terms, positive and negative relationships. In fact, one could easily align Foulkes's categories with Propp: moving toward, with ("being like" or "with"), and equivalence ("identical to") could roughly be equated with the helper, donor and princess functions, depending on the story context; moving from and moving against with the hero-villain conflict; and creating (developing, discovering) and means (or medium through which a relationship is sustained) with the dispatcher, donor and hero functions; obviously the dreamer would qualify as the hero and there is even a sense in which Propp's false hero appears in dreams as the ego of

the most bizarre of dreams, if only because character function seems to be the one element of dream structure that is not distorted by the dreamwork. If you are being chased by a stalk of celery in a dream, there is no doubt that it is serving the function of villain or one of the villain's helpers, and for plot purposes it would matter little if the celery suddenly changed into a tomato. And if you find yourself rescuing a lobster in distress, the endangered crustacean is at least temporarily serving the function of a thousand and one sought-after princesses in the folktales. Presumably, a dream would understand what the deconstructionists have been telling us: that no single image, not even a so-called primal image, can account by itself for its affective power. There is always a limitless history behind every dream image, insofar as all images are members of a symmetrical set, in Matte Blanco's term. Therefore, the dream has an endless bank of images that belong in the same functional category (of, say, helper or dispatcher). As a consequence, the dream tends to produce composite images that may be thought of as a means of solving the representational problem of competing urgencies or expressing the many in the one. But it is the *function* that insures that the dream remains stable and tells its story even as landscapes or characters become fused or replace each other, like players in a basketball game.

---

the dreamer displaced into another dream character (see Foulkes's chart of categories, p. 237). It would make an interesting project to compare Foulkes and Propp as fellow-structuralists working in two very different traditions with two different (but related) kinds of narratives (Propp does not appear among Foulkes's references). I have chosen to bypass Foulkes here for two reasons: (1) for my purposes, his coding system (based in Chomskian grammar) is far too complex to begin to survey here; more important, (2) it is a system for "deciphering dreams on the basis of information about [their "private meaning" to specific dreamers] rather than on the basis of suppositions about dreamers [or dreaming] in general" (p. 219). My interest here is not interpretive or motivational but phenomenological and comparative. Moreover, not being a psychoanalyst, I would hold out for the possibility that dream objects, characters, and animals are not always codable as latent father, mother, sibling, spouse, or peer symbols, but may be what they seem to be. Whereas Foulkes would score "The elephant attacked me" as an instance of parent-ego aggression (p. 220), I would hope that it is possible to dream that one was being attacked by an elephant (and possibly even being rescued by Mother or Dad). Foulkes may, however, agree, inasmuch as it is always the associational complex that influences the coding procedure in his system.

For purely illustrative purposes I greatly simplify Propp. We might reduce Propp's list to still more basic gerundive categories such as *seeking* and *finding* (which would belong primarily to the sphere of action of the protagonist-dreamer) and *helping* and *hindering* (which belong primarily to the sphere of action of the others—villain, donor, helper). In short, *seeking* something (even if only a bathroom or your car keys or a way home) is normally undergone by the dreamer in most dreams. Dreams do not normally have villains, but there is usually a villain function in dreams, some obstructive or hindering agency that impedes the dreamer's desire. Donors (a person or animal, for example, who gives the hero a magic weapon) seem to be a specific function in folktales, but when they are present in dreams they can usually be subsumed under the *helper* category. The princess might simply be thought of as the goal sought after or conclusion desired, and I suppose that a psychoanalytic approach might even retain the princess's father in an oedipal role of some sort. As for the dispatcher, the agent who sends the hero on his quest, this would seem to be the element in the dream, often absent as an entity, that produces the dream situation. For example, most dreams (or at least dramatic and epic dreams) find the dreamer *already* in a situation of quest, or desire, or frustration; how this comes about we only rarely know, since dreams seem to begin at the point where the dreamer has already been dispatched in a particular direction or project (if only purchasing a train ticket to get home). But it might be useful to retain the principle of dispatcher, thinking of it very broadly as the energizing factor in the dream or, to use Boss's term, the fact of the dreamer's "thrownness" into the world of the dream. Stories, of course, normally introduce the dispatcher as part of the exposition, as when M dispatches James Bond on an urgent mission, armed (through a donor) with the latest weaponry (which will prevent his otherwise certain death at the climax).

These might seem so general as to be worthless (like dividing people into such categories as tall or short, male or female, or young or old). But it is necessary to begin at the bottom, and I am inclined to think that they may be to narrative structure what angles, arcs, squares, and circles are to the structure of painting and architecture. At least I think dreams tend to specialize—when they are not purely lyrical in form—in narratives involving *seeking* and *finding* (or, more often than not, *not finding*) and being *helped* or (more often than not) being *hindered*—as when the vehicle you are driving refuses to behave and goes off a cliff. So the virtue of Propp's categories, or of my reductions of them, is that they allow us to break down a narrative structure (be it epic or dramatic) into what Freud might call cathectic units—persons or things that contain or release an emotional charge by virtue of what they do to you, or for you, or what you do to or for them.

Let us try to trace this general idea into the basic "narrative" structure of daily life which is the source of dreams and fictions. Presumably, we might assume that dreams and fictions use not simply the content of waking experience but the form of waking experience as well. To take a common life pattern, frustration arises when there are more hinderances about than there are helpers. For example, let us say that my wife's birthday is coming up. So I am dispatched on a quest that begins with finding a parking place on a busy Saturday afternoon at the shopping center. After some work, I make it to the third floor of Robinson's (where I am very much like Theseus entering the labyrinth). There among the clerks and crowds I encounter both helpers and hinderers—Ariadnes and Minotaurs—people who assist me ("Oh yes, we have that in red and it's on sale") and people who frustrate me ("We're out, but we'll have a new shipment next week") or redispatch me to another store ("Try Macy's"). Eventually, I manage to find the magic sweater. But alas, when I reach the parking lot I realize that it is almost identical to the magic sweater I bought last year. So back to the store (in the morphology of shopping this is called *returning the magic gift*), and so on to the next episode of my quest.

Now, by way of transition, let us look at this same structure in still another kind of household narrative: the improvised bedtime story parents tell later that same day. This is a fictional form that must be about ten minutes long, have suspense, a crisis or mild endangerment (nothing that will cause bad dreams), and of course a happy ending. Here one needs a heroine (little Amanda), helpers (squirrels and birds), Mr. Turtle (who takes Amanda and her pet dog Bentley across the lake to the mystery house), villains (snakes and spiders, the smart fox), and, of course, a princess, or sought-for object (a lost kitty or a new friend for Amanda). And you may find yourself relying on what Propp calls the "trebling device" (1970: 74): three attempts at a task before it is completed (Amanda tries the front door of the mystery house, then the back door, and finally Bentley sniffs out a hidden side entrance). Three is simply the most efficient number of repetitions needed to dramatize frustration and success or failure. It is a miniature variation of the narrative principle of beginning, middle, and end.

These may seem simple examples. But I suggest that they are bottom-rung experiences out of which emotional frustration, anxiety, and gratification arise, and such emotions take us to the cathectic base of fictions and dreams. Children read stories in school, they want to be told stories before they go to sleep, and they tell themselves stories during sleep. And however different, the stories (if you go down far enough into them) are all alike. They are all structural variations of the quest for the birthday sweater, the lost kitty, the lost way, or all such experiences in which there is emotional longing and disequilibrium—something to be done, to be got through, to be found or avoided: in short, a desire separated from its goal. And in each case the story unfolds through the intervention of helpers and hinderers, other words for which might be friends and enemies, conductors and resistances, flow and congealment, progress and stalemate/reversal—or, in Peter Brooks's theory, life and death, plot itself being "the internal logic of the discourse of mortality": "We live in order to die, hence . . . the intentionality of plot lies in its orientation toward the end even while the end must be achieved only through detour. This reestablishes the necessary distance between beginning and end, maintained through the play of those drives that connect them yet prevent the one collapsing back into the other" (1985: 22, 108).

Brooks's theory of narrative is useful for my purposes because it attaches plot so basically to the rhythm and cycle of life. His model for the theory is Freud's *Beyond the Pleasure Principle*; the main parallel is that between, on one hand, the life of the organism and its preparation for the "return to the quiescence of the inorganic world" (p. 107) and, on the other, the life of the narrative and its struggle toward its own ending. The metaphor (if we can call it such) is particularly useful in connection with the dream because, as I have been saying here, the dream is both a narrative and a form of organic life in its own right; that is, the dream stands midway between life and fiction, having some of the characteristics of both. To come back to Boss, the dream is a living fiction in which something happens to the dreaming person which isn't really happening outside the dream. But this is only one aspect of the parallel. For, in addition to possessing the sensory character of lived experience, the dream narrative borrows from life its particular form of plottedness. By this I am not referring to life's adventurousness or the sense of drama that occasionally inheres in everyday events. I mean, rather, the tendency of the life routine to produce the sense of "a tension" or "irritation," in Brooks's words (p. 103), or of being in the midst of something pending, surrounded, as it were, by helpers and hinderers who appear, as such, only when we find ourselves "in situation." For the terms *helper* and *hinderer* already imply such disequilibrium; to use them at all is to convert the neutrality of the world to a directional involvement in our immediate personal needs. Being "in situation," either in empirical or in dream life, amounts then to being "in narrative" or "in the middle," and this is the condition of life that dreams seem to specialize in reproducing. Thus we may now say that Hall's dream of the young man—"I remember being at a train ticket window. I guess I was buying a ticket. A girl at the ticket window kissed me in a way that seemed to give promise of better things when I returned from wherever I was going. I got on the train and it looked like the inside of a boxcar. I knew I was on the wrong train and I believe I tried to get somebody to pull the cord of the air brake" (1966: 164)—is really a paradigmatic dream structure. Here we have the dream protagonist on a quest to get someplace; he encounters a donor-helper(-princess?) who performs a service of a promising nature; he is hindered in his progress by boarding the wrong train and he immediately tries to find somebody to help him get off. Moreover, it is typical of such dreams that the dreamer does not know (or remember) where he was going; for the organic motive behind the dream, apart from its specific theme of misconduct, is that it represents a situation based on tension and desire.[3] It isn't the destination that counts but being in the situation of desiring to reach a destination—being, you might say, destinationless. Every episode in the dream contributes directly to this tension, not precisely in the narrative sense that one thing leads sequentially to another or that one thing foreshadows another or is the cause of the other's effect, but in the sense that each event unfolds, as events in life do, with an open-ended contingency. The difference between the dream plot and the plot of waking life, however, is that the contingency of dreams springs from the logic of association rather than the logic of interaction between individual and world. Put simply, the next event in my waking life depends on a convergence of forces in the world over which I have only partial control; the next event in my dreamlife depends on a similar convergence of forces, but these are all housed in my memory of the world and are called forth in the form of composite images by the evocative power of the image in progress. Thus, the sequence of dream events tends not so much toward the "And then" structure as toward "And suddenly" or "I found myself." Transitions or bridges between events are unnecessary in dreams because dreams, unlike waking fictions, require only a felt intelligibility. Unlike the reader of a story, the dreamer does not require transitions, because each new event is all-emersing—as it were, a new thrownness into a complete world. This is what sometimes makes it impossible to place certain events in the night's dreamlife.

[3] An even better example of this kind of dream, a veritable obstacle course of impediments, occurs elsewhere in Hall's collection. It is the dream of a young woman: "I was trying to buy a train ticket for home. People kept getting in my way and keeping me from the ticket window. I had only a few minutes to catch the train. When I finally did get the ticket I couldn't find the train. I kept getting on the wrong tracks and going on the wrong trains. At last I found the right ramp and got on the train. I found my sister's boy friend on the train and kissed him. There was only one thing wrong, the train was going the wrong way" (1966: 139–40). This, I must admit, comes close to a comic dream.

This tension, then, is the stuff of the most uneventful life—being among the things, the impediments and challenges, that constitute our situation. A novel such as Kafka's *Trial*, whatever it may reveal about Kafka's Oedipus complex, is about the same frustration we all experience in the grocery line or in dealing with the bank, the Internal Revenue Service, or the clerks at Macy's. The corollary to all this is that the size or the seriousness of the experience is not important. We write stories and novels about people to whom nothing happens on a Saturday (or any other) night. And most dreams, in the light of day, are about events so boring they would put you to sleep, if you weren't already. Psychoanalysis would explain this by saying that the triviality of the dream is a disguise of repressed latent content. That there is a latent content in dreams I have no doubt; I would describe it, however, as being existential and ontological before it is pathological or neurotic. In short, if we could hypothesize a perfectly healthy person with no hang-ups, no neuroses, no childhood traumas—a dubious conception, of course—we could presume that he or she would dream about the things we have been talking about *simply because they constitute the narrative of life*. Certainly, invoking the quantum physicist's law of complementarity, dreams can be looked at from both points of view (as both particles and waves), but I think the psychoanalytic theory tends to overlook the fundamental power and ubiquity of the trivial, how it accumulates into patterns of concern and tension, and how the trivial carries with it our deepest psychic investments, being, so to speak, the rhythm that corresponds most dependably to the organic heartbeat. The truth is that the trivial shopping trip carries as much emotional current as the quest for the Golden Fleece, just as the peasant's shoes in Van Gogh's painting carry as much affective power as David's *Death of Socrates*.

Let us come back to the improvised bedtime story. What is happening when I make up a new story for Amanda? First, it cannot possibly be a new story in the sense that I start from scratch. I know in advance what a story is and I have some sense of how to organize one around a beginning ("Once upon a time"), a middle ("And then"), and an end ("They lived happily ever after"). And I will certainly apply some measures of appropriateness which I know, in advance, would interest a young woman of five. Finally, I will probably build into the story a lesson of some sort ("Always be kind to others"), or at least the story, in resolving its tensions, will also imitate the resolution of tensions one would desire in life. The more one thinks about it, the more a story's newness consists primarily in putting new images (characters, a scene) into old combinations (character functions, a desired goal) and attendant patterns of development. The art of storytelling, as Brooks's theory suggests, is the art of detour, of keeping the ending from collapsing into the beginning. But even though some of us are better at the art than others, it is an art we all know by virtue of having absorbed the rules of story construction from childhood on. Beneath even that, however, is the larger base of the narrative of life itself which the narratives of stories simply put into more efficient and heightened form (I deal with this problem more thoroughly in the following chapter).

My claim is not that all dreams follow such a basic pattern; for there are dreams, or segments of dreams, that consist in little more than a landscape or an activity (like Globus's grotto dream, or a dream in which I am simply flossing my teeth and discover a huge cavity) or a seemingly endless repetition of a task. Dreams, let us say, tend toward a narrative structure. Moreover, the problem introduced by our poor memory of the content of our dreams suggests that even short dreams, like Globus's, may be the detached parts of narrative dreams we have forgotten. But even this hypothesis is unnecessary: narrative is a persistent characteristic of dreams, and a persistent characteristic of dream narrative is that its consistency—its aesthetic coherence, so to speak—is the evolution of an emotional tension as opposed to the evolution of a causal sequence. In the essay I quoted earlier, Maurice Blanchot suggests that the true "depth" of the dream is that it is all *surface* (Leiris, 1987: xxvii). I interpret this as referring to an undecomposable emotional content in the dream. Under it, or behind it, is simply more of the same thing: a history of similar emotion-laden events, any one of which might be capable of carrying the full emotional import of that particular history. This is not to imply that the dream is therefore uninterpretable or that its possible meanings are exhausted in its surface, only that the part is holographically endowed with the power of the whole. The business of the dream, then, is not to point cryptically to, or away from, the primal source of a particular emotion but to enact the emotion in its entirety as a psychic state that can only be represented cubistically—that is, as a fusion of past and present experience. Cubism is the all-at-onceness of an object; the dream is the all-at-onceness of an emotional history. Hence it is not surprising that my father (now deceased) should show up in a dream with Amanda (now five) and that Amanda should thereupon turn into a young boy oddly like myself. The logic of such a transformation lies purely along the plane of resemblance and the interchangeability of parts.

I must add that I am not advocating a method of interpretation. I am simply offering a commentary on the structure of dreams in relation to two adjacent kinds of narrative: that of life itself, from which the dream borrows both its content and its contingent plot structure, and that of fictions, which are in a manner of speaking waking dreams designed for other people. These are the three basic kinds of narrative, though one might hold that a fourth is the daydream, which is more volitional and less bizarre (in the sense of transformational) than the dream and on the whole less sustained and orderly than either the dream or the waking fiction. In any case, I am suggesting that the common denominator of all these narratives is some variation of Propp's functional categories. These have been refined and altered by subsequent theorists such as Souriau, Bremond, Greimas, Todorov, and Scholes, but the indispensable categories remain the same in all cases: the hero, the goal or objective, the helper, and the opposing force or hinderer. These, we might say, are the life (and death) forces of all narrative, including that of life itself. Perhaps it should be added that the categories of helper and hinderer must be conceived as extremely protean and not necessarily distinct from each other, as in the case of the duplicitous friend (who might be seen as a variation of Propp's false hero). Indeed, Calvin Hall offers the fascinating possibility that people who get into our dreams are usually a fusion of both extremes:

[The dreamer] invites those people for whom he has mixed feelings of affection and antagonism. They are people about whom he
has divergent conceptions and with whom he has not achieved a
stable relationship. They are the focal points of unresolved tension. When the tension abates, the appearance of the person in
one's dreams diminishes, when the tension increases his entrances
are more numerous. Those people toward whom the dreamer
feels both love and hate or fear and hate occupy the center of the
dream stage. Putting it in another way it can be said that we do
not dream about people with whom we have achieved a stable and
satisfying relationship. (1966: 30–31)

On one hand, this strikes me as rather categorical, since the endangered loved one (for example) is a steady fixture in dreams, along
with loving parents, grandparents, and best friends. But, on the
other hand, one might ask with whom we manage to achieve a
stable relationship, tensions being what they are in the waking
world. Then too, it is possible that even the absolutely stable friend
or wife or husband might qualify for a role in a dream on the basis
of the dreamer's fear that the stability *might* vanish. To whom has
the thought not occurred, "I'm lucky to have a friend like X,"
which is a dialectical thought in that it contains an awareness, at
least subliminally, of the opposite possibility ("I'm lucky" = "It
could be otherwise"). And these are the possibilities we carry into
our dreams—not active fears directed toward specific people, necessarily, but possibilities born of life in a highly unpredictable
world. Value something highly and it is apt to be taken away from
you in a dream. Hall seems to be saying something different, on the
basis of a thorough study of thousands of dreams, and he may be
right. But we might allow the alternative view that the helper-
hinderer (or friend-enemy) hybrid is another variation of how
Propp's categories might be blended to form a tension-producing
affect. One's dreams may contain not only helpers and hinderers
but helper-hinderers as well.

One more variation seems worth considering, and I can express
it best by returning to Globus's grotto dream, which I have called
an example of the lyric structure. Here Globus finds himself swim-

ming from the ocean into a rocky grotto: "I gaze up, and against the dark vaulted ceiling I perceive a starry display of luxuriant, green, luminous growth, which I experience with a feeling of pleasurable awe" (1987: 93). Globus offers an elaborate discussion of this dream's genesis in the facts of his personal life and concludes that "the symbolism of ocean, grotto and primordial life suggests that at a deeper level, there is a wish for rebirth gratified in the dream. Thus, this is a very satisfying dream "at both material and spiritual levels" (p. 96).

Since I do not know Globus personally, any interpretation of the dream I might derive from his discussion would be an uninformed one at best. But I do think we can see how the dream, peaceful as it is, rests on a somewhat unstable basis, or at least wherein it involves our Proppian functional categories. I suggest that the pleasurable awe of the luxuriant grotto is derived from the dream's subversion of a situation of profound endangerment. Swimming from the open ocean into a grotto is risky business for the best of swimmers, and Globus confesses that he doesn't really like to swim. He mentions this in connection with his swimming pool at home, which is one of the main determinants of the dream. The pool "ha[d] been an expensive and untrustworthy companion . . . for many years. (I have often referred to it as my 'worthy adversary!')," and with the recent birth of twins it had become a virtual nemesis in point of "protect[ing] them from falling into [its] clutches." Finally, Globus is a little amazed at the confidence and excitement with which he is able to swim around in the grotto so adventurously: "In waking life, I would have been worried about sharks!" (pp. 95–97). I am certainly not telling Globus anything he doesn't know in suggesting that all these negative determinants are hardly left outside the dream or that the exhilaration he felt must owe something to the dream's triumph over such an awesome force of nature as an ocean grotto, together with a lingering understanding that exhilaration itself is no stranger to terror. This must be the case with many dreams of flying over a city or countryside (in my own experience, Niagara Falls) or standing securely on the edge of a deep ravine and feeling a sublime oneness with nature vaguely mixed with horrific vertigo. Such dream experiences do indeed rise above the terror factor but mainly in the respect that a figure stands against a ground: it is the ground that allows the figure to emerge as a shape. The figure depends on the ground, one might say, for its independence, and the same principle can be carried over into emotional configurations. Thus "experiencing awe at [the] primordial life [of the grotto] . . . and feeling refreshed" (p. 97) appears to be an instance of what Sartre calls appropriation, or one's "conquest" of an element ["enormous masses of water, of earth, and of air"], the possession not of "the element for itself but the type of existence in-itself which is expressed by means of this element" (1966: 746–47). Globus's peace and contentment in the grotto, then, seem to be based on the resolution of a tension through a "synthesis of self and not-self," as Sartre says. The enemy, or nemesis, is still present, but the anxiety has been brought to a state of lyric rest.

Here, then, is another possible dialectical situation in which an equilibrium is achieved by a tension of opposites. I think Propp would be puzzled to hear that his functional categories of helper and villain had been applied to materials so remote from folktales. My purpose, however, is to examine various forms of narrative conduct, and I am claiming only that tension is a "cooperative competition," in Kenneth Burke's term, whereby a narrative might sequentially adapt some variation of the helper/hinderer principle (one undoing, or at least complicating, the work of the other), or it might fuse the two into an oxymoronic unity. But both spheres of action are indispensable to narrative development: they are the systolic and diastolic forces of the narrative quest.

So far I have dealt primarily with matters of overall or generic narrative form and with some of the agencies through which form is expressed. I want now to apply these principles to a problem that takes us to another level of dream narrative. To this end, I want to examine a theory put forth by David Foulkes. Foulkes is concerned with the problem of the mnemonic instigation of dreaming and with how a dream can organize its narrative materials as well as most dreams do. The basic problem is this: does mnemonic activation (the arousal of the memory content on which the dream is based) precede or follow the planning of the dream? Is it memory→planner, or planner→memory? This is the inevitable chicken-egg problem of all dream theory: how does the dream get planned from moment to moment? Where does the planner live, in the dream house itself or outside it? Foulkes argues for a memory-to-planner model: "Mnemonic activation must have general priority over planning processes, which interpret this activation" (1985: 150); otherwise we would have no explanation for "the peculiarities [the bizarreness] of dreams" (p. 149). That is to say that the planner, were it exclusively in charge of dream formation, would hardly allow disorderly elements to occur in the dream. But the planner, in its turn, has access to the contents of "symbolic memory," or to such things as "scripts" derived from waking situations; a script is "a generalized representation of an ordered sequence of events" (the most widely cited example being Nelson's "restaurant" script; p. 117). The script is learned in waking life and stored in the symbolic memory:

> Once a certain script has been adopted (e.g., a restaurant script), there is a much higher probability of associative facilitation of certain concepts (e.g., food, dishes, etc.) than of others (e.g., bathtub). Thus, since any interpretive schema itself is an activated component of symbolic memory, the path has already been partly cleared by the selection of such a schema for the production of a relatively coherent dream scenario. In this sense, there *is* some interaction between mnemonic activation and dream planning, and this interaction can only facilitate the integration of mnemonic elements into an effective dream plan. (p. 150)

Mnemonic activation, then, is probably random in some respects, in the sense that we typically cannot predict the topic or theme of particular dreams we will experience; but "the system being activated is not [random because] activation spreads according to pre-existing patterns in symbolic memory" (p. 151). In other words, the planner seems to be lodged in the symbolic "control booth" of memory itself. Thus, a dream carries its own gyroscope that keeps it, more often than not, from going off the rails and "jump[ing] around unpredictably over time." This process of "scriptual coherence" is not perfect, of course, but "the mundaneness of most REM dreams suggests that, once a script or other generalized-event knowledge structure has been selected to organize dream experience, the momentary representations and the sequences of the dream conform fairly well to the pattern implicit in that structure" (p. 169).

My own feeling is that Foulkes is overly concerned with accounting for bizarreness, which he sees strictly as a symptom of disorder in the dream. But, that aside, what I find useful about his theory, and consistent with what I have been saying, is his notion that form and content, process and product, the planner and the material to be planned, are all stored in the memory banks and operate in a reciprocal way, if indeed they can be separated at all. Despite lingering homuncular language ("The planner is . . . continuously faced with decisions about which mnemonic units to process and how to process them" p. 149), we have the beginning of a theory that explains dream organization without an "it" that is somehow psychically distinct from the dream and supervises it from afar out of some ulterior motive that presumes a system even more mysterious than the one it is intended to explain.

In terms of my own discussion about the narrative character of dreams and fictions, it remains chiefly to expand the idea of scripts and other "knowledge structures." I deal with this more fully in the next chapter, but here I suggest that the planner or planning mechanism is experience at large; that is, the formal organization of dreams is nothing more or less than the patterns imprinted on the mind by life in the waking world, which, I have been arguing here, also form the basis of all stories and fictions. The difference between waking experience and fiction and dreaming is really one of degree of organization rather than of kind. The very concept of mimesis, or imitation and representation, carries with it the planner that functions in all narrative forms. If we assume (and all theories do) that dreams and fictions borrow their content from the experience of life, what prevents us from assuming that they borrow the form as well? (Cezanne, for example, did not paint simply nature's rocks, trees, earth, and sky but their formal relationships as well.) It might immediately be argued, as Foulkes perhaps would himself, that life is not organized or that it is haphazard, subject to accident, boredom, long stretches of inactivity and vacuity—anything but planned. But all this is beside the point. As I have tried to show through my adaptation of Peter Brooks's theory of plot, there is in waking experience a constant presence of desire, an organismic seeking to take the right path, do the right creatural thing, in order to avoid pain, boredom, inconvenience, and frustration. We may even hypothesize that, if animals dream, their dream planners (as Jouvet's experiments with cats suggest) are based on the prototypical experience offered by their *Umwelten.* They do the things in dreams that they do in their environments—or rather, they dream about the things that *matter* in their environments—not the long stretches of boredom or waiting for the next kill but the aspects of life in which desire emerges most critically. Desire is not simply a state of want but a narrational enzyme. If dreaming occurs in virtually all animals, it seems likely that these dreams are narratives. There is, therefore, no skill involved in the making of dream narratives and no need for planners. Animals instinctively know, or are taught by life, how to organize their dream narratives. It is quite possible that, lacking language, their grammar of dreaming is less sophisticated than our own, but grammar in one *Umwelt* wouldn't work in another one anyway. We would assume that predation dreams occur most often among animals, just as dreams of social interaction occur most frequently in human beings. So my model would look like this:

life experience (desire)→dream→day dream→fiction and art

Here we see a relative increase in formal organization as we proceed from left to right, though one might plausibly argue that day-dreaming is a less organized experience than most REM dreaming. I place it in this order primarily because it is a relatively volitional and self-regulated activity, or can be; moreover, the daydream contains its own editor and possibility of revising the image sequence (as when one imagines a personal athletic achievement or a scene with the beloved and then improves on its possiblities in a revision)—in short, the Walter Mitty syndrome.[4] Moreover, one might say that fiction writers and storytellers are engaging in an orderly form of daydreaming. At any rate, with this possible ambivalence, the degree of organization increases, in one sense at least, with the necessity of making the narrative intelligible to others. As the narrative "goes public" it takes on what we might call semiotic refinements, and desire is more and more subdued to plausibility, genre interests, and literary requirements such as suspense, character consistency, reversal, and climax.[5]

But the spine of the narrative—and life offers many different spines on which to create narratives—remains essentially the same in all cases. The dreaming brain does not have to be instructed, any more than the novelist does, on how to create a car chase, an embarrassing cocktail party, or a visit to a Tibetan museum. Nor does the dream have to "think" very hard to imagine a personalized situation dominated by fear, lust, frustration, or primordial awe. For example, we must assume that early cave people dreamed.

[4] Here we should note Freud's essay "The Poet and Day-Dreaming." For Freud the "first traces of imaginative activity" occur in the child's play in which the child, like the poet, "creates a world of his own or, rather, re-arranges the things of his world in a new way that pleases him" (1973 [1908]: 143–44). It might be advisable to include *play,* then, as a fifth member of my model, except that it tends (as Freud says) to disappear in adulthood and reappear as daydreaming. Suffice to say that play supplies a certain education in plotting that teaches the child how to restructure experience imaginatively, whether in daydreams, dreams (which presumably get "better" or at least differently organized, partially as a consequence of the child's wide experience in play), and fiction. It is hard to say what any one of these things owes to the others, here I am interested strictly in the increase of organizational facility.

[5] We might add that this principle of degree of organization seems to obtain within the category of fiction and art itself, to put aside the others for a moment, that is, fictions can produce narratives that do not occur in dreams. We do not dream in the style of a Robbe-Grillet novel or in the style of *Finnegans Wake.* Moreover, most people don't read *Jealousy* or *Finnegans Wake* because they find them virtually incomprehensible. In general, the public would find such works bizarre and disorganized.

What might they have dreamed about if not the trials and successes of a life of hunting and gathering, much as we see depicted in their daydreams on the walls of Lascaux. Where did this narrative skill come from—this ability to put the hunt before the kill, the cause before the effect, the preparation before the achievement (in short, the art of plotting)—if not from a creatural understanding, born of the interplay of time and space, that life itself is a narrative, a series of probable successions of events as basic as the act of walking, or putting one foot-event after another? There is no reason, then, to assume that forms of order are not stored in the same way other mnemonic materials are stored, or to assume that memories are contents as opposed to forms of order, or that specific memories are not order-prone in specific ways (as, for example, a sexual memory would carry instructions for the formation of sexual scenarios). In this connection, however, there is another order of narrative structure that remains to be examined; I take that up in the following chapter.

4

Scripts and Archetypes

David Foulkes, among others, has suggested that one of
the purposes of dreaming may be to interconnect particularized and
generalized knowledge "in a way waking experience typically
wouldn't permit." To this end, narrative offers "a basic form of
comprehension" and "becoming human is . . . learning to understand and to be able to tell 'stories'" (1985: 202). I would like to
follow this notion further from a comparative poetic perspective. I
am less concerned with claiming that it is the purpose of dreaming,
or one purpose among others, than in examining its implications
for the relationship of dreams to waking fictions. In short, I want to
depart from a common denominator and try to see exactly what it
is that is common, or being shared. I trust Foulkes would agree that
most of what he says about dreams in this connection could be said
of waking fictions as well. There is no doubt that different degrees
of organization are involved, but that seems a secondary matter
relating to the different working conditions of consciousness in
either case. The main idea is that both dreams and fictions are,
more often than not, narrative in form. So the question to be asked
about dreams might be, how would the self tell a story if it didn't
have to be heard by someone else? But behind that question is a
more fundamental one: why would the self—waking or sleeping—

want to tell a story in the first place? What have such falsehoods to do with understanding and generalized knowledge?

The possibility immediately emerges that the function of dreaming is not simply to create a narrative *about* the dreamer's problems and waking experience—as if the dream were a sort of self-tribunal or confessional or a self-understander—but to use the problems and experience to create a narrative, the narrative being the final cause, the problems and experience simply the material causes through which the narrative can only be made. Let us take the case of the artist. A novelist may write from one of two standpoints: out of a need to express a social or personal theme in displaced or fictional form, or simply to write a novel. (After all, people become writers because they enjoy creating narratives, not because they have bigger problems than nonwriters.) Of course, these are not mutually exclusive motives. But can we say that one motive is more urgent or deeply rooted in the psyche than the other? Some people write narratives and all of us read the narratives of others because, among other things, they seem to satisfy a universal craving for a unified, closed, and imaginary analogue to life in an open-ended and accident-prone world. As Hayden White has put it, the need is "not only to narrate but to give to events an aspect of narrativity" (1980: 8). I am not promoting one motive over another, only suggesting that a comprehensive theory might consider dreams and fictions as differentia of a common genus and hence that the procedures and possible motives of one might be seen, mutatis mutandis, as operating in the other.

At least one corollary follows from this speculation. If we can see the dream as springing in any sense from a creatural need to make narratives as ends in themselves, as a way of plotting the possibilities of experience somewhat as scholars create models and systems that plot nature or history, we might extend to the dream the same creative freedom enjoyed by the novelist who is always thinking in what we may call an eclectic mode that is at once hypothetical and autobiographical. He writes in the autobiographical mode to the extent that he uses the materials of his experience as a basis for story construction, characterization, and so on, and he works in the hypothetical mode to the extent that he does not try to be faithful to these materials but to perfect them according to the principles, conventions, and intuitions that govern the making of art. The writer's mother, along with all the mothers he has had occasion to observe, may provide much of his understanding of how mothers behave, but the mother who appears in the fiction is a more or less deliberate composite whose characteristics are based on the needs of the fiction. Thus, the better to create a behavioral horror, a novelist would have no scruples whatsoever about using his mother's gentle and loving manner to characterize the victimization of prison inmates by a sadistic "motherly" warden. This would be a case, then, in which a known reality would be creatively edited and put to reverse use without the least implication of resentment, hatred, or all the repressions usually associated with purely autobiographical writing. Of course, if our novelist made a lifelong habit of editing his mother thus, as Kafka did his father, one might begin to have suspicions that the real theme of the work lay outside purely aesthetic considerations. The point is simply that art carries a mandate that insists on the maximization of all incoming materials to the end of realizing the emotional and affective potentials of the work.

So, too, I dream about my friend Paul hypothetically. I dream Paul possibilities—not just likely possibilities (though these are probably the most frequent) but improbable possibilities, even impossibilities. It is far from likely that Paul would betray me in real life. But should the theme of betrayal somehow arise when I am dreaming and Paul happens to be at hand, the dream would not hesitate to cast him in the role of betrayer. And he would betray me *as* Paul, that is, in Paul's voice, with Paul's wit, Paul's quiet considerate way. Really an improbable Paul, but Paul even so. And what such a dream might be doing for me, thematically, is revealing, not an unconscious fear that Paul is capable of betraying me or that he is a displacement of someone else whose potential for betrayal I have repressed, but the paradox that is the persistent topic of literary tragedy—as summed up succinctly in Caesar's famous "Et tu, Brute!"—that the world's potentiality is most thoroughly demonstrated in its capacity for unexpected reversal, the terminal discrep-

ancy of the *peripeteia*. In short, my dream of Paul—"Et tu, Paul!"—
would be a version of one of the oldest story structures in the
world. An analyst might want to ask, "Yes, but even so, why Paul?
Why not Dan or Leonard or Jim?" And it is quite possible that with
a little associational searching we could find something about my
relationship with Paul that triggered his role in a betrayal scenario.
God knows, Paul and I have our differences, and he regularly "betrays" me on the tennis court by winning. The point is that it is just
as possible (as in fiction) that he might serve as betrayer on the
dialectical ground of contradiction that astonished Oedipus so
much when he found out who his real mother was (and, as many
people have pointed out, Oedipus couldn't possibly have had an
Oedipus complex). To put it another way, the maximization of a
betrayal scenario would, in most cases, involve a maximal degree of
unexpectedness because it carries a higher degree of interest as well
as a more thorough demonstration of the stakes of betrayal. The
Oedipus story may have far-reaching psychic ramifications for all
human beings, but it is also one of the world's most thorough
stories.

So the dream may, as one of its possible functions, be doing
much the same thing as the fiction writer who makes models of the
world that carry the imprint and structure of our deepest concerns.
And it does this by using real people, or scraps of real people, as the
instruments of hypothetical acts (a bit of mother here, a confusion
of father and teacher there, a friend cast as foe, and voila! a Franken-
stein). In other words, the relevance of the dream's content to the
dreamer's personal life may be less significant than the function it
serves as a structuring principle. It may be that the narrative is the
important factor and the content only secondary, and that dreaming
is an exercise in pure storytelling whose end is nothing more (or
less) than the organization of experience, even to the point of altering people and loved ones for the sake of the perfection of the plot. I
take it this is at least partly what Foulkes means in saying that
narrative is basic to human comprehension and that "dreaming
affords the opportunity for this kind of comprehension to be exercised in conditions more demanding than those we typically are

likely to encounter in our extrinsically-structured waking lives" (1985: 202)—except, of course, in art and waking fictions where the same conditions apply. This is the thrust of my argument here.

All this borders on the principle of the archetype as a structuring device, and as an extension of what I was saying in the previous chapter about scripts I move now to that topic. By *archetype* I intend something rather different from Hunt's notion of an archetypal dream as one with an "uncanny-numinous quality and aesthetically rich structure [and a] powerful sense of felt meaning and portent" (1989: 129); different too from Globus's "predispositions inherited in evolution" or "inherited tendencies towards ways of being in the world" (1987: 140–41); and finally, different (in emphasis at least) from James Hillman's notion of the archetype as "a rich image" that gets deeper "as we go deeper into it" (1977: 80). I am not denying the value of these usages or even their possible relevance to the idea of archetype I develop here. In the present instance, however, it is not so much depth that concerns me as form. And I can best approach the problem by citing a characteristic archetypal experience from my own life.

A few years ago I was rereading *Cyrano de Bergerac* for a class, and it suddenly dawned on me that I knew this plot from another source. Here, it seemed to me, were the basic ingredients of the myth of Philoctetes, the Greek warrior who was exiled from the Troy-bound army because of an offensive wound; in exiling Philoctetes, however, the Greeks had inadvertently exiled Hercules' famed bow without which Troy could not be taken—hence the necessity of somehow bringing Philoctetes, bad smell and all, back into the society of his fellow warriors. Several important points must be screened out to make the Philoctetes story fit Rostand's play, but this much at least captures what Edmund Wilson some years ago identified as the archetypal interest of the Philoctetes plot: the pariah/savior who stands in what we might call a minus-plus relation to society. Like Philoctetes, Cyrano is, on one hand, physically offensive because of his grotesque nose but, on the other, gifted in the skills of swordsmanship and eloquence which are indispensable for successful campaigns in this courtly world. In short, what *Cyrano* has in common with the Philoctetes story is, as Wilson says, the idea of "genius and disease," superior strength and disability, bound inextricably together.

Following the experience, I began seeing Philoctetes everywhere: in all those tales, for example, that center about ugly people, or ducklings, who are discovered to have beautiful souls; in that broad class of fairytales and novellas in which frogs are converted to princes and kitchen maids are discovered to be of royal birth or, by virtue of their undeserved hardships, to have attracted the patronage of fairy godmothers; moreover, are not many stories of overcompensation based on just this principle of the gifted pariah? And what of the genre of the moral tale? Consider the story of Rudolph, that lovable Horatio Alger of the reindeer world, whose grotesque electronic nose saves Christmas by piloting Santa's sleigh through the foggy night. Any shelf of children's literature is bound to turn up at least one story titled "The Little Train That Could," "Tommy Saves the Town," or "Judy Saves the Space Program"—all of which are designed to teach the wonderful lesson that inferiority or "wounds" are only skin deep and that you had better think twice before you write off the weakling, the young, the different, or the outsider.[1]

It would be absurd to say that these fictions have anything to do

---

[1] This same story situation, referred to by some anthropologists as the myth of Cinderella or the outcast hero, is also prevalent in the mythology of North American Indians, where it serves quite different social functions. According to Dmitry M. Segal, it refers to "the facts of social organization of primitive tribes, to the great importance of the collectivity in primitive social organization, to the enormous significance of the transition from the state of exclusion from the collectivity which goes with being young (synonymous with rejection), and to the entry into the collectivity" (1972: 220). The Cinderella situation is also widespread in the folklore of the Ulithi Atoll in the western Pacific, as documented by William A. Lessa: "The reversal of fortune by heroes who conquer the odds and emerge triumphant constitutes an important stylistic theme in Ulithian stories. The winners are tender-aged, deformed, insane, poor, low-caste, scorned, or otherwise without apparent prospect of success. . . . Out of my original collection of twenty-four tales I have ascertained that almost half have as their dominant idea the triumph of the handicapped underdog" (1972: 99). There are significant differences between these tales and the Philoctetes situation, of course. My point is that the situation of the outcast or handicapped hero is

with the Philoctetes myth being somehow imprinted on our consciousness or inherited in any collective biological sense. Yet archetypal (or mythic) criticism, at least that of unintentional myth,
tacitly or openly makes some such assumption and rests on little
more evidence of debt than I have mustered here.[2] My suggestion is
that it would be much more reasonable to view all these fictions as
tragic, comic, folkloric, and didactic variations of a *social* tension
that is as old as society itself. In short, society unavoidably consists,
among other things, of insiders and outsiders, and in the drama of
human relations there are always times when you can't tell which is
which. The Philoctetes-Cyrano situation is thus a highly versatile
model of an inevitable problem and another possible variation of
our helper-hinderer principle, or perhaps more appropriately the
hero-villian combination. Reverse the emphasis—put the plus before the minus, the savior before the pariah—and you have Christ
and Ibsen's Dr. Stockman, the exile or destruction of the strong
man who stands alone and becomes the enemy of the people he
would rescue from their own sins.

   If this is true, where does that leave the archetype? If you think of
the similarities in these stories as springing from the realm of social
problem putting, what Kenneth Burke calls "literature as equip-
ment for living" (1957: 253–62), what happens to our concept of
the archetype as the persistence of the archaic world? I am not
denying that there is at times a subtler relation between myth and

---

endlessly useful: thematically, it is a way of dealing with a whole set of perennial
social problems concerned with the reabsorption of the rejected outsider into the
group; and, as pure fiction, it gratifies our natural interest in stories with strong
pathos (an undeserving victim), a maximum reversal (coming from behind to win),
and a liberal dose of poetic justice.

[2] By unintentional myth I mean the possible presence in a work of literature of
mythic materials (fragments, structures, images) not intended by the author. It is a
moot point whether an author knows (and how he knows) he is dealing in myth. In
any case, I am not concerned with the conscious use of myth and archetype we find
in Racine (Euripides), Milton (the Bible), or Joyce (Homer). I realize that Sophocles's *Philoctetes* and other Greek plays are not myths at all but self-conscious literary
works that may have grown out of myths. Rightly or wrongly, however, such plays,
along with the Homeric epics and the Bible, constitute the chief source of archetypes
in later literature to which myth criticism addresses itself.

fiction or that a poet might consciously or unconsciously create a work that depends for its deepest effect on an oscillation with myth; I am simply suggesting that what we often call an archetype, imbedded in a later fiction, may not be an archetype at all—or, if it is, that archetypes, so broadly defined, are impossible to avoid in literature, having much the same inevitabilty as the curve, the straight line, and the angle in painting and architecture.

I am suggesting, then, that what we call an archetype has no original version and requires no mysterious or deliberate awareness of earlier variations. But somewhere along the line studies of the recurrence of myth and archetype in later literature tend to fall victim to what we might call the homing instinct. Once the idea of priority exerts its pull, along with the assumption that the archaic world is somehow more primal and closer to nature, the critic can only view the newer term in the archetypal metaphor as a post hoc displacement of the original and not as a thing in its own right which may simply have adapted a standard design in the structural order for altogether different purposes. The paradigm of this kind of thinking, and certainly its scientific authorization, was established by Freud. It appears most succinctly in his comparison of Oedipus and Hamlet. *Oedipus* is nearer to its raw source in "primaeval dream-material," as expressed in Jocasta's line about men "ere now" dreaming of laying with their mothers. But in *Hamlet* "the changed treatment of *the same material* reveals the whole difference in the mental life of these two widely separated epochs of civilization: the secular advance of repression in the emotional life of mankind" (1973 [1900], 4: 264 emphasis added). In other words, what Freud poses as the operative difference between the epochs of Sophocles and Shakespeare is the advance of a defense mechanism: the psychic materials of myth simply sink deeper beneath the crust of a censored exteriority where they magically exert their influence in symbolic forms. This concept of living myth made it possible to explain any recurrence of an old structure as the persistence of primal psychic energy or—what amounts to the same thing—its corruption by the discontents of civilization. If we are looking for an explanation for the persistence of archetype in literature and, we may now add, in dreams, we can find it directly in the structure of a mind that doesn't have to remember (biologically, genetically, or in a collective memory) in order to imitate. The archetype is given by the empirical world, and more specifically by the value relationships that inform human conduct. There are archetypes everywhere; indeed, it would be impossible to write a meaningful fiction or dream a dream that did not somehow lean on an archetypal model as its organizing principle, since the principle of archetype is simply a special reference to the tensions arising from the value structure itself. Archetype is another way of accounting for a world that does not change: the origin of the archetype can be found in the institutions of contemporary society. Would one therefore look on the remains of early man's shelters, marvel that they too had roofs, just like ours, and conclude that our roofs must have their origin in theirs?

At this point, we may return to our original question: why should a species like our own need to create fictions in the first place or to dream dreams, both of which persistently return to familiar structures and require such functional elements as helpers, hinderers, dispatchers, princesses, and heroes? How might this be explained by an alien observer? These people, our observer might say, lead brief oxygen-dependent lives, they reproduce sexually, they live in families and communities, and they work toward individual and collective goals. But our observer might go beyond this and theorize that these fictions and dreams—remarkably similar in their content—are not simply ways these people amuse or instruct themselves; rather, they need fictions and dreams as complementary means by which they constantly monitor and index the diversity of their experience. Through narrative they might, in a sense, *remember* experience—not in the trite way that we say a novel is an accurate account of life in a certain historical period but, rather, the kind of remembering that has to be done over and over. If something is to be remembered at all, it must be remembered not as *what* happened but as what has happened *again* in a different way and will surely happen again in the future in still another way. And by this means, as Roger Schank suggests in his essay on memory models, a "commonality" can be built up among various versions of the same experience that might serve as the basis for forming a new knowledge structure or for modifying or confirming an old one. Any new case of something, Schank says, verifies a hypothesis we carry around in our memory waiting to be verified and then verified again (Schank and Seifert, 1985: 72). Or, as Schank puts it in another book, "man is . . . a processor that only understands what it has previously understood" (Schank and Abelson, 1977: 67). So we keep writing the same old stories and having the same old dreams because we keep having the same old experience in different ways. And each different way constitutes a moment of adaptation of what I am suggesting are fundamental archetypal situations attended by such emotions as fear, anger, frustration, sadness, and the like, which may be defined as the psychic consequences of experience.

Schank, I might add, is a computer scientist; but he is describing a functional process similar to those described by neuroscientists of memory processing such as Jonathan Winson (1990) and Gerald Edelman (1987). The technical part of this is way over my head, but it seems worth our time to look at what scientists are saying about the synapses that produce our fictions and dreams. In this respect, Edelman is especially inviting because his highly experimental work on neuronal group selection leads him, finally, to wonder whether "every perception [may be] considered to be an act of creation and every memory an act of imagination" (1987: 329). This is not a metaphor or a sop thrown to the humanists. Imagination, for Edelman, is that absence of precision in neural networks that makes all pattern recognition possible. In more specific terms, Edelman defines memory as "a form of recategorization based on current input" (p. 265). It is disjunctive (meaning that it distorts) and it is transformational (meaning that the brain stores nothing, not even your memory of your mother's face, as it is or was on a certain day). Thus memory is a "continually active process [through which the brain partitions] a world that exists 'without labels'" (p. 266). By this Edelman simply means that the world itself is not prelabeled. Each species comes along, like Adam and Eve, and labels it according to its own needs.

What is becoming apparent, then, is that the formation and

maintenance of long-term memory seems to involve a continual revision of our knowledge structures through their linkage with new experience. We tend to take the achievement of memory for granted, somewhat like a paid-up mortgage. But it seems plausible to assume that the brain has a continual task of keeping established networks in good working order by running characteristic programs, or what Schank calls scripts. Scripts, as I discussed them in the previous chapter, are high-level memory structures that are capable of self-modification; they are based on repeated experience and they "make information experienced in one situation available for use in another" (Schank, 1986: 11, 9).[3] Otherwise, for example, it might even be possible to forget to feel terror, like the child who has not yet learned the danger of water or height. I am not claiming that stories and dreams qualify as scripts in Schank's sense. But on almost every page of Schank's book I am provoked to think of narrative as a contribution to our formulation and recognition of patterns of experience. Stories and fictions might be thought of as ways of sharing knowledge structures, dreams as a way of organizing private knowledge structures. If the dream seems bizarre, that is possibly because in the dream we are literally watching our thought process as it searches, indexes, combines, and correlates information and creates or revises scenes that will be useful predictors of future experience. The dreamer is thus an involuntary artist who takes the labeled world to sleep and reclassifies it—that is, returns it to more basic categories of perception that are, on one hand, shared by all human beings but, on the other, unique to the dreamer's own experience. And if we can't make sense of the dream when we awake in the morning, that is because it conflicts with the pragmatic labeling system we reinherit when we open our eyes.

In saying all this, I have no wish to restrict either dreams or

---

[3] A fuller definition of *script* is offered by Schank: "A script is a structure that describes appropriate sequences of events in a particular context. A script is made up of slots and requirements about what can fill those slots. The structure is an interconnected whole, and what is in one slot affects what can be in another. Scripts handle stylized everyday situations. They are not subject to much change, nor do they provide the apparatus for handling totally novel situations. Thus, a script is a predetermined, stereotyped sequence of actions that defines a well-known situation" (Schank and Abelson, 1977: 41)

stories to a pure storage function. In the first place, it is far beyond my knowledge to make such an assumption; in the second, even the speculations of neuroscientists are based on what is at best suggestive evidence. I am simply impressed by the sympathies between recurring patterns in dreams and fictions and our most recent theories about memory processing. It is at least possible that the principle of "Once upon a time" may, after all, be a seductive mnemonic device, and a rattling good story or dream an exercise in circuit maintenance. Perhaps there are still other, more basic uses in stories and dreams. In any case, experience itself dictates the form our plots take, in fiction as well as dreams. Plots may be considered as causal structures that recur often enough to have worn a kind of cowpath into the neural memory. There is no predetermined master plot or strict structuration in brain plotting. Dream plots tend to replicate situations—fear, escape, apprehension, pleasure, shame, pride, humiliation, being lost, feeling desire—that either have a significant rate of frequency in life (however diluted) or are essential to survival. A dream of climbing a cliff and experiencing vertigo, endangerment, and fear of falling is a condition of existence, even if one has only been as high from the ground as a step ladder. The dream tends to "purify" such structures: it perfects or maximizes them, making danger even more dangerous, desire more desirous, and humiliation more humiliating. It could be that where these more negative emotions are concerned the dream serves as a kind of premonitory warning to make the dreamer aware of the stakes of life in the waking world: "Stay out of situations like this, the penalty of relaxation is—danger."

This leads me to a consideration of the relevance of scripts to archetypes in dreams and fictions. Foulkes, as we have seen, is also taken by the notion of scripts as a basis of dream planning. He seems, however, chiefly concerned over whether the dream follows the script as written in the world of social usage: "How is [the dream] like, and how is it unlike, waking evocations of relevant script knowledge? Do the deviations suggest the simultaneous activation of unrelated scripts, or are they more an indication of a greater possibility of omissions or alternative slot-fillers in the operative script?" (1985: 168) I would not say these are irrelevant matters, but in my view scripts would form a grounding function in the structuring of dream and fictional narratives. Scripts are culture-based and are formulated after the fact of existence and desire; in a word, we are "thrown" into a world held together by scripts. Consequently, beneath scripts something deeper is at work, even in scripted situations themselves. Being socially ordained by manners, custom, social harmony, and the like, scripts tend to be restrictive and civilized; hence they create tensions or become the very ground from which tensions and frustrations emerge. Embarrassment is a strong theme of dreams, for instance, and embarrassment occurs in life precisely as a failure to follow scripts—the personal script, so to speak, rubbing against the social script (as when a person who speaks first and thinks afterward gets into trouble by "putting his foot in his mouth"). Freud's dreams of success and professional frustration arise from pressures caused by certain scripts, among which the current notions of Jewish physicians must have figured highly, by his own admission. The famous Irma dream bristles with scripts and the penalties for abusing them, as does every dream in Freud's or anyone else's book. It is, after all, a script revision that gets Philoctetes in and out of trouble on Lemnos; it is a set of conflicting scripts concerning friendship, romance, and personal honor that leads to Cyrano's plight in his love for Roxanne. The story of *Antigone* is one of two equally weighted high-priority scripts (family burial rites versus state law) in direct confrontation, *Hamlet* is a story in which a man is trapped between the demands of (at least) two behavioral scripts, and so forth through world literature. Dreams and fictions tend to be about the wages of getting out of step with the scripted world, of differing interpretations of the same script, or of a collision of personal goals with established scripts.

What I have here been referring to as archetypes are really narrative equations concerning predictable conflicts in our scriptual life. An archetype, considered as a narrative structure, involves an interaction of social scripts and personal desire or "flaw." If scripts teach us how to move appropriately through life with the least friction, they are also the source of bane. Means designed to keep us in step quickly become means through which we *may* fall out of step. Thus, every script gives rise to a potential antiscript. If you were stubbornly to decide to reject every script that figures in the conduct of your life for a single day (assuming you could identify them all), you would have no recourse but to remain at home behind closed doors in a catatonic funk—and even that would entail the observance of a kind of "Do not disturb!" script. In short, scripts provide both the plot structure of dreams and fiction and their affective energy. The simplest narrative is built on a scriptual base. For example: "Mother had told Mary not to wander from the backyard, but the sight of the brightly colored kite flying over the meadow was too much to resist" has already announced a departure from a script in the direction of a more powerful antiscript (desire, curiosity).[4] Let me apply the general idea to two specific texts, one a fictional text and one a dream text. It is difficult to deal with fictions in this connection because they are too long to quote. But, in the hope that a sample might make the point, I have chosen the familiar opening of Tolstoy's *Anna Karenina,* which goes like this:

> Happy families are all alike; every unhappy family is unhappy in its own way.
> Everything was in a state of confusion in the Oblonsky's household. The wife had discovered that the husband was carrying on

[4] I am aware that I am taking the notion of scripts beyond the dimension and usage described by Schank. Schank is mainly interested in scripts as the basis of mnemonic economy or the means by which the brain stores implicit knowledge structures that need not be processed freshly in each new situation. Scripts provide "connectivity" and a basis of "understandability" of stories (Shank and Abelson, 1977: 40). I am concerned with scripts as a source of psychological and narrative tension and disequilibrium and I see no reason why one cannot treat the concept as giving rise to personalized patterns of desire or to reactionary and deviant behavior. As Schank says, "the actions of others make sense only insofar as they are part of a stored pattern of actions that have been previously experienced. Deviations from the standard pattern are handled with some difficulty" (p. 67). Precisely, and such deviations are the basis of fictions and dreams. Finally, I am simplifying Schank to some extent. A full treatment would have to consider what he calls goals and themes (including role themes, interpersonal themes, and life themes), a theme being "essentially a generator of related goals. When a theme is identified it makes sense of a person's behavior by providing a prior context for his actions" (p. 132).

an affair with a French girl, who had been a governess in their family, and she had announced to her husband that she could not go on living in the same house with him. This state of affairs had now lasted three days, and not only the husband and wife, but all the members of their family and household, were painfully conscious of it. (Garnett trans.)

If we extract the emotional content of this passage—and by extension of the entire novel—we arrive at notions of happiness, unhappiness, hurt, anger, frustration, and pain.

What a world of implication lies behind the simple phrases "happy families" and "unhappy families"—one to be desired (as in the expression "the pursuit of happiness"), the other avoided. Might we not assume that the story of the happy family would involve a greater number of helpers or (in principle) princesses (that is, rewards and successful quests), and that of the unhappy family a greater number of hindrances, trials, tests, and failures? And may we not further say that the famous opening statement, "Happy families are all alike," could be construed as Tolstoy saying to his reader that there is really no story to tell about happy families, since happiness is a state of having, not a condition of longing and desire. Happiness has no narrative, and therefore it requires no narrator. To put this another way, the happiness script holds no more story interest (tension, disequilibrium) than the narration of a perfectly normal dinner in a restaurant where everyone follows the predetermined, stereotyped sequence of actions expected in the restaurant situation. Such a story, as the Soviet writers used to complain, would be a drama without conflict in a society without flaw: a perfect script with perfect players. And since happiness is so boring (to all but the happy few), this novel will spend its time with the unhappy Oblonskys and the (soon to be) unhappy Karenins among whom confusion, anger, fear, desperation, and pain are rampant, due primarily to the violation of the marital script on which family happiness is presumably based. And the novel will be a description of this unhappiness (which we label a tragedy in literary study) as it hypothetically occurred in mid-nineteenth-century Russia in the urban upper class. And as we read the novel late in the twentieth century, we think, "Yes, that's *right!* That's the way it *is!* That's what *happens!*" In other words, in Schank's sense, something has been verified, an old knowledge structure has been enlarged and renewed; it has accommodated a new variation, and in some imponderable way we are a little more alert (though no happier) for having read it. So it turns out that even unhappy families are, in a deep way, all alike. If you think away all the local historical references, all the Russian-ness and nineteenth-century-ness, you are left with a massive evolution of scriptual tensions involving fundamental principles of manners and morals.

Let us turn now to the text of a dream:

> I have been dispatched to give some sort of a public lecture. In the remarkable shorthand of the dream, the scene takes place on the night of the event. I am walking to the Great Hall with colleagues, friends, and family. They are all cordial, supportive, curious, or at least obliged to hear what I have to say, and the band is playing a gay tune. But every step I take drives a stake into my heart because, alas! I have neglected to prepare the lecture. I try to jot down some thoughts as we near the Great Hall. In desperation, I steal a book from a passing student, hoping to find a subject. But of course the book is unreadable. Even as I am being introduced, I am still groping. Finally, the moment comes. I rise. And now my notes have disappeared and my mind is a total blank. I am terrified. But, thanks to a merciful feature of the dream, I suddenly awake and it is all over but the memory.

Here is a narrative of devastating efficiency in which I fail to follow a script so habitual that it would seem to be second nature in my profession. I am caught scriptless, so to speak, in one of society's more tightly scripted rituals. Here is one of the true archetypal dreams of the teacher, the other one being the dream in which one has the lecture but no one shows up to hear it. I take it that such dreams are based on our principle of catastrophic expectancy, or, to follow Schank's notion of verification, catastrophic wariness; for one conceivable value of such a dream may be that it updates an old memory program "based on current input," as Edelman would say. One of the persistent fears of a teacher's life—as of the actor's, the skydiver's, the metropolitan window washer's, and the surgeon's—is that the scriptual routine can never be counted on and there is always the possibility of the unexpected intrusion and the consequence of disaster. If I persistently had such dreams (that is, if I were neurotic), I might go to an analyst and together we might uncover all sorts of forgotten experience from my past that could lead to an understanding of my fear of the lecture situation. Where I would part company with psychoanalysis, however, is in the assumption that this or any other dream has undergone a censorship of a repressed content. I suggest that the dream is, pure and simple, a representation of the fear of humiliation, one of the prime stakes of social life on this planet. But to find the cause of the humiliation in one's personal life—and surely, as Tolstoy would say, every humiliated person is humiliated in his or her own way—does not explain why it should be such a persistent and universal response to so many situations—why, in other words, all humiliated people are *also* all alike.

It would be an exaggeration to say that all dreams and fictions are fundamentally about scriptual violations or scripts in conflict. It is unlikely that the dreams of very young children are script-based. For example, this dream of a three-year-old girl cited by Piaget—"I dreamt there was some wood under the beds and the kitten went and laid on it" (1951: 178)—can probably be better associated with what Piaget calls sensory-motor schema, the representation of a generalized situation prior to conceptual life in a "socialized" world (p. 215). One suspects, however, that something *like* a script, in Schank's sense, is beginning to be apparent in the following dream of a five-year-old girl: "I dreamt I was going to school all by myself in the tram (she laughed with pleasure at this idea). But I missed the tram and walked, all alone (more laughter). I was late, and the mistress sent me away, and I walked home all by myself" (Piaget 1951: 178). Here, at the relative beginning of scriptual life (and untested reality), laughter comes easily (for whatever reason), even though underneath the dream we sense the rudiments of danger,

punishment, and isolation—in short, the emergence of social structures and obligations designed to assure safety and order. Finally (to
continue the theme into later life), here from the collection of Calvin Hall is another dream of a schoolgirl at a considerably later
stage of scriptual exposure:

> I dreamed I was with a crowd of schoolgirls getting on a bus. Just
> then a very tall man came up in back of me and tried to pick me
> up. I got on the bus just in time before he could catch me although
> I don't remember him chasing me. All at once we were driving
> down the street in front of my house and I felt if I could just get off
> here at my house I would be safe. (1966: 138).

In these three dreams, then, we follow a kind of evolution from
innocence into the world of standardized behavior and its deviant
possibilities. Beyond the dreams of children, moreover, there are
certainly asocial adult dreams that have little to do with scripted
models of this sort: primordial dreams, dreams of natural phenomena, sublime landscapes, dreams of telekinesis, premonition, pure
volition, diagnostic dreams, religious dreams, feverish dreams,
problem-solving dreams, mechanical repetition dreams, nonsense
dreams, and many archetypal dreams in Hunt's sense of the term
(dreams containing "uncanny numinous emotion, geometric and
mandala-like patterns, flying, mythological/metaphysical thinking, encounters with mythological beings, monsters, or strange
animals"; 1989: 128).[5] All these forms owe little to the tensions of
interpersonal reality and thus little to the scripts that control its
traffic. For the most part, such dreams seem to fall closer to the
lyric mode than to fully narrative (dramatic and epic) structures.
Indeed, we might advance a tentative rule of thumb to the effect
that the more narrative the dream the more likely it is based on
scriptual models, for the simple reason that interpersonal themes
require structures capable of dialectical opposition. This rule can

[5] It occurs to me that even these dream forms may be said to be based on a form of
scripted knowledge of still another kind. How would one know what a mandala was
without having seen one? or a sublime landscape? or a mythological being?

probably be applied safely to literary forms as well. On the extreme opposite of fully interpersonal and narrative forms such as *Anna Karenina, Oedipus Rex, Farewell to Arms,* and *Gone with the Wind* we might place certain works of Poe ("Descent into the Maelstrom," "The Pit and the Pendulum"), Artaud (*The Spurt of Blood*), Kafka ("The Burrow," "The Country Doctor"), Beckett (*The Lost Ones, Footfalls, Not I*), much surrealism, and the various forms Northrop Frye might classify under the category of the archetypal masque, which "at its most concentrated becomes the interior of the human mind" (1957: 291). Many of these fictions fall short of normal story expectations (at least those at the other extreme) and might be considered as being closer to action sequences than to stories (*Not I,* for example, begins in the full career of Mouth's monologue and ends with the fading of lights and sound, under which the story continues without cessation). In short, it is impossible to arrive at any definitive set of criteria for either dreams or stories: dreams often imitate the forms of fiction (the detective, mystery, and adventure dreams) and fictions (in the modern period at least) often strive to capture the precise form and atmosphere of the dream (insofar as they can be reproduced in the waking state). One can hardly say that such fictions are unsuccessful because they do not follow Ricoeur's, or any other, criteria. Rather, it seems appropriate to alter one's conception of what is behind such criteria as beginnings and endings to include what Minsky (1988: 122–23) calls a function, as opposed to causal closure; such fictions begin at the onset of an emotional tension (in progress), much like dreams, and end at the point where it has been either circumscribed (see Chapter 2) or established as never-ending.

In some respects, it may seem a self-fulfilling prophecy to claim that scripts are at the bottom of much dreaming and fiction and that we have simply offered an elaborate description of what is more conventionally called conflict and tension—hardly news in the world of narrative. My larger interest in scripts and archetypes, however, is to illustrate my claim that dreams (especially) imitate not only the content of experience but the forms of action that flourish in waking life as a consequence of inevitable behavioral patterns. When we say, simply, that a narrative normally has a conflict we are to some degree ignoring the question of how and where a conflict originates in repeated experiential structures, especially in dream narrative where the possibilities of advance planning, sorting out possible agents, and sharpening thematic focus are highly unfavorable—as if the dream were interested in such matters. If we attach dream narrative to scripts—that is, to stereotyped patterns of behavior in the waking world, as opposed to some mysterious creative ability—it seems to me we have explained how dreams are able to get from point A to point B and beyond (barring intrusions owing to other influences) and remain with relatively good incidence on the subject without the guidance of a homuncular editor. For example, in Hall's schoolgirl's dream the plot essentials circulate about the miniscript of safety in numbers ("a crowd of schoolgirls," ". . . just in time"), which prevents the tall man's attack, and the dreamer's hope that the bus will stop in front of her house where she would be safe. In short, the world offers—indeed, is "scripted" to contain—ports of safety against such counterbehavior as the tall man's. Hall claims that this dream represents "a seduction wish on the part of the dreamer" and "a conflict between freedom and security" (1966: 138), a reading that can hardly be derived from the dream alone; but that does not explain how a dreaming brain can plot such a coherent tension using imaginary materials, unless the routines and rituals of the world are indelibly recorded in the memory. You might feel that this is such elementary plotting as to be achievable by a rodent that dreams it is being pursued by a cat, and you would be right, but that would equally be a matter of a scripted memory, a pattern the rodent had evolved in the form of a knowledge structure ("This is the old cat script, and I'm out of here!").[6] One gets considerably more respect for the value and complexity of such "elementary" scripting after reading

---

[6] Indeed, there is an interesting parallel between a script and what Gerald Edelman calls a scene. A scene is a form of categorization through which some animals correlate unconnected parts of their world in order to make "adaptive changes in behavior that satisfy value": "By a scene I mean a spatiotemporally ordered set of categorizations of familiar and nonfamiliar events, *some with and some without necessary physical or causal connections to others in the same scene.* The advantage provided by

of Schank's frustrations in trying to program a computer to tell a simple story about life in a fictional animal community:

> *One day Joe Bear was hungry. He asked his friend Irving Bird where some honey was. Irving told him there was a beehive in the oak tree. Joe threatened to hit Irving if he didn't tell him where some honey was.*

Our program had to have quite a bit of intelligence to generate this story, but it obviously didn't understand what it had created. It didn't know that Irving had told Joe where the honey was. To solve this particular problem, we had to add the information that beehives contain honey:

> *One day Joe Bear was hungry. He asked his friend Irving Bird where some honey was. Irving told him there was a beehive in the oak tree. Joe walked to the oak tree. He ate the beehive.* (Schank and Seifert, 1985: 65)

The miracle of narrative formation, it seems to me, can be explained by no other agency than some variation on the principle of scripted, schematic, or archetypal behavior, which we may think of as the grammar of memory in that it provides the combinational

---

the ability to construct a scene is that events that may have had significance to an animal's past learning can be related to new events, however causally unconnected those events are in the outside world. Even more importantly, this relationship can be established in terms of the demands of the value systems of the individual animal. By these means, the salience of an event is determined not only by its position and energy in the physical world but also by the relative value it has been accorded in the past history of the individual as a result of learning" (1992: 118). Scenes and scripts are obviously different things, or at least they pertain to two different levels of learning. Scenes, in Edelman's sense, relate to organisms with only a primary consciousness—that is, a consciousness that is "bound to a time around the measurable present, lacks concepts of self, past, and future, and lies beyond direct descriptive individual report from its own standpoint"; whereas scripts, in Schank's sense, pertain to acquired social behavior among animals (humans) possessing a "higher-order consciousness [with] direct awareness . . . , language and a reportable subjective life" (p. 115). Either extreme, in any case, bears out Edelman's central thesis about consciousness: the brain is basically a categorizing mechanism and man, to paraphrase Kenneth Burke, is the categorizing animal par excellence.

patterns with which memory can condense experience into narrative form. Thus the logic of storytelling is largely a matter of plagiarizing the world of social usage and abuse. This is all but a tautology (the storyteller writes about what people should and shouldn't do), but it reminds us how much all good stories rely on our memory of "how things are done" in the world and how the interest of a plot lies in its manipulation of codes that are all but invisible, like the windows through which we look out at reality.[7] To claim, either way, that dreams do or do not follow this logic obviously opens us to all sorts of mixed-level comparisons, not the least of which is that gray area, mentioned above, in which dream structure and content are indistinguishable from fictional structure and content. Does this mean, then, that dreams faithfully follow the scripts "written" by society? What can be said about dreams that use the scripts of the waking world "irresponsibly"? Foulkes makes an interesting speculation in suggesting how a dream might violate scriptual coherence while remaining thematically coherent "in terms of character persistence and sequential self-other behavioral interchange." For example, he says,

> I could dream that I was sitting in a restaurant, was served rocks, asked the waiter about them, whereupon he undertook to show me a mountainous area just outside the back door where he obtained them, whereupon we set to prospecting for gold-colored rocks, whereupon we inadvertently opened up a cave from which a small child emerged holding a dog in her arms, etc. In this "dream" each event flows smoothly from the preceding one, even though there is no waking script to which the unfolding of dream events seems to conform. Thematic coherence, in this sense, does not presuppose scriptual coherence, which is adherence to a pattern of temporally sequenced events with which we are familiar in our waking lives. (1985: 169)

---

[7] An amusing instance of this idea is found in Laura Bohannan's "Shakespeare in the Bush" (1966), in which Bohannan tells a group of African tribal elders the story of *Hamlet* and is corrected at each stage by the elders, who find the behavior of the characters in the play either incomprehensible or morally outrageous.

The point to be made about this hypothetical dream, however, is not that it doesn't follow the sequence of events we expect in a restaurant script but that it splices the restaurant script to a prospecting script. What we have, then, is a case in which one script contains, or gives way to, another and produces what we may call a superscript that has a larger contextual coherence. And this is exactly how fictional narratives are built up. All in all, Foulkes's dream is just the sort of thing that might happen in one of William Saroyan's restaurants, not to mention the outrageous restaurant in *The Cook, The Thief, His Wife and Her Lover,* and if I'm not mistaken there is a similar structure in *The Treasure of the Sierra Madre,* which begins in a restaurant, or at least a bar (although no one was served rocks), and heads promptly for the Mexican hills . I am also reminded of the scene in *The Godfather II* in which Michael Corleone orders pasta in the Italian restaurant, goes to the bathroom, and on his return violates all rules of proper restaurant deportment by gunning down his luncheon companions. There is a script in Foulkes's dream, then, but it is composed of three subscripts (if we toss in the buried-child motif). Apart from the improbability of being served rocks in a restaurant, the dream is perfectly faithful to the restaurant script as far as it is relevant. And that is really my point: dreams both violate and enchain scripts, just as we violate and enchain them in the movies, in fictions, and in life.

I am not suggesting that Foulkes fails to understand this. As he says later on, "just as in speech, we can change topics or digress in midcourse, so too in dreaming the operative schema can change (e.g., from restaurants to transcontinental train travel) as mnemonic activation changes" (1985: 172). But I am puzzled about why the change from a restaurant schema to a prospecting schema in his dream should be a failure of scriptural coherence simply (I assume) because rocks were served rather than baked potatoes or coq au vin, especially since he goes on to say that dreams are "thematically guided by considerations of meaning coherence rather than appearance coherence" (p. 173).

To put this another way, what Foulkes has really produced in his restaurant dream is what Benjamin Hrushovski would call a shift in field of reference (FR). If the dream were a literary text the rocks, as Hrushovski would say, "cannot be accepted" because we can think of no hypothetical FR that would accommodate restaurants and being served rocks, at least short of a bizarre comedy (1979: 372). One could, however, claim that a dream differs from a literary text precisely in having a different FR system of "expectations." Not being semiotically designed for external understanders, the FR of a dream is bound only by the dreamer's unique storehouse of associations (what goes with what) in which, presumably, rocks and food could have salient metaphorical connections; therefore, the progression from restaurant to rocks would make perfect thematic sense, though only an intrepid delver into the dreamer's psyche could discover what it was. This is an almost self-evident extension of Freud; but, if true, the argument that dreams are chaotic, random, or disorganized to the extent that they "serve rocks" now and then may turn out to be a confusion of apples and baked potatoes.

Finally, there seems likely to be little cause to make dreams, fictions, or biographies out of behavioral scripts unless the scripts also contain, by inference, the basis for improper departures and reversals of expectation. Again, a script is really a dialectical structure erected against certain potentialities for disorder: a script is built, as it were, on the ground of its own nemesis—a restaurant script, by inference, is really saying, "Don't do such-and-such here," "No bare feet allowed." Harold Pinter's plays, as we have mentioned, are about the weasel under the cocktail cabinet, the ways scripted behavior gets twisted into a tool of psychic harassment; Dylan Thomas was an infamous violator of cocktail party scripts and that is what makes his life story so interesting. Life, we might say, is one script after another: we follow one script on the way to a party, another when the host opens the door and welcomes us, and another when the police car stops us on the way home. The issue is not conformity to a single script or to expected behavior in any single instance but how scripts converge into archetypal patterns (repeated sequences of actions) and provide dreams and fictions with blocks of structure that can be joined or violated in endless ways.[8] In dreams, of course, the joints between scriptual blocks are apt to creak a bit by waking standards of probability (Foulkes's rocks), but that, as we have seen (Chapter 1), has nothing to do with probability in the dream *Umwelt*. I am sure Foulkes invented his restaurant dream to illustrate how irresponsible dreams can be where scripts are concerned, and his invention is well conceived to that end. Indeed, it follows excellent imaginative standards including an unforeseen mediation (the rocks) that changes the situation, dispatches the hero and his helper/donor on a quest leading to a surprising discovery (a little "prince" and his dog). It may seem somewhat nonsensical, but from the structural and presumably affective standpoints (were one to dream such a dream) it is really a very old pattern. How might Foulkes have arrived so casually at such a narrative? In all likelihood, by following a scriptual enchainment that he, like most of us, learned many bedtimes ago and now knows by heart. The original might have run like this: (1) Little Johnny was on his way to school. (2) On the path in front of him he suddenly saw a strange moving rock. (3) He followed it through the trees and up a long hill. (4) Eventually he came to a huge cave. He followed the rock inside. (5) There he discovered— (you name it).

Foulkes's mock dream is a perfect instance of how unavoidably we fall into the old forms of sequencing in making up the simplest, or silliest, of stories. It should be much more difficult for the brain to invent an absolutely chaotic story since its cognitive programs are designed to make sense at one level or another. To produce nonsense the brain must *avoid* making sense, and that is about as hard as standing in a corner and trying *not* to think of rocks on your plate. And even if we do succeed in making up a nonsensical story, a hearer of the story will go to great lengths to make sense of it.

[8] Mark Blagrove (1992) treats such scriptual deviations in dreams from a structuralist perspective. I must add, in agreement with Blagrove, that the idea that when dreams fail to follow a social script they become deviant from it a puzzling one. The incorporation of several scripts into a single dream and of frequent violation of scriptual behavior seem the most natural things in the world, in complete keeping with the practice of fiction as well. But this does not in the least diminish the value of the script concept as a way of examining dreams.

Freud believed that to make true sense of a dream we must disman-
tle the deceptive sequence of its events and images and examine
them piecemeal. This might be a useful diagnostic strategy for
determining instances of displacement, condensation, and repetition; I am suggesting the virtual reverse as a way of understanding
how dreams and fictions are made: that the archetypal axes, or
"gestalt structures,"[9] of most dreams offer us a way of looking past
the often peculiar surface features that tend to promote the notion
of nonsense (or symbolism) to see the respect in which dreams
manifest the brain's pervasive attempt to make sense of experience.[10]

All in all, my sense of how scripts and archetypes are interrelated
is quite similar to Albert S. Bregman's concept of ideals and descriptions. An ideal, he says, is "a control pattern in the brain
. . . [that] specifies a permissible relationship among a set of perceptual, conceptual, or behavioral variables [and it] specifies rules
for assigning these variables to real factors in the situation (sensory,

[9] I borrow this term from Mark Johnson's *The Body in the Mind*: a gestalt structure
is "an organized, unified whole within our experience and understanding that mani-
fests a repeatable pattern or structure" (1987: 44). Johnson equates the gestalt structure with what he calls an "image schemata" or schema, which is very similar to
Schank's notion of script though in some respects much more versatile and appropriate to my own line of discussion here. For instance: "A schema consists of a small
number of parts and relations, by virtue of which it can structure indefinitely many
perceptions, images, and events. In sum, image schemata operate at a level of mental
organization that falls between abstract propositional structures, on the one side, and
particular concrete images, on the other. . . . It is important to recognize the dynamic character of image schemata. I conceive of them as *structures for organizing our
experience* and comprehension." Finally, "I am identifying the schema as a *continuous
structure of an organizing activity*" (p. 29). From the standpoint of my own discussion
this latter statement is a perfect definition of a dream: it is a continuous structure that
organizes psychic materials, usually into a narrative form.

[10] Archetypes, as I am defining them here, seem to be highly relevant to the
concept of vigilance that has been discussed by Liddell (1950), Ullman (1961, 1969),
Snyder (1966), Tolaas (1978), Ullman and Storm (1986), and many others. Accordingly, vigilance would involve the formation and maintenance of knowledge structures that pertain to dangers and tensions faced by the individual in the waking
world. I have no idea how this process might work functionally, and there is consid-
erable debate among theorists about how it works and what vigilance may be
protecting against (see Tolaas's 1978 critique of Snyder and Ullman). Ullman has

behavioral, or thought patterns)" (1977: 276). Ideals, he says, could also be called concepts, paradigms, schemata, frames, Platonic ideas or, though Bregman does not use the word, scripts. A description—or what I am calling an archetype—"is a composition created out of elementary [ideals] to serve as a map or model of a world situation." Ideals "are altered as they enter into composition with one another" in the formation of a description (pp. 252–54). For example, Bregman offers the illustration of a dream, "the imaginative construction par excellence":

> Suppose one dreams of a purple dragon. The purpleness and the dragon shape are not just two separate aspects of the dream experience. For example, the purpleness never leaks outside the boundaries of the dragon form. Thus it is a dragon-shaped purpleness which changes location and shape as the dragon moves, and not just a nonspecific purpleness. We have to say that the idea purple was not just brought in as an independent element of the dream but specifically as a property of the dragon. . . . The result is a construction. All experiences are constructions and the difference between imaginative ones (including memory) and perceptual ones is that the latter are being 'driven' by a complex, detailed sensory input and the former are not . . . . People have often been struck by the nonsequiturs in dreams, but the coherence is even

---

suggested that a dream is "a metaphorical explication of a circumstance of living explored in its fullest implications for the [dreamer's] current scene" (1969: 700), but he does not make it very clear how a dream negotiates its way from one phase of its master metaphor to another. In any case, it is clear that archetypal structures— however one defines them—bear on permanent concerns and are not repeated in all societies simply because they form the basis for good stories. There may also be some overlap between archetypes, in my sense of the term, and the concept of personal myths as discussed by Jung (*Memories, Dreams, Reflections,* 1973) and more recently by Stanley Krippner (1986). My interest here, however, is not in personal applications to individual behavior but in organizational patterns that are steadily observable in dreams and fictions. I am tempted to suggest (without the least biological backing) that vigilance may be the wrong, or at least an incomplete, term for what dreaming does for us. I am completely unable to understand what many of my own dreams may be protecting me against; but I can see that most of them are related to concerns I have in social and private life.

more striking. It is no trivial achievement to make the dragon
color move with the dragon shape and to make the dragon move
forward at a speed proportional to the length and number of his
strides. (p. 274)

So too with the dream's alteration and interweaving of scripts into
archetypes, though I have no wish to exclude the possibility that an
archetype and a script might in some cases be the same thing. I am
simply observing that most of the archetypes that come to mind
seem to be a composite of interrupted or combative scripts (as in
Foulkes's restaurant dream). The main idea, however, is that dream
descriptions or narratives are not created ex nihilo but through the
"cooperation of ideals" stored in memory through countless expo-
sures to similar experiences. A dream, as Bregman might say, is
always a mixture of something old and something new: what is old
is the structure, what is new is the incoming variant, though it is
likely that some incoming variants are less variant than original,
giving rise to the need for a new description/archetype. Although
Bregman does not mention it, we might entertain a possibility that
the day residue on which a dream is based carries, in some way, an
ideal quality that insists on being instantiated in a dream. "As the
pressure of an ideal becomes stronger," Bregman says, "it becomes
more visible to other ideals. Such a postulate would have the effect
that if an ideal A was achieving success in its bid for instantiation,
ideals that were defined in terms of A (such as sub-ideals, super-
ideals or co-ideals) would also grow stronger." Thus a dream might
be thought of as a cooperative competition between ideals in which
the fittest survives and attracts companion ideals "which are maximally consistent with one another" (p. 280). The whole process
bears some resemblance to the "coattails" principle in politics in
which you reward campaign helpers when you win an election.
This also seems to bear on Montague Ullman's (1969) concept of
the dream as a "metaphor in motion."

In contrast, strong competition among ideals may well be the
cause of some dream bizarreness. For example, assuming that
Foulkes's dream was a real dream, we might explain the serving of

the rocks as a stronger ideal (prospecting) winning out over a weaker one (eating). There is no reason to assume that dreams might not suffer the same competitive motivations as a waking person trying to decide between two choices on a menu. "Contradiction exists when the instantiation of one ideal in a description precludes the instantiation of another one, either because they call for different transformations of the same variables [a rock is, as Polonius might say, "very like" a baked potato] or because a super-ordinate ideal will not permit them both to exist at the same time (e.g., seeing the same person as both friendly and unfriendly)" (Bregman, 1977: 281). In short, the dream may have wanted to go prospecting all along and didn't really want to waste time over lunch, and the rock served as a perfect symbolic transition from one script to another.

A final note, by way of transition to our next problem: Foulkes goes on to suggest that the "generalized semantic constraint" scripts may exercise on dream structure extends (rather than refutes) "the principle that the dream is formed more to say something (anything) well rather than to convey some particular message. That is, we can use evidence of scriptual coherence better to argue that the dream is keeping events generally consistent with waking expectations about what happens in situation X than to argue that the dream reflects an intention to use dream imagery to say something very specific about the situation or anything else" (1985: 169–70). This analysis is thoroughly in keeping with my own belief about what dreams may be "saying." My only cavil might be with the implication that dreams are concerned to say something "well." Do they have a choice? Are they in any way guided by qualitative motivations in, say, the sense that a novelist would strive to write well? Still, I can take the point as a metaphorical way of saying that the dream successfully follows the structures of our life in reality—having in a sense no other structures to follow—rather than pursuing an agenda aimed at a conscious interpretation of what such structures may mean to the dreamer. This leads us directly to the question of meaning in dreams and fictions.

5

Meaning in Dreams and Fictions

Behind our preoccupation with meaning in dreams lurks an implication that they must be rescued from the threat of meaninglessness. Surely dreams must be meaningful because they are too real and too personal to be otherwise, and as Harry Hunt puts it, "it feels ungracious to regard the dream as anything but an intentional communication of some sort" (1989: 9). Even in a dream in which your much dreamed of Aunt Sarah does something completely unlike herself, you are apt to wonder on waking—such is the authority of the dream—if there isn't more to Aunt Sarah than you had thought. Even when dreams are disorderly we are led to regard the disorder as a form of code or symbolism. Both order and disorder, then, reinforce the notion that dreams have meaning.

Normally we don't argue whether linguistic constructions (literary texts, for example) have meaning. We might claim that one meaning is better than another or that there are contradictory meanings or no end of possible meanings, and so on. But literary texts are safely assumed to mean because they are produced by waking individuals who wouldn't bother writing unless they had something to communicate to other waking individuals, and this something is almost always referred to as meaning. The problem with dreaming is that there is no apparent receiver and hence the whole dimension of intentionality—one of the subconditions of meaning—acquires a questionable status.[1] Indeed, as Freud said, the dream itself is "a matter of no importance"; only the dream thoughts (and waking thoughts about the dream) are important, and "the faintest possibility that something [recalled by the dreamer] may have occurred in the dream shall be treated as complete certainty" (1973 [1900], 5:516–17). The dream, then, is an occasion for talking about something exterior to or beneath it.

Let us look further into the question of meaning. Obviously this is a central problem in philosophy that we cannot explore properly here. I am concerned strictly with respects in which *meaning* may or may not be an appropriate term to apply to dreams, especially in their connection with stories and literary texts. Apart from the meaning that arises from "intentional communication," we tend to use the word in any transaction in which something makes sense or tells us something about itself (perhaps inadvertently) or about something else (as when clocks tell us the time). On one hand, the implication is that meaning is distinct from the vehicle that means, but on the other, it is *in* the vehicle in an ambiguous way, rather like vitality in an organism. This ambiguity of location, shuttling between medium and message, is what makes meaning such a slippery notion. For one thing, it opens the possibility that meaning

[1] I use the term *intentionality* here in a sense quite different from the phenomenological usage in which all mental acts are intentional, all consciousness consciousness *of* something. In this sense, all dreaming is intentional and involves what phenomenologists call the doctrine of intentional inexistence; to take the familiar example (because analogous to the dream), if I am thinking of a unicorn, "the object of the thought about a unicorn *is* a unicorn, but a unicorn with a mode of being . . . that is short of actuality but more than nothingness . . . and that lasts for just the length of time that the unicorn is thought about" (*Encyclopedia of Philosophy*, 1972, 4:201). So too a dream involves intentionality and occurs in the mode of intentional inexistence: "short of actuality but more than nothingness," though it would depend on how one chooses to limit the idea of actuality. Also, the term *intentionality* has been applied to all thoughts, beliefs, desires, and "inner episodes," but, as William S. Robinson says, "having intentionality in general (and thus also, being intentional, in general) has nothing specially to do with being done as a result of an intention to bring something about" (1988: 84).

As I am using the term in the present context, intentionality means what most nonphenomenological interpreters mean by it: the idea that there is what we may

may be simply a manifestation of orderliness in something. In this regard, most dreams could be said to possess a degree of order, if only in that they tend to follow a plot line involving a restricted cast of characters. But if orderliness is a characteristic or a precondition of meaning, can't we claim that rock crystals or machines or solar systems have meaning? Still, when we refer to meaning in dreams we are assuming not only that they are orderly but also that the order has a coherent personal theme, or, in Gordon Globus's view, that they are "instantiations of a unifying concept" (1991: 38). But, here again, one could claim that a machine or a solar system has a unifying concept, though one might be using the term *concept* in a loose or metaphorical way. This raises another question: how do metaphors have meaning? Granted, the author of a metaphor, unlike the author of a dream, more or less deliberately creates a qualitative horizon of possible associations, but is this horizon rightly considered as meaning, at least in the conceptual sense, or as an intentional ground on which meaning may be derived—a kind of incipient or latent meaningfulness perhaps? Is the meaning created by the poet of a different order from the meaning created by the reader? (I return to this question later.) And if this is the case with the metaphor, is the meaning created by the dream (if any) of a different order from that created by an interpreter? Milton Kramer points out that "meaning does not exist in dreams but is brought to them from some external system of meanings" (1991b: 149). And, as William Ray puts the same idea in relation to literary texts, "a sequence of words can mean nothing in particular until someone

---

call a semiotic or semantic motivation in the dream, as there is in literature; dreams intend to mean, or are intending agencies: they are deliberately about something. Thus, the source of meaning and meaningfulness is placed in the dream as object (text) rather than in the perceiving interpreter (subject) or in the interaction between dream and interpreter. What I am basically critiquing here is the cul de sac this idea of intentionality (usually implicit in the argument) creates. As William Ray says in his critique of Norman Holland, "when one liberates the notions of intentional object and intending subject from one another, one runs the risk of falling into pure subjectivism, pure objectivism, or both. . . . Meaning becomes a random subjective event triggered by an object beyond knowledge; criticism [or dream interpretation], an occulted process of narcissism and self-replication" (1984: 75–76).

means something by it" (1984: 3). Presumably, this "sequence" might include even a series of random words or shapes—if you are clever enough to detect a pattern, as when you see a fanged serpent in a Rorschach blot. Perhaps this is better referred to as illusion rather than as meaning. Still, this is what the blot "means" to you,[2] and it falls into the same class of mismeanings represented in macro by the old Ptolemaic reading of the solar system which, until Copernicus, was based on a similar set of observable "facts." "As meanings vanish in favor of certain relationships among terms," Nelson Goodman says, "so facts vanish in favor of certain relationships among versions" (1978: 93). Then too, we should add that such illusions are the associative stuff all dreams are made on; so there is a kind of falsity, or mistakenness, at the very heart of whatever meanings dreams may have. But it is a falsity founded on a certain order out of which real meanings might arise. For instance, I might find evidence of a unifying concept in your illusion of the serpent in the ink blot, assuming I could locate such serpentine illusions in other aspects of your behavior, beginning with your dreams.

To round out the point, when the analyst or the physicist, or anyone else, finds a unifying concept that explains a certain psychic or physical phenomenon, the phenomenon itself is only as meaningful as the system of meanings to which it is submitted. One might justifiably argue that a dream is different from a rock crystal or a solar system in that it is a product of human thought and has strong personal connotations for the dreamer: "No natural phenomenon," Mikhail Bakhtin says, "has 'meaning,' only signs (in-

---

[2] This is not as casual a conception of meaning as it may seem. For instance, George Mandler's notion of *meaning analysis* would fit this sort of personal interpretation. The cognitive-interpretive system of the brain "takes [any] item of input and, locating it in terms of its particular characteristics, attributes, and features, immediately notes (or activates) the relations of that particular item or set of events to other structures and sets of events. Thus the relation of a particular input to existing structures gives us an organization that is specific to that particular item and gives us the organization of that item within the existing structures or its meaning" (1975: 26–27). By such a progress a simple, innocent ink blot might snake its way into one's private depository of serpent meanings.

cluding words) have meanings" (1987: 113). But that does not solve
the problem of where meaning begins and ends and through what
agency it is produced. Moreover, how can we be sure that the order
in dreams, personal as it is, is so different from the silent order of
the solar system, the rock crystal, the machine, or the Rorschach
blot? Perhaps dreams should more appropriately be studied as natural phenomena, instances of "dumb" biology (which is orderly)
rather than "smart" psychology. In short, respecting this matter of
meaning, are dreams more like literature or more like the digestive
system?

It is evident that most of our notions of meaning in dreams have
been profoundly influenced by psychoanalytic interpretation in
which the dream is considered *as if* it were an intentional speech act
(Lacan: "The unconscious is structured like a language"). The
meaning is simply whatever psychic values in the dream are identi-
fiable with the dreamer's total experience and can be deployed in
the interest of diagnosis in which the dream is a carrier of symptoms, no different from other kinds of symptomatic acts (such as
Dora toying nervously with her reticule in the session with Freud).
It is not a question of dismissing psychoanalytic interpretation but
of getting out of the orbit of its assumptions in order to examine
the nature of meaning from other possible points of view. As a
transition to this end, I want to look at two discussions of meaning
that try to get beyond standard psychoanalytic interpretation in a
provocative way. The first is an essay by Meredith Anne Skura on
meaning in dreams and literary texts titled "Revisions and Rereadings in Dreams and Allegories" (1980). Skura suggests that the
proper literary parallel to the dream is not the "chance encounter"
of surrealist art, which is too "disjointed" and illogical (meaningless?); rather, the dream is closer to the allegory, with which it
shares several characteristics: both "insist on a gap between what
the text seems to mean and the extra meaning it seems to imply."
Thus dreams, like allegories, can be interpreted in many different
ways: "Interpreters in both realms try to cross the gap by stripping
away the sensuous surface and get down to (or up to?) the simple
abstractions which supposedly generate it." Moreover, dreams and

allegories "make use of pictorial narratives for nonmimetic but perfectly natural purposes," even to using "the pictures in contradictory ways"; finally, both present experience "from several different points of view apart from the objective mimetic one" (pp. 364–69). As for the difference between dream and allegory, Skura concludes that it rests in the different ways the two forms shift interpretive points of view:

> In the case of the dream and the dreamer, the switch takes place when we move from the isolated dream-as-dreamt to the larger network of associations and contexts. This is a move from the naïveté of the sleeping dreamer to the wariness of the wide-awake interpreter; it is a move from one kind of reading to another. The allegory, by contrast, encompasses the clues for the switch within the bounds of the text; but the switch is the same. The real difference between dream and allegory is not so much that the latter is more artful but that it is more self-conscious. While in the dream the need to switch just makes understanding more difficult, in the allegory this difficulty is part of what the text is about. (p. 378)

Now, it may be that Skura is using the term *meaning* as a kind of shorthand for the dream's susceptibility to interpretation. She is, after all, coming at the problem from the psychoanalytic side. Above all, she is concerned with establishing that the gap in dreams and allegories—contra Freud—"is not between the surface and some other, truer meaning but between different ways of reading the surface" (p. 366). Like the allegory, the dream shuffles between instance and a system of meanings or a language outside it. There is no single secret meaning. There are only various (perhaps endless) ways of reading either kind of text, and the texts themselves (of both dream and allegory) are actively involved in defeating the primacy of a single meaning. The allegory is simply more self-conscious about its procedures than the dream, putting the difficulty of understanding into the text itself—whereas in the dream the difficulty of interpretation occurs only when the dreamer awakens and inherits all the semantic expectations of the double-minded

world. We should probably add that there is no attempt at interpretation within the dream state.

This is an attractive argument for two reasons: first, it seeks to
release the dream from the grip of Freud's single "infantile-
regressive" determinant and to see dreams as being "multiply determined" (p. 354); second, whereas Freud virtually ignored the
surface, or narrative sequence, of the dream in preference for the
"fragments" of thought "imbedded" in it, Skura's approach depends on an interplay between the narrative and the symbolic codes
beneath it. In short, she is concerned not simply with motives but
with "modes of representation" (p. 347). In this respect, her position has much in common (to a point) with that of Pierre
Macherey—my second text—on meaning in literary works: "The
work," Macherey says, "does not contain a meaning which it con-
ceals by giving it its achieved form. The necessity of the work is
founded on the multiplicity of its meanings; to explain the work is
to recognize and *differentiate* the principle of this diversity . . . : the
work is not *created* by an intention (objective or subjective); it is
produced under determinate conditions . . . : the work would be
full of meaning, and it is this plenitude which must be examined
(1978: 78).

The part I am not sure about here is whether Skura would agree
that the work is not created by an intention but is produced under
determinate conditions—which for Macherey involves the work's
submission to "the necessity that determines [it] but which does not
culminate in a *meaning.*" Necessity, I take it, is "what [the work]
does not and could not say [about itself]: just as the triangle remains
silent over the sum of its angles" (pp. 77–78). Since this parallel or
difference is crucial, let me quote Macherey further on this theme:
"It is not a question of confronting the work with some external
truth: rather than passing a normative judgment, we identify the
class of truth which constitutes the work and determines its meaning. This truth is not there in the work, like a nut in its shell;
paradoxically, it is both interior and absent. If this were not the
case, we would have to concede that the work was actually *unknow-
able*, miraculous and mysterious, and that criticism was futile" (p.

78). Though Macherey isn't at all concerned with dreams, I find his idea (or this part of his idea) just as useful in understanding dreams as it is in understanding literary works. Like a book, a dream "is not the extension of a meaning; it is generated from the incompatibility of several meanings, the strongest bond by which it is attached to reality, in a tense and ever-renewed confrontation" (p. 80). Without claiming that all dreams are necessarily based on a conflict of incompatible meanings (for instance, what about lyric dreams?), one may say that the dream is generated from a reality that is itself constantly "incomplete" (in Macherey's term) and in-the-making, a reality that is therefore without a meaning precisely in being composed of many meanings bumping along interdependently in the current of any human destiny. Reality, then, is not meaningless: it is *made of* meanings, but it does not have a meaning. Looked at dramatistically, human reality *tends* toward the confrontation of meanings; differences more often than not lead to oppositions (as when we can think of equally valid reasons for marrying or not marrying or for buying or not buying a car). And it goes without saying that such confrontations are apt to find their way into dreams which are "incomplete" constructions reflecting an incomplete reality.[3] What is important to note here is that meaning is seen not as a conceptual construction ("This means so-and-so") but as an experiential one; the meaning is not susceptible to an interpretative reduction but only to a display, or a circumscription, that does not displace the work's "fullness." For Macherey, meanings invariably take the form of historical ideologies confronting each other, but there is no reason to confine his theory of meaning to a Marxist orientation. For instance, this seems to me more or less how Skura is approaching Freud's botanical monograph dream, which, she argues (contra Freud), opens out on "nothing less than a series of crises in Freud's life" (1980: 361): it does not solve any of them, it simply contains them as a dreamed equivalency. In other

---

[3] Here might be still another explanation for why dreams are so casual about beginnings and endings (see Chapter 2): dreams begin in medias res because they are about life in medias res rather than about completeness (solutions to problems and so on).

words, what she offers is not an interpretation but an indication that stops short of a typical psychoanalytic resolution. I am tempted to say that she offers what Macherey calls an explanation of the dream: unlike interpretation, explanation does not reduce the work "to a meaning, whether manifest or latent"; it assumes that the meaning is "indistinguishable from the actual elaboration of the work" and proceeds to show how "the work unfolds in more than one plane" (Macherey, 1978: 159–61).[4]

Like Macherey, then, Skura is conducting an argument against normative interpretation that would wrest a single secret meaning from the dream or work. The question I would pose, however, is where her theory leaves "the dream-as-dreamt"—the experience undergone by the dreamer which, while it was occurring, was attended by none of the confusion or gaps that arise when the dreamer becomes a wary wide-awake interpreter looking back at the dream from the larger network of associations and contexts. I have doubts about whether the interpretive switch within the allegorical text is, after all, the same as the switch from dream-as-dreamt to waking interpreter. Isn't the latter a switch from experience to interpretation involving two entirely different classes of truth that may determine very different kinds of meanings than Skura is dealing with? And if one uses an exterior class of truth (or system of meanings) to interpret the interior dream-as-dreamt, is this not in effect to privilege one form of truth over another, on the theory that the dream, as a consequence of censorship, has less access to its true associations and contexts than the waking interpreter? Does it not finally deny that the dream-as-dreamt may mean something *else* in the context of its own interior determinant conditions, something an interpreter (at least one who has not dreamed the dream) could not possibly recover?

---

[4] I draw this parallel with some reservation. Macherey's theory of explanation, which is opposed to interpretation, is not a simple one to elucidate. Moreover, Macherey writes as a Marxist with one methodological foot in phenomenology and the other in Freudian psychoanalysis, with a central concern for the work's "ideological moment." In any event, I am not implying that Skura shares his notion of a principle of disparity inhabiting literary works (or dreams), only that she seems to share his strong bias, within a psychoanalytic context, against the reduction of works to specific meanings.

At the center of Skura's theory, it seems to me, there is a kind of impasse or reluctance to go as far beyond Freud as she might on the evidence of her own argument. I gather that she feels the dream is still in the business of censoring at least part of its content: Freud, she says,

> looked for the reproduction of a single, explanatory wish—and saw only censorship if he failed to find that wish. We, however, can see that the dream's indirections do not always disguise but sometimes express something otherwise inexpressible. The dream [the botanical monograph] is not about a single wish (which it has failed to represent), but about a whole network of associations, thoughts, and images related to each other and represented in the dream in the strangest, most diverse ways. (1980: 363)

I find this a convincing adjustment of Freudian "singularity," but why the qualification of "not always" and "sometimes"? It is not clear why the least vestige of censorship should be necessary to this process of creating such a rich network of associations. On one hand, Skura is able to account for the quality of dream images (either "primitive" or "adult") on the basis of expressive condensation, or multiple determination, but on the other hand she seems to feel that the censor is also at work "vying for the same dream space, pulling it into different patterns, and making different use of it" (pp. 354–55). But the only detectable evidence for this tug of war is the seeming confusion and gaps in the dream as viewed from the waking side of the switch: "Dreams always seem to mean more than the wakened dreamer can tell" (p. 355). Exactly. But such confusion, as I have maintained throughout and as we see in Skura's discussion of Freud's botanical monograph dream, can easily be explained without invoking a principle of censorship. It seems far more likely that the gaps and confusion were a function of the switch to the interpretive mode itself. I can, for example, visually alter the appearance of the world by simply closing one eye and flattening it to a monocular image; but the world out there goes on being its binocular self without alteration. Does the act of interpretation flatten the meaning of the dream in a similar way? Does interpretation remove the binocular fullness of the dream-as-dreamt by substituting the experience that is thought to have determined the dream for the experience of dreaming itself? This process effectively amounts to the production of meanings of a particular kind. But are these meanings the meaning of the dream or the meanings of conceptual "exterior" thinking? And what is the relation of one to the other?

Perhaps I am worrying a point that may have been intended only in a psychoanalytic context where meaningfulness is virtually taken for granted because it is what you can wrest from the dream. After all, Skura is hardly writing an essay about cognitive processes. But it is on just this ground that the question of meaning will finally have to be settled if we are to get the little man out of the dream machine (though I am not sure Skura is interested in that problem). To come back to my opening question, is it necessary that dreams mean anything—in any sense approaching the way allegories mean—in order to serve their purposes as a psychic mechanism? Perhaps dreams are, after all, only a kind of psychic digestive system, with no more awareness of what they are doing than the stomach has. And suppose that what they digest (experience) turns out, from the interpreter's point of view, to have several meanings, or many meanings (as the stomach, in Menenius's tale, is "the storehouse and the shop of the whole body"); is this the work of the dream, or does it have strictly to do with the openness and inevitable subjectivity of interpretation itself? It seems to me we must take very seriously Milton Kramer's statement that "meaning does not exist in dreams but is brought to them from some external system of meanings" (1991b: 149). Just what are the implications of this statement?

Let me offer a hypothetical situation that might ground the problem more directly in the "incomplete reality" of everyday experience. Suppose I find myself worrying that something I said may have disturbed my friend Mark during our conversation yesterday. This thought nags at me all day long. I go over and over the conversation, reliving the scene in order to determine whether my fears are justified. In what way does this incident have meaning?

Certainly, it tells me something about myself: it speaks of my concerns, my personality, my need for harmony in relationships, and so forth. I may even remark to myself that I am "always" worrying about these situations. It is true that I do that, but is this meaning or is it simply behavioral description, self-awareness—in a word, understanding? What could such worrying possibly mean except that I am worrying (as usual)? Now suppose that same night I have a dream about this concern in which Mark and I are talking, and I see he has a disturbed look on his face and there is some incident in the dream that establishes the verity of my waking fear. Or perhaps there is no such incident and I feel relieved (in the dream) that nothing seems to be wrong (a wish fulfillment, in short). What is just as likely is that Mark will not appear in the dream at all, but John will appear in his stead. Moreover, it is possible that John is not just picked out of the blue but that John and Mark (perhaps without my awareness) share a common context in my past experience that we might call the "fear-of-disturbing" situation. In other words, what I said to Mark may bother me so much because it is a reprise of an incident involving John and Dan and Dorothy and god knows who else, the idea being that there certainly must be a history of such incidents; otherwise, what bothers me so much about *this* one? So all of the incidents appear, so to speak, as an indistinguishable fusion in a scene that may itself be a composite of sites in which past similar situations have taken place. (Of course, this would be a very tidy notion of how dreams work.)

What I think is occurring in both cases is that I am not producing meaning, I am thinking: the meaning is right there in the act. There is nothing behind or underneath my worrying beyond the extensivity of my history and personal reactivity in this ever-incomplete reality I occupy. Nor is my dream trying to communicate something to me or remind me of the incident; that would be tantamount to reminding myself of an incident that I am already thinking about. Something in external reality may remind me of the incident and it will come to mind, but that does not involve the production of meaning either. In any case, my concern arises from a doubt about the conversation with Mark; I am trying to determine what happened in the event, not what it means. And though a psychoanalyst might delve more deeply into my concern and discover things about me (and the concern itself) that I did not know, my acts of worrying and of dreaming are no different in kind from my wondering how I am going to lift a refrigerator onto the bed of a pick-up without a helper (an equally likely topic for a dream based on a similar history of frustration).

Let us take a somewhat different illustration of the problem. It occurred to me some time ago that it might be revealing to study certain kinds of waking experience that have a dreamlike quality. Like Kleist's Prince of Homburg, I sometimes have experiences of which I think, "This is like a dream." But what sort of experience might this be? Here is an example that occurred on a recent afternoon:

> I am in the backyard waiting for my wife to come out to our deck. Having nothing better to do, I walk to the avocado tree to see how the new fruit is coming along; but on inspecting, I can find none of the small round green balls we had seen earlier. I walk around the tree, disappointed. Have they all fallen to the ground? And then beneath one of the leaves I find one hanging, about the size of a fingernail, then another, and another, and soon I am finding them everywhere. It is as if they had been deliberately hiding from me and have now come out in number. I am mystified by this but pleased that we will have a good crop. Then I look down over the hill. The sunlight is filtering through the oak trees. I notice that the path I constructed several years ago is virtually grown over with iceplant and I feel guilty that I have not been a better tenant of my land. I hear the shrill song of a mockingbird in the neighboring pine tree. Suddenly, I am filled with a deep regret that life is passing and I am missing things going on behind my back.

This event, I'm afraid, has everything but an orchestral accompaniment. It is what one might call an epiphany in Joyce's sense[5] or an

---

[5] Joyce's concept of the epiphany is found in *Stephen Hero*, the first draft of *A Portrait of the Artist as a Young Man*, and throughout the *Portrait* itself.

adventure in the sense of the term defined by Hans-Georg Gad-amer:

> An adventure . . . interrupts the customary course of events, but is positively and significantly related to the context which it interrupts. Thus an adventure lets life become felt as a whole, in its breadth and in its strength. Here lies the fascination of an adventure. It removes the conditions and obligations of everyday life. It ventures out into the uncertain. . . . There is an element of this, in fact, in every experience. . . . Because [the experience] is within the whole of life, in it too the whole of life is present. (1985: 62)

My experience in the backyard, then, has the peculiar quality of being framed and set apart from the continuity of the day; otherwise it would not have occurred to me to save it for future reference. But how is this true? Have I not given it that quality as a consequence of a certain symmetry that accidentally provokes the emotion that ends the sequence? It is one of those events that seems to stand out of time and become significant enough to tell others and in telling it—which is to say, framing it—we begin at the beginning and we end at the end, these being nothing more than the limits that enclose the felt coherence of the experience. Indeed, so coherent does it seem that one might plot it along these lines:

waiting→diversion→discovery of loss→recovery→realization

Thus, I have given it a shape, not unlike that of a minitragedy, which moves, as Georg Lukács says, out of empirical reality into essential reality: "Something necessary and essential [is made] out of the accidental; the periphery [is transformed] into the centre" (1974: 157). But, as Lukács goes on to suggest, isn't this an illusion? Isn't it born of a sense of awe that events beyond my control (the disappearance of the fruit into the tree foliage, the song of the bird, the beckoning path) could be sequentially instrumental in producing a powerful emotion? These seem to enclose the event—indeed, they *make* it an event, an adventure. It is true that the sequence of perceptions that brought on the realization—lending it this shape so unlike the flow of accidental life—in no way possesses an intelligence or significance of its own: the avocado fruit was not *hiding*; the mockingbird was not mocking *me*. There is no poet *above me*. It is I who have self-ishly bestowed on contingent reality a significance, even to the point of seeing a complicity between the causal series and my own personal situation. Whatever meaning there may be in the event I have put there myself; it is not to be found in the series. Reality has helped me to make meaning—if that is what I have made—by accidentally deploying itself in what we construe as a meaningful pattern. Indeed, when we have such intervals in waking life—in which the empirical induces a sense of essentiality—we are in a sense creating meaning out of meaningless things. Again, as Kramer says, meaning is brought to them. *The event* did not mean anything but I mean something *by it*, or it meant something *to me* whereas another person might find it senseless.

It is easy to see how this same event may have occurred as a dream. Dreams have a way of personifying things like avocado buds, the cry of mockingbirds, and the sad condition of paths (which, on some dream occasions, actually talk to you sadly). And if this were the case in such a dream, one would immediately assume that the causal series had been thematized by the dream itself. The dreamwork has "set up" this sequence in order to prepare the way for the dramatic emotional fulfillment of its "semantic significance," as Hunt says (1989: 167).

But isn't it possible that the causal series of the dream, precisely like the causal series in my waking adventure, had no such design? I dreamed it, or part of it, without any such thing in mind. This is not to say that I dreamed it arbitrarily or carelessly. Surely it is possible that a dream may recall an event because it was pleasant, strange, provoking, asymmetrical with the day, or somehow similar in kind to something else whose power it unlocks. In my dream, I may have found myself in the backyard (as easily and naturally as on campus, downtown, someplace in the past). Or the backyard may have stuck in my mind from the day residue as a result of any number of things—the drift of a conversation there the evening before, the fact that I look into it from my study window, and so on; moreover, the avocado tree is also in the backyard; and I had just been examining the new crop of fruit; fruit at this stage, being extremely small, tends to be elusive and gets lost in the tree; mockingbirds tend to sing at this time of year; the overgrown path is directly below the tree, and so all these events fall out as a normal metonymic ensemble (though dreams don't require, or even produce, empirically faithful ensembles). And wouldn't it be plausible, within the dream, for me to have the same emotional reaction to this ensemble purely on natural—as opposed to thematic—provocation?

In short, any one of these image/events might have occurred through a causal logic that has nothing to do with provoking my epiphany. The epiphany may be the effect of a causal order every bit as independent of it as the causal order operating in my waking version of the same experience. What may easily have happened is that I reacted to the sequence in the dream in a perfectly waking way, just as I did in the afternoon reality; in both cases I was the same person having the same experience that life was passing. What has happened is that, on waking, I convert the dream experience into a *story*; I reflect on it and, since it carries the remarkable authority of dream experience, I endow it with an intentionality: it is the dream that has prepared this experience *for* me. Thus, I have made the dream the author and have taken for my dreaming self the passive role of a character who simply experiences what the dream offers. But this is surely a simplistic view, all the more so because it drives a wedge between dream and dreamer. In the dream proper such intentionality need not have been present in order for the dream to come about. I, the thinking self within the dream, the protagonist of the dream, am the source of the intentionality. Or, to cite an example from Ricoeur: "Christopher Columbus's voyage can be said to be the cause of the spread of European culture, in a sense of the word 'cause' that has nothing to do with Columbus's intentions" (1984, 1:131). Just as European culture spread as a by-product of Columbus's voyage, my emotional realization could have occurred as a by-product of the "causal" ensemble and not the other way around—not as a consequence of a deliberate dream emplotment but something more like a partnership between dreamer and dream, which is finally only my brain thinking in this odd dualistic way that allows me to create images and then to react to, and thereby change, them. Is this not, moreover, how art is made—through this evolving conversation between the work in progress and the artist who sees the possibilities of the work only as they unfold? For instance, Henri Matisse in "Notes of a Painter": "If I put a black dot on a sheet of white paper the dot will be visible no matter how far I stand away from it—it is a clear notation; but beside this dot I place another one, and then a third. Already there is confusion. In order that the first dot may maintain its value I must enlarge it as I proceed putting other marks on the paper" (1965: 258). The idea is expressed even more relevantly to the present discussion in Joanna Field's description of the state of concentration required for drawing in *On Not Being Able to Paint:*

> It was a mood which could be described as one of reciprocity; for although it was certainly a dreamy state of mind it was not a dreaminess that shuts itself off from the outside world or shuts out action. It was more a dreaminess that was the result of restraining conscious intention, or rather, a quick willingness to have it and then forgo it. Quite often there was some conscious intention of what to draw, at the beginning, but the point was that one had to be willing to give up this first idea as soon as the lines drawn suggested something else. (1983: 71–72)

However different the dream may be from the artwork, it seems reasonable to assume this fundamental similarity in the method of creation: both depend on a reciprocal interplay between the dreamy mind and its bodily product (dream image, drawing), each as Field goes on to say, "taking the lead in turn in a quick interchange or dialogue relation" (p. 73). The notion of a conscious or unconscious intention of what to draw or what to dream, brought to the process in advance and maintained throughout it, is simply unnecessary. The pattern of coherence that results in either case is a consequence of dynamic negotiation between image and its potentialities for advancement.[6]

I am not advancing this as a theory that would diminish the diagnostic value of dreams. Indeed, I do not offer it as an explanation of the causality of all dreams.[7] I am inquiring about possibilities that may be overlooked in our understandable zeal to apply hermeneutic logic to dreams. We should not assume that dreams are intentional because they have a certain order and personal content, or because meanings can be derived from them; meanings can also be derived from bird innards and tea leaves. That a particular dreamer tends to repeat certain dream motifs or situations (dreams of enclosure, guilt, impotence) and that an analyst can identify themes and recurring symbols that emerge from very real perturbations does not at all indicate that dreams are one bit more intentional than waking experience in which one can find the same tendencies operating. As in the episode with my friend Mark, what concerns me in the waking world is likely to concern me in my

---

[6] Finally, in this vein, I cannot resist the remarks of the artist Howard Warshaw: "We no longer think of the subject matter as something static, something posed 'out there' and subject to empirical examination. In working from the human figure today my notion of the subject matter would include the figure as part of a process going on while the drawing is being made. A process consisting of an active dialogue between the changing events on the page, the changing character of the draftsman's vision, and the consequent changes of revelation pertinent to the figure" (1980: 181). I hope it is clear from my discussion here that I am not denying that such reciprocal creation can have psychoanalytic meanings for the person (Picasso's reciprocal creation yielding one form of personal "obsession," Turner's or Francis Bacon's another). I am strictly interested in investigating the dreamwork's role in creating such meanings. I am conceiving of the dream itself, as an experience, as standing in the relation of empirical reality to the waking person. The difference is, obviously, that my thought cannot influence the flow of empirical reality as it can in the dream reality.

[7] For example, feverish or restless dreams that obsessively repeat the same motif seem to suffer from an impairment of the reciprocal process, thus creating what Joanna Field refers to as "chaotic scribbles," dreams dreamed "when the disruptive forces were for the time being in ascendance." At the same time, "meaningful drawings [or dreams] might certainly be looked upon as the expression of a tendency of nature inside one to form wholes, a formative pattern-making tendency" (1983: 74). It goes without saying that this pattern-making tendency, in dreams and in waking life, can be interrupted and confused in countless ways.

dream, and one version of the concern is no more significant than the other. So there should be no surprise that dreams have a certain symbolic order. Diagnosis and interpretation are equally possible in either of these cases—which is to say that, if we did not dream, analysts could study our waking experience with equal validity and by much the same methods. A diagnosis does not in the least require a dream that knows what it is doing, or disguises what it is doing, or is telling a thematized story. Indeed, as Freud said, the dream is not important; what analysis tries to find is a meaning in the life of the dreamer; but inadvertently, in some cases at least, the meaning gets attributed to the dream itself, perhaps because it is much simpler to say, "Your dream means this," than to say, "This is how we might use your dream to understand your situation." To put it another way, the kinds of stories lived in dreams are lived in life as well. One can use the dream to discover unconscious or repressed materials, but in being so used the dream may be functioning catalytically, like a Rorschach blot.

Let us suppose, as I have been doing throughout, that dreams are simply extensions of empirical life, with respect to their organizational logic: some things are planned (I want to go to the hardware store today), some partly planned (I may stop at the pharmacy), some unplanned—all of these sets continually impinging on each other and changing the direction of the day's narrative. Certainly day experience doesn't really mean anything (in the sense of intending to project a theme[8]); but then it is not chaotic either. It has a logic, or at least a shape, that might best be thought of as a continual tension—or, in Field's term, reciprocity—between motive ("Today I must get to the hardware store"), on one hand, and motion or contingency ("Suddenly, who walks up to me but John!"), on the other. But let us see how this might operate in a dream. Let us assume that something in the day residue comes to the fore as the main determinant of the dream. Here we are absolutely in the dark

---

[8] I am putting aside the possibility that a person might deliberately live his or her life with the full intention of projecting a theme or lifestyle or of "making a statement" (Oscar Wilde, Andy Warhol, Madonna). These indeed mean, as Hamlet might say, for they are actions that a man (or a woman) might play.

because we know very little about why dreams choose the residue they do. In any case, the dream surfaces in the dreamer's consciousness; it has not been planned in advance by any mental agency, it is only incipiently *about* anything or it is about something only with respect to the potentially evocative force of the day residue. The dream wants, so to speak, to go to the hardware store, nothing more; so it puts a black "hardware" dot on the blank field of the mind. By this I mean that it has an emotional vector quantity (as they say in mathematics) that is based in a desire centered in some way in the day residue (or so we assume) but not yet an inkling of a story to tell. It goes without saying that a desire is not so many unattached ergs hurling themselves in any old direction. But there is a great difference between claiming that dreams know what they want to do next and saying that they are orderly within certain parameters. As we saw in the case of Hunt's dream of the Tibetan museum, each dream image tends to delimit the range and quality of the ensuing images. Thus, the dream becomes both deterministic and unpredictable. Or, to invoke another principle from Rudolf Arnheim's *Entropy and Art,* the dream, like all systems (natural, social, or psychological), abides by an anabolic tendency that overcomes disorder and entropy by contributing "the structural theme of a pattern, and this theme creates orderly form through interaction with the [catabolic] tendency to tension reduction." It is this tendency that establishes "'what the thing is about,' be it a crystal or a solar system, a society or a machine, a statement of thoughts or a work of art" (1974: 31, 49). What such a principle implies, in short, is a continual self-modifying operation that keeps a system from falling to the countertendency toward simplicity, rigidity, and eventual collapse. The operation requires no supervising agency, no intentionality, no homunculus in the works; or, if it does, then we must say there is a homunculus in the structures of rock crystals and immune systems as well.[9] To put it in a slightly different way, one

[9] Arnheim's book is well worth studying in connection with dreams, as are most of his other books. For instance, the following excerpts seem provocative: "When a system changes, especially when it grows, its new size, complexity, function call for a correspondingly modified order. . . . There may be transitional stages

may say that between two alternatives—staying on an established subject or chaotically changing subjects—the first is the easier course for the brain because its inertial inclination is to make order rather than disorder. There is no reason, then, to assume that a dream organizes its parts in advance or even knows where it is going from moment to moment. Indeed, if such were the case the planning would amount to a form of precognition: it would have to have taken into account, in advance, the dreamer's reactions to dream events before they occur. For the dreamer is also a causal force in dreams, contributing the momentum of a personality that unleashes itself at each stage in its own reactive and characteristic way, thus changing the current of the dream, just as the same personality changes the current of waking life by being dependably itself.

We do tell stories not in order to produce meanings, in the sense that a machine produces products, but in order to experience something that can mean what it does only to us. Thus, the meaning of my avocado dream (assuming I had a dream rather than an adventure) is the experiencing of the sensation that my life is passing. The meaning—repecting what provoked the dream—is the dream it-

---

of disorder, at which changing requirements are in conflict with outdated forms. The incomplete, clashing structures in states of disorder create tensions directed toward the realization of potential order" (p. 26). "The structural theme must be conceived dynamically, as a pattern of forces, not an arrangement of static shapes" (p. 33). "The artist's striving toward orderliness is guided by the perceptual pulls and pushes he observes within the work while shaping it. To this extent, the creative process can be described as self-regulatory. However . . . it is necessary to distinguish between the balancing of forces in the perceptual field itself and the 'outside' control exerted by the artist's motives, plans, and preferences" (p. 34).

Perhaps the peculiar mechanism in dreams by which we seem to anticipate and direct the events of the dream may be related to this internal drive toward orderliness. The dreamer does not at all want the monster to see him, but the dream, following the theme of fear, "objectively" causes the monster to see the dreamer. In other words, the order, the "self-regulatory" creative process, does not inhere in the dream as a response to the dreamer's desire to remain safe; it inheres in the logic of possibility. When the dreamer thinks, "I hope it doesn't see me!" the dream realizes that possibility: it continues realistically the theme that in all likelihood introduced the monster in the first place. Though the dreamer is terrified, the dream has shaped the dream in line with expectations. It is a little like standing in a corner and trying *not* to think of a pink elephant. The opposite of the desired effect is thus produced

self; it is no more transmissible than the meaning of a religious vision, and the semantic explanation of it, here on the page, is embarrassingly maudlin and conceptual. As Stanley Fish has put it, "the information an utterance gives, its message, is a constituent of, but certainly not to be identified with, its meaning. It is the experience of an utterance—*all* of it and not anything that could be said about it. . . . that *is* its meaning" (1980: 77–78). In effect, we may say of dreaming what Samuel Beckett said of Joyce's writing: it is not about something, it is that something itself.

The best case for this conception of meaning I know is made by Eugene Gendlin in his analysis of felt meaning in relation to metaphor. Since so much of my argument here depends on this basic idea, I want to follow his discussion of felt meaning in a specific occurrence in poetic imagery. Of Robert Burns's line "my love is like a red, red rose," Gendlin says that there are many different ways roses and girls can be alike ("fresh, blooming, eventually passing, beautiful, living, tender, attractive, soft, quietly waiting to be picked, part of greater nature") but each draws out only "some true aspect" of the resemblance. Moreover, as readers, "our drawing out these meanings [is] a further creative process, for we [do]

---

by the very conjuring of the undesirable possibility. As David Lodge says, contrast is "a kind of negative similarity" (1977: 81).

It seems to me that we might also approach this process of image transformation through J. L. Austin's theory of speech acts, though we are really dealing with perceptual or thought acts. Particularly relevant is Austin's concept of the perlocutionary act, a speech act that brings about or achieves something, "such as convincing, persuading, deterring"; for example, "He persuaded me to shoot her" (1975: 109, 102). The equivalent of a perlocutionary act in dreamwork would be one, then, that carried a certain *force* (another Austin term) that "achiev[es] an object [or] produc[es] a sequel" (p. 121)—namely, the transformation of the image (as when in a dream you think, "Please don't shoot me!" and your thought "persuades" the person to do so). This is a very sketchy proposal, I realize, and I am not sure how far we can treat dream acts as we do speech acts; but it might be worth further examination, since it is possible that the same mechanism may be operating on a different level. There is, after all, a kind of communication taking place between the dreamer and the creatures spawned by the dream, and there are achievements and sequels following dream thoughts. Anyone interested in pursuing such a line of thought (afield of my concerns here) should read Ted Cohen's (1975) critique of Austin, which distinguishes between *direct* and *oblique* perlocutions and discusses their relationship to metaphor formations.

not *explicitly* note any of these even when we read the metaphor. It is clear that, *for us,* the metaphor *is not based on these* likenesses. Rather, the likenesses . . . [are] based on the metaphor—on the experiencing together of 'my love' and 'red, red rose'." As for the creator of the metaphor, Gendlin continues,

> The first *creator* of the metaphor begins with his undifferentiated experience (of his girl), which the metaphor will help him to specify. He specifies his experience by asking himself, 'Now what is that like?' He, too, does not yet have the likeness at that point. He asserts that there is a likeness between something unspecified in his present experienced meaning (of the girl) and something (as yet not found) in his experience in general. When he finds it (a red, red rose) he has *only then* fully created *the specific aspect* of the experience of his girl. . . . In other words, the likenesses exist only as the new meaning is created. The likenesses do not create the new meaning . . . . Hence, a metaphor is a *creation* of meanings *and* of likenesses. One of these does not create the other, but they are tantamount to each other. (1962: 142–43)

Granted, the dreamer is not like the poet in the sense that the poet is able to ask himself, "Now what is my love like?" and go leisurely in search of a likeness. Moreover, it is difficult to say how the image came about (what part literary convention played in the choice or how many images Burns may have discarded before settling on the rose), since the poet is always planning ahead and to a degree writing "backward," a privilege denied the dreamer. But Gendlin's point is persuasive, even so: the creation of metaphor is not preceded by an awareness of likenesses because there is nothing, in advance, for the likenesses to be *like*.[10] It is a little like eating your cake before you actually have it. But, you might ask, suppose you began your thinking with a specific attribute in mind and then went about finding a metaphor to suit it. Wouldn't that be an instance of

[10] This is similar to Max Black's view that "it would be more illuminating . . . to say that [a] metaphor *creates* the similarity than to say that it formulates some similarity antecedently existing" (1954–55: 284–85).

the likeness preceding the image? For instance, I might ask myself, "What is my love like?" and decide "Well, she's fresh and blooming. I've got it: she's like a rose!" If, however, you think that *fresh* and *blooming* got you to rose, there is no proof that that was all that got you there, or that the smell of a hidden rose isn't what got you to *fresh* and *blooming* in the first place, inasmuch as your mind was already wandering in a flower garden. In other words, *blooming* at this stage isn't a likeness but something nearer the genus itself, with only the differentia to be named. This might seem a stacked case, however, since *blooming* is something of a leading image. But suppose *blooming* hadn't occurred to you and the only attribute you had in mind was *fresh*. The likelihood in this case, however, is that *fresh* would get you no closer to *rose* than to vegetables, cheese, or air. I agree that it is possible to move from *my love* to *rose* through a specific transitional channel in which an attribute like *fresh* figures in the discovery. But in Gendlin's theory they couldn't be called likenesses before you had the complete metaphor in mind.[11]

This leaves open the question of where the rose (of all things possible) came from, which is in effect to ask where *creation* comes from.[12] And this is precisely where Gendlin's concept of felt or

---

[11] Gendlin's argument is similar to that of Donald Davidson in his influential (and controversial) discussion of metaphorical meaning in *Critical Inquiry* (1978). The meaning of a metaphor, Davidson says, is exactly what it says in its text: "We must give up the idea that a metaphor carries a message, that it has a content or meaning (except, of course, its literal meaning) . . . . A metaphor does its work through other intermediaries—to suppose it can be effective only by conveying a coded message is like thinking a joke or a dream makes some statement which a clever interpreter can restate in plain prose. Joke or dream or metaphor can, like a picture or a bump on the head, make us appreciate some fact—but not by standing for, or expressing, the fact. . . . what we attempt in 'paraphrasing' a metaphor cannot be to give its meaning, for that lies on the surface; rather we attempt to evoke what the metaphor brings to our attention. . . . When we try to say what a metaphor 'means,' we soon realize there is no end to what we want to mention" (pp. 45–46).

[12] For simplicity I put aside the very important factor of literary fashion, which to an extent dictates the kind of metaphors poets are likely to choose in particular periods (nature imagery in Romantic poetry, technological or scientific imagery in the modern). There is also the problem of the influence of ryhme and meter; having found "June" in his second line ("That's newly sprung in June"), Burns is committed to a second metaphor that is compatible—hence "tune" in line four and "melodie" in line three.

experienced meanings enters the picture. In short, in *my love* there is a felt meaning that is specified only in the discovery of something that can carry an appropriate qualitative likeness. It might have been a "melodie" (as in the third line of Burns's poem), a bird, a cloud, or another flower—anything in nature that might serve to approximate certain felt qualities of *my love*, but each would arouse a different set of likenesses (and your love may be like all of them as well). But only with the specification (*rose*, in this case) do more or less precise meanings begin to flourish and (in turn) delimit themselves in what we may call a circle of implications.[13] It is a matter of dropping down into the brain's store of categories and finding one (*roses, roseness*) that seems qualitatively isomorphic with your sense of your love. In other words, the brain has nothing specific in mind, it simply scans categories of experience on the frequency of a felt gestalt, which might even be conceived as a certain lack, or set of contraints, as when you try to decide what it is you want to do by enumerating the things you don't want to do; or, when you scan a physical environment for something that has to be long and pretty rigid if it is to serve the purpose of the lever you need to lift a stone. For example, Burns's particular sense of his love (but not everybody's) would probably exclude the attributes of such categories as *octopus, potato, window, cellar,* or *muskrat* but might include those of such categories as *swan, bird, moon, cloud, sunrise,* or *Sunday.* How *rose* is selected is anyone's guess. The point is that there must be a strong intermediate step between undifferentiated love and the red rose that finally delimits its range of characteristics.

George Lakoff and Mark Johnson, who offer a linguistic variation of Gendlin's notion of felt experience, would explain this act

[13] Robert Fogelin suggests that "likeness statements" (metaphors, similes) are useful because they help to solve "what might be called the ineffability problem," or what Gendlin would call a felt meaning that has not yet been brought out of the blue: "By comparing a person with a bulldozer, we invoke a feature space dominated by bulldozer-salient qualities. But under that reading, the comparison seems plainly false. In order to avoid attributing a pointlessly false statement to the speaker, the respondent now prunes the feature space of the falsifying features and, if the metaphor is *sound* . . . , then the comparison, figuratively taken, is true" (Fogelin, 1988: 79, 89).

by saying that underlying the choice of any metaphor is a preconceptual structure—a structure based on our preconceptual experience of the world, from which all conceptual structures arise. This
is a complex argument advanced over several books (most notably
Lakoff and Johnson, 1980; Lakoff, 1987; Johnson, 1987); but one of
these structures is called an image schema (see chapter 4), which is a
"gestalt structure" midway between an abstract proposition and a
concrete image (Johnson, 1987: 29, 44). In the case of *rose,* one
might speculate that Burns was motivated by any number of kines-
thetic constraints—fragility, verticality, sensuality, fragrance,
roundness, softness, symmetry (though I think even this is pinning
it down too finely)—the bundle of them forming a metonymic
structure in mental space that might include all kinds of love-ly
qualities, none really specified in his conscious mind any more than
his love's qualities were specified as the cause of his first falling in
love with her.

In any case, the poet knows the image is right before he knows
what is right about it; if he doesn't know what the likenesses are, he
knows, experientially, something of what *roseness* is from observation and other literature.[14] At this point in the process, roseness
would be an instance of what Ignacio Matte Blanco calls "knowledge without parts" (1975: 288). Only when *rose* is specified does
the felt meaning begin to release itself in particular directions and,
like Cupid's arrow, curve back on "my love," creating new meanings. This is what we might refer to as a kind of "secondary revision," a step toward conceptual coherence, in the creative process.
First there is the preconceptual meaning, then the conceptual, and
you can't get to the conceptual, or symbolic, without the prepara-
tory stage of the preconceptual structure, what Gendlin calls "felt
or experienced meaning." And when one adds the interpreter to
this process, the creativity is repeated all over again. For example,

---

[14] Along this line, we might add to the possibilities C. K. Ogden and I. A.
Richards' notion of the *engram,* or all the original traces left by roses, roseness, and
rose experiences from Burns's past, which presumably have what we may call a high
correlation with the engram of love, lovers, and loving (Ogden and Richards, 1923:
52–53).

Gendlin notes that you are likely to discard any idea that the red
rose image suggests that *my love* grows out of the ground—unless it
should creatively occur to you (which it probably didn't to Burns)
that "she is deeply rooted in her native country and its culture, she
is earthy, she appears suddenly and noiselessly as if out of the
ground" (1962: 169). And once *that* meaning occurs to you, you are
inside the same creative loop that began with the discovery of the
rose—which is to say that interpreters are quite literally as creative
as poets when it comes to the sheer cognitive act of finding meanings in things. Things suggest other things, but then these other
things bring with them contexts and engrams of their own that
change the meanings of the original thing, like Matisse's black dots
on the paper or my chain of dictionary synonyms. Indeed, is is not
necessary for there to have been an original meaning, or even an
aura of appropriate intentions, for an image to provoke an interpretation. If I randomly say "My love is like a bar of soap," a whole
host of slippery cleansing meanings will come pouring into the
scene (a shower in which my love is living up to her likeness).

I trust it is clear how all this may apply to the dream, conceived as
a *process* of creation. The dream does not go in search of metaphors
in the conscious sense that the poet might. And it is obvious that
dream imagery and dream narratives, having no surviving text, are
open to even greater interpretive ranges and abuses. But one might
well claim that when a waking poet does go in search of a metaphor, or a metaphor suggests itself, then the poet has entered a state
analogous to the dream: he or she is *open* to suggestion; the mind
claims a certain exemption from pragmatic concerns, becomes
available to the influx of associations we tend to dampen in daily
life. After all, one is not apt to discover metaphors while perform-
ing brain surgery or defusing a land mine. Gendlin's concept of felt
or preconceptual meaning as a kind of open closedness[15] in the

---

[15] For example, a more precise definition of the preconceptual: "The preconceptual is not constituted of actual defined existent contents or meanings. These are *not*
interpenetrating units, forms, meanings, orders that—if we could only represent
them all—could be equated with a moment or aspect of experiencing. All these
meanings 'exist' in a sense, but it is not the sense of marbles in a bag. These 'implicit'

imaging process seems to me an economical way of explaining both the order and the seeming disorder in dreams. In the dream we are virtually at the site of pure creativity, where the associative process is not hampered by matters of comprehensibility or conceptuality. The dream does not make metaphors in the sense of a string of images with a theme (as in Burns's poem); rather, it produces likenesses that are also felt meanings. These meanings are, however, based on the entire history of the dreamer, and as such they occur as a chain of events guided, as I discussed in earlier chapters, by the same conditions of narratability that apply in the daily life of the dreamer. Within the chain, however, the dream is bizarre or constantly subjected to associational revision: it has, one might say, likeness fever (Sarah may become Aunt Julie; my car may become a ship; my love may literally become a rose), and one can never fully identify all the associations that may have produced the "bizarre intrusion."[16]

If we accept Gendlin's discussion of the creative process as valid, it becomes virtually supererogatory to claim that dreams have many or even endless meanings or that a dream could have any antecedent plan; the very nature of creativity involves the uncover-

---

meanings are not complete or formed (under cover, as it were). When they become 'explicit,' they become different from what they were, when they are 'implicit.' They were 'preconceptual' aspects of this protean type of order, and only as they interact with symbols do they become completely formed. Thus upon the symbols that will interact with experiencing depends just what aspect of it will (then be said to) have been there. This 'implicit' preconceptual complexity awaits future symbols" (1962: 28–29).

This idea really refines the problem before us in another way: the preconceptual meaning, or structure, that brought on the rose image in Burns's poem was not simply a preconceptual model of roseness; roseness was only one of its potentialities, which, being made explicit, now seems to limit the implications of the preconceptual structure. But when Burns adds, in the next line, that his love is also like a melodie, the process occurs all over again and roseness becomes a kind of ground to the melodic figure.

[16] Kenneth Burke is saying something very close to this in his discussion of the ramifications of the symbol in *Counter-Statement*: "A theoretically perfect Symbol would, in all its ramifications, reveal the underlying pattern of experience. . . . The underlying pattern is observable when an apparently arbitrary or illogical association of ideas can be shown to possess an 'emotional' connective" (1953: 158–59).

ing of likenesses that are also meanings, though not the sort of
meanings interpreters arrive at when they claim that dreams mean
something specific within the horizon of implications. It is not a
question of dreams meaning one or several things but of meaning
itself being noncondensable to interpretations. For example, if you
take the entire first verse of Burns's poem—

> O, my luve is like a red, red rose,
> That's newly sprung in June.
> O my luve is like a melodie
> That's sweetly played in tune.

you really have an interplay, as Field would say, of metaphors and
specified likenesses. But even though Burns pins down the meaning of *rose* and *melodie* to specific attributes, one cannot claim that
the meanings stop with the specifications. Burns is playing two
different roles here under the cap of the poet: he is by turns a
metaphorist and an interpreter of his own metaphors: "That's newly sprung in June" is an interpretation of "rose"; "That's sweetly
played in tune" is an interpretation of "melodie." At least the lines
suggest part of what Burns *says* he means in using the figures. But
the beauty of metaphor is that once it's out of the bag you can't
limit its connotations simply by naming a few that occur to you,
either as poet or as reader. A rose that's newly sprung in June
carries the whole perceptual aura of roseness with it. This aura, a
term I am using roughly in Walter Benjamin's sense,[17] is the locus
of felt meanings, which are not the same thing as specified meanings or interpretations. Moreover, when you say that your love is
like a red rose and then add that it is also like a melodie, you have
created still a third metaphor because we are invited to consider not
only what your love has in common with roses and melodies but

---

[17] The term *aura,* for Benjamin, is a thing's "unique existence." It is also its
"authenticity," or "the essence of all that is transmissible [about it] from its beginning, ranging from its substantive duration to its testimony to the history which it
has experienced"—and, I would add for present purposes, the history we have
experienced through it (1977: 221).

what melodies and roses *do* to each other (the melodie of the rose), quite apart from being like my love. As Robert J. Fogelin says, "metaphors, as renegade comparisons, defy standard constraints." Each metaphor in a poem helps to establish "the level of specificity at which [each other] metaphor is to be read" (1988: 112). Indeed, interpretation is something of an act of violence committed on the image insofar as it converts an experience into a concept, which is to say that it arrests the radiation of meanings. And this is the central limitation of dream interpretation, as it is, in Fish's view, of literary interpretation: it substitutes one kind of meaning for another; it puts an event in the place of a history of association and more pertinently an explanation in the place of an understanding. Meaning, as George Lakoff puts it, "is not a thing: it involves what is meaningful to us. . . . Meaningfulness derives from the experience of functioning as a being of a certain sort in an environment of a certain sort" (1987: 292). For like the poets we dream about things whose meaning we already know in an emotional and preconceptual sense, and that is no doubt why we dream about them and why dreams make a certain kind of essentialized sense. The dream is the instantiation of a felt meaning—which is the cause of the dream, not its effect—brought into sleep from the day's experience, and what meaning one gets out of it on the waking side by way of interpretation is itself a new meaning (because a new symbolization) that leaves the experience behind in the act of conceptualizing it for waking understanding. If you dream that you are dancing, you may be dreaming about one of several things: how easy it is to dance, how graceful and perfect your effort, or how self-conscious and awkward; your dream dance, then, is the dancing of a feeling about dancing, which is to say about one of dancing's meanings to you. In any case, to paraphrase Yeats, you can't tell the meaning from the dance.[18]

[18] I am here altering Burke's well-known phrase "dancing of an attitude," from his *Philosophy of Literary Form* (1957: 10). On this note, the perfect complement to Gendlin's theory of felt (experienced) meaning is Burke's essay (in the same volume) "Semantic and Poetic Meaning." For example: "The semantic ideal would attempt to *get a description* [or meaning] by the *elimination* of attitude. The poetic ideal would

My position respecting meaning in dreams is somewhere between those of Foulkes, Globus, and Boss. Foulkes substantially
argues that dreams are meaningless (I qualify this in a moment), but
that they are not on that account fully random or worthless. Rather,
they struggle to deal with bizarre intrusions and radical shifts of
focus cast up from the symbolic memory by submitting them to
scripts and knowledge structures learned in waking life. In the
process, dreams manage to offer "rich clues to the nature of the
human mind, in general," and specifically to the ways it assimilates
and processes information by means of narratives (1985: 204–5).
Globus has argued vigorously against the "new science" of dreaming (including Foulkes in this group) by claiming that radical shifts
of focus are not signs of meaninglessness or chaotic disorganization
but, on some occasions at least, products of a "unifying concept
that affects both the memories [that get into the dream] . . . and the
dream narrative." Globus's approach, much like Freud's, consists
in submitting dreams to a search of day (and life) residue that finds
its way into the dream by a process he refers to as abstract specification, the generation of a model of reality according to a wishful
self-command (1987: esp. 40–45).[19] Boss, on still another extreme,
believes that dreams are given to the dreamer precisely as waking
life is given to us. The image appears (or uncovers itself) as things
"unhide" themselves in the empirical world (like my avocado fruit).
For Boss, no creativity is involved: being itself gives the image and
the dreamer simply responds, as in waking life itself.

---

attempt to *attain a full moral act* by attaining a perspective *atop all the conflicts of attitude.*
The first would try to *cut away,* to *abstract,* all emotional factors that complicate the
objective clarity of meaning. The second would try to derive its vision from the
maximum *heaping up* of all these emotional factors, playing them off against each
other, inviting them to reinforce and contradict one another, and seeking to make
this active participation itself a major ingredient of the vision" (p. 128). In short, the
more meanings (within a circle of relevant likeness) you can load into the red red
rose or any other figure, the closer it comes to the poetic ideal and the more useless it
is to a semantic diagnostic interpretation.

[19] For example, in connection with a dream Globus cites as a case in point: "It is as
if a rule were being followed: select instances of recent memory that come under the
concept 'loss of attachments' or select attachments and narratively show them as
lost" (1991: 37).

Widely different as these approaches are, each has something to be said for it. I have already discussed Foulkes's notion of scripts and knowledge structures (Chapter 4). As for Globus's notion of a unifying concept, I have experienced so many instances of unity in my own dreamlife (as in the lobster dream) that I have no need to be persuaded that he has a point—in terms of certain dreams at least—and that physiologists would do well to examine their own dreams before writing them off as random nonsense. My only reservation is the strictly semantic one that the term *concept*, as I have been examining it in relation to preconceptual meaning, tends to throw us back on the notion that dreams themselves—rather than inter-preters—think in conceptual terms (as opposed to experiential); that is, in some mysterious way dreams form unifying concepts that serve as a mechanism of image selection. "It is," as Globus says of his dream illustration, "as if a rule were being followed: select instances of recent memory that come under the concept 'loss of attachments' or select attachments and narratively show them as lost" (1991: 37). To be fair, this statement is intended as a meta-phorical one ("it is *as* if") rather than as an illusion to a concrete mental process Globus is advocating. And the same may be true for Globus's use of the word *concept*. But the metaphor has the unfortu-nate implication of bifurcating the dream into administrative and

---

Along this same line, Don Kuiken is developing an approach called systematic phenomenological dream interpretation, or "numerically aided phenomenology." In a paper presented to the Association for the Study of Dreams conference in 1991, he illustrates the method by examining a dream of my own from *The Rhetoric of Dreams*—the so-called bathroom dream (States, 1988: 161–66). I must say I was flattered that Kuiken had chosen a dream of mine for such public scrutiny; however, given the intimate circumstances the dream depicts (I was uneasy from the begin-ning), having it return to me, thus aired, made me feel as if I were still *in* the bathroom and had forgotten to close the door. In any case, Kuiken's interpretation was completely convincing to me (and I might add, gentlemanly) and the method—tracing "meaning structures" or "transformations of a common theme" through the sequence of dream scenes (Kuiken, 1991: 9, 11)—strikes me as being a useful way of locating emotional order, or meaning, in dreams without claiming that the dream is being intentional or tendentious. In other words, it is one thing to claim that dreams have a thematic or meaningful organization (Kuiken's point), quite another to attri-bute it to what Daniel Dennett calls a "central meaner." Dennett, of course, finds such a notion completely untenable (1991: esp. 228–38).

executive processes, or, if you will, of endowing it with a super-logic that somehow precedes and oversees its creation. In my own experientialist or preconceptual view of dreaming, this is unneces-sary: the dream itself is all there is of dreaming, and the concept it follows is no different from the concept it draws from the dreamer's waking life. In short, if you are concerned about loss of attachments during the day, you are apt to dream about them, sooner or later, at night, even though no concept has been formed in either instance. As for the mechanism that produces the dream sequence, no skill in selecting or plotting is required beyond the immense mapping ca-pabilities of the brain, which have been plotting the dreamer's ex-perience since birth, both in and out of dreams. If this were not the case we would inevitably have the same problem explaining how the dream concept goes about giving instructions to the dream-work. Who, or what, in the ever-regressing line of cellular hier-archy, gives instructions to the instructor?[20]

My own defense of the meaningfulness of dreams in the face of their so-called random conduct also invokes a literary precedent. Abrupt changes in scene and characters are as common in fiction as they are in dreams, and before we conclude that they signal ran-domness in dream construction we ought to see if they bear any structural resemblance or purpose to those of fiction. The assump-tion is that fictions require such changes (when they do) to unfold their story in a logical order. Take a simple example: Y is on her way to X's apartment. The scene shifts from Y's car (en route) to the apartment where X is setting up a hidden recording device in preparation for Y's arrival. This is information we must know in order to understand what is at stake in the next scene. The rule,

---

[20] See Gerald Edelman on this point (1992: 16–30). As a sideline to this matter of concepts in dreams, I should add that it is perfectly possible for the dreamer to think conceptually within a dream. Like most other students of the dream, I'm sure, I often "get ideas" while dreaming—sometimes even ideas about dreams if I have been puzzling over them during the day. I then form concepts in the dream: "This must mean this, . . ." Unfortunately, ninety percent of the time my concepts turn out to be worthless imitations of the structure of conceptual thought in the light of day, like Hunt's detective dream. All this, however, is quite different from the idea that dreams have a conceptual basis.

then, is that the continuity of fictions is based not on the persistence of a single perspective or a chronological sequence of events but on a maximization of affect—the presentation of the scenes in the best order for satisfying the reader's expectations—even though that order may involve bizarre interruptions of scenes in progress. Fictions are constantly saying to us, "Before you can appreciate this, I must tell you *this*."

A dream hardly has such a problem, since it doesn't have to satisfy anyone's expectations. But there is a possibility that a dream does move from place to place and from person to person (even fusing scenes and people) according to a different principle of form, one concerned less with advancement of a "syllogistic" kind than with "qualitative progression" or the use of "repetitive form," to invoke Kenneth Burke's well-known terms. Repetitive form "is the consistent maintaining of a principle under new guises. It is a re-statement of the same thing in different ways" (1953: 125). Indeed, the literary form that comes closest to this kind of ordering is the anatomy, which consists of a heaping up or cataloguing of things belonging to the same category, and the basic idea is a spatial circumscription of events in the category rather than a temporal evolution. Even more specifically, the dream may be likened to the Menippean satire (a near-neighbor of the anatomy), which, as Northrop Frye says,

> deals less with people as such than with mental attitudes . . . . At its most concentrated the Menippean satire presents us with a vision of the world in terms of a single intellectual pattern. The intellectual structure built up from the story makes for violent dislocations in the customary logic of narrative, though the appearance of carelessness that results reflects only the carelessness of the reader or his tendency to judge by a novel-centered conception of fiction. (1957: 10)

I am not suggesting that there is any formal resemblance between the dream and the Menippean satire, only—to come back to my premise in Chapter 3—that forms are themselves the consequence of certain fundamental ways the brain orders human experience.

There is nothing in the least satirical or intellectual about the dream, and the dream does not appear to be in the business of making catalogues of mnemonic material. But the dream does seem to be a thought process that requires "violent dislocations in the customary logic of narrative" *in order to follow its particular logic*, which is the logic of association and resemblance.

This seems to me what Globus is referring to in his notion of the unified concept in certain dreams.[21] In short, randomness is a highly debatable notion: the scientist's idea of *random* may, in some instances, involve the poet's (and the dreamer's) principle of order. The point, then, would not be to credit sudden jumps in sequence, place, or character composition to disorderliness in the dream but to determine what sort of emotional or conceptual material binds the jumps into a unified whole. My personal experience is that the evolution of a particular dream, and perhaps even of the dreams of a night, often involves non sequiturs of time and place but rarely of emotional tenor. If I am frustrated or paranoic in one part of the dream, I am likely to be in all other parts as well. Not taking such things into consideration seems to me to reflect, as Frye might put it, only the carelessness in our tendency to judge by a reality-centered conception of the dream.

I do feel, however, that Globus is confusing, or overestimating, what Foulkes means by saying that dreams are meaningless. As I see it, Foulkes is referring strictly to intentional meanings, or dreams as coded messages, the kinds of meaning I have been at some pains to question here. "It does not follow," Foulkes says in another part of his book, "that, since dreams are constructed to convey no particular message, they are meaningless. There are broader senses of meaning than apply to the case of deliberate

[21] Montague Ullman makes essentially the same point in "Dreaming as Metaphor in Motion": "Dreaming involves rapidly changing presentational sequences which in their unity amount to a metaphorical statement (major metaphor). Each element (minor metaphor) in the sequence has metaphorical attributes organized toward the end of establishing in a unified way an over-all metaphorical description of the new ideas and relations and their implications as these rise to the surface during periods of activated sleep. . . . Incongruity of elements, inappropriate relations, displacement, are all well known attributes of dreams" (1969: 697).

message-encoding" (1985: 192). And again, at the end of the book, "Dreams are not meaningless. To the contrary. . . . [But] intelligent use of dreams for self-knowledge depends on understanding what kinds of information they might, and might not, contain" (p. 214). Finally, we should say that Foulkes's *Grammar of Dreams* (1978) presents an elaborate scoring system for latent dream structures, or for what Foulkes refers to as "private meaning." In fact, the system is based on the kind of free associational interpretation used by Globus in his "dream illustration" (1991: 35–39). The problem here is once again the word *meaning*. I have no idea how Foulkes might regard Gendlin's concept of felt or experienced meanings (as against encoded meanings), but it does not seem incompatible with his position. And I suspect that Foulkes would agree that dreams might have a unifying concept (what he might call a knowledge structure), but that such a concept constitutes meaning, in the encoded or intentional sense of the term, is quite another matter. This is perfectly consistent with my own belief and I must confess that Globus's notion of abstract specification seems elusive and, from what I can understand, not really much different from the kind of organizational mechanisms Foulkes discusses (scriptual coherence, syntactical intentionality). As for Boss, Globus seems right in complaining that Boss's Dreaming Dasein theory leaves us in a "Heideggerian fog" as to how Dasein goes about giving us dream images (1987: 169). As a point of focus, let us look briefly at one of Boss's dream samples.

A twenty-nine-year-old single woman dreamed of seeing her analyst (always clean-shaven in life) with an unkempt, wild growth of beard. Boss's explanation is that the beard is real (in the dream *Umwelt*); it has been given by the dream and was not, so to speak, dreamed up in the patient's creative workshop: "As far as the dreamer's perception is concerned," Boss says, "all that really happens is that a decidedly bearded analyst manifest himself in the light of her dreaming existence. . . . Furthermore the dreamt beard is not at all experienced by the dreamer as being only an 'image' of a beard but as being a real beard made of the stuff actual beards are made of. . . . it is a growth emanating from an existing male"

(1977: 65). This is an intrepidly phenomenological perspective, but as far as perception is concerned there can be no doubt that this is what took place in the dream, from the dreamer's point of view. Although it may be inadequate as an interpretation of the beard's meaning, it does bracket the dream experience on purely perceptual grounds (here, we are back with Boss's sleeping skier of Chapter 1).[22] Globus finds Boss's "disdain of mechanism" (p. 169) wanting, to say the least, and would undoubtedly (if the patient were his own) run a search through her recent memory for an explanation as to how the analyst got thus bearded in his own den.

But again, I think Globus is not doing full justice to the underlying assumption of Boss's phenomenological approach. Boss is not denying, in this or other instances, that waking day residue finds its way into the dream. He is saying that what the woman dreamed in the beard dream is not what she thought of her analyst in waking life: "While awake, she had always stressed that she saw her analyst exclusively as a rational, intelligent, trustworthy, unbiased medical advisor" (p. 64)—a statement, I realize, that is guaranteed to raise a psychoanalyst's eyebrow. Dreams, for Boss, offer their own versions of waking relationships and there is no reason to assume that the dream version is less meaningful than the waking version or that the dream has disguised a *real* meaning—in short, that the woman's repressed feelings about her analyst come out in the dream in the wild growth of beard. Even if the dreamer, on waking, makes a connection between the dream and the waking version of the attitude, it does not prove that the dream has released a repressed attitude or is repressing one. Here is Boss's explanation of the dream: "As a dreamer, the patient receives more information about her analyst than her waking self ever perceived. No longer is

---

[22] This is not to say that Boss does not, in his own way, interpret the dreams he cites, both here and in his earlier book, *The Analysis of Dreams* (1958). Indeed, his "therapeutic applications" (1977: 65) of dreams to the "bearing" of his patients (or the patients of other analysts!) seem no different (and in many cases more arbitrary) than those of standard Freudian or Jungian psychoanalysis. The case for a disjunction between Boss's concepts and his method (of interpretation) is made by Gendlin (1977).

he locked into the frame of the intellectually superior, distant medical guardian. Now he appears in her dreaming as a sloppy, uncouth bearded man. Her dreaming response to that man, ending in terrified flight, is worthy of notice" (p. 65). In short, in Boss's phenomenological approach, which considers the dreamworld as given in the same way the waking world is given, the dream is its own source of truth, which may be used to enlarge, or even reinterpret, reality ("In your dreaming," he goes on, "your eyes open to something vital, unpolished, inherently masculine about him"; p. 65), as opposed to reality informing a hidden meaning in the dream. Here we are back with Jonathan Culler's paradox of origin: "If either cause or effect can occupy the position of origin, then origin is no longer originary; it loses its metaphysical privilege" (1985: 88). Thus, we can begin from either end of the cause-effect operation with equal justification. There is no reason, then, to treat the waking attitude (fear, desire) as the origin of the dream image, in the sense that the image's meaning coincides with, or disguises, the waking attitude, conscious or unconscious. The dream image, as Gendlin would say, means what is experienced in its presence and that is all it means. No doubt we have all experienced dreaming about someone in a way that readjusts, if only temporarily, our attitude toward that person in waking life (for instance, that odd intimacy you feel on encountering someone you have dreamed about the night before). Psychoanalysis would likely say that in such a case you had unconsciously felt that way all along and the dream simply realized it—that, indeed, is why you dreamed the dream. The phenomenological explanation would treat the dream as the cause, or point of origin, of the new attitude: the dream was creating a meaning, not passing one along, and that meaning (a new attitude) might exert an influence on waking life, or it might not.

One other possible approach to the beard problem amounts to a compromise between the positions of Foulkes and Boss. Dreams, Foulkes says, "seem to be guided, once they're under way, by narrative schemata or thematic scripts that have a logic of their own, and that use knowledge to their own ends rather than simply reflecting the inherent organization of knowledge in symbolic memory" (1985: 205). If we were looking for a thematic script that might cover the sudden appearance of beards on clean-shaven faces, we could find it in a script category we can call "mutability: subcategory, people's looks." These would be instances of unexpected change in appearance, such as seeing people who have aged since you last saw them or people who have radically changed their appearance—the sort of thing that usually produces a minor shock and gets talked about on the way home from a party ("What do you think of Bob's new moustache?"). This may seem frivolous, and it may have nothing to do with the beard in question; but such incidents are almost invariably remembered and they happen often enough in a lifetime to form a category of their own in the dictionary of recurrent situations. They certainly happen in dreams, the most typical cases being bizarre metamorphoses in the appearance of loved ones, the sort of thing Freud treats under the principle of contradiction where "any element [can be represented] by its wishful contrary" (1973 [1900], 4:318). Of course, Freud reaches different conclusions about the cause of such images, and the woman's beard dream might finally be explainable on the grounds of a wishful contrary or some subliminally held attitude about her analyst's impeccable grooming habits. I am suggesting a moderated phenomenological approach that might combine Foulkes's notion of thematic schemata and Boss's principle of givenness—maybe even Globus's unifying concept. One would assume that what is given in the dream must somehow be based on one's experience of givenness in the waking world. Dreamlife, then, would be a structural replica of waking life in the sense that it would consist of similar kinds of experience patterns and similar responses to them, greatly transmogrified by the conditions of dreaming. Such patterns are the source and axis of our emotional life, and it would be hard to think of an emotion that wasn't built around some such structure. For instance, if you made a list of all the situations in which you've been angry, you would probably find a pattern of some sort, or a system of patterns—not simply of what you got angry at but in how you handle anger, your reactive pattern. And, presumably, if you were angry in a dream, the emotion would express itself in this pattern. But to come back to the beard, among the things that waking life gives to dreamlife would be encounters with the reversibility of the known, or, more precisely, what we would retain is the structure of such encounters. As dreamers we are like colonists who inhabit a new world but bring along all the forms and response systems we learned in the old world.

Needless to say, I am not interpreting the woman's dream per se but trying to account for one possible basis of such dreams. The metamorphosis of the analyst is only one of countless thematic categories retained from the waking world. I assume we take notice of such things, and in turn dream about them, because they constitute a species of surprise in our relation to world continuity. What is the shock behind such occurrences, however minor, but the shock of awareness of the underlying mutability of all things in tension with the counterwish that things remain as they are? Actually, we are back with Peter Brooks's notion of narrative as the "condition of deviance and abnormality": "Deviance is the very condition for life to be 'narratable': the state of normality is devoid of interest, energy, and the possibility for narration" (1985:139). Hence the dream, as ur-narrative, specializes in the art of deviance. The creatural requirement for something's admission to a dream is that it surrender its stability and its autonomy as an identity.

These remarks should not be taken as a preference for one interpretive avenue to the exclusion of another. Ultimately there is no incompatibility between my amended notion of givenness as an explanation for the analyst's beard and any possible psychoanalytic reading that would locate the cause in the personal situation of the patient. Let us say, for instance, that the woman had become annoyed (disappointed, envious, frustrated) at her analyst's fastidiousness and self-control ("He's perfect, I'm a mess!"); and one night she simply went to sleep and endowed him with an unkempt and wild growth of beard. Here the intricacies of transference (which Boss is precisely denying in his discussion of the dream) have indeed found a perfect metonymic container in a classic wish-fulfillment dream. But where did this splendid mechanism of conversion come from if not from being-in-the-world itself, long prior to this particular annoyance and its aftermath in a dream? In essence, the wish fulfillment involves the manipulation of a thematic schemata given by reality, stored in memory, and ready to hand should a dream ever require it (although not stored for that purpose). Thus, the relationship of an existential (or phenomenological) and a psychoanalytic reading of dreams would be complementary or intertwined, similar perhaps to the relationship of such things as form to content, style to subject, sense to reference, process to product, or language (*langue*) to speech (*parole*). They are, in a sense, made of each other.

E. H. Gombrich once said that artists don't go into the field to paint what they see but to see what they already know how to paint. The same may be said of the theorist of dreams, who has almost invariably been taught to look at dreams from the standpoint of a particular methodology. Boss would even extend this principle to the patient in analysis:

> The analyst's theoretical expectations, which cannot stay hidden from the patient for long, are particularly active in codeterming [*sic*] the direction 'free association' takes. This helps explain why the 'free associations' of patients in Freudian analysis regularly head toward instinctual desires, while in Jungian patients they lead to archetypal structures and mandalas. And if patients in Daseinsanalysis were encouraged to practice 'free association' (in the Freudian sense) no doubt they would keep coming up with typically existential ideas. (1977: 31)

So one's theoretical expectations dictate what one is able to say about the dream, just as they dictate what we say about art. If we take the four strongest interpretive methodologies being practiced today—or at least those common to both the literary and dream realms—we see how the yield of meaning is predicated directly on the assumptions of the approach. The four I suggest (see the table at the end of this chapter) are psychoanalytic, semiotic, phenomenological, and structural, and I have thrown in deconstructive as an extreme approach derived historically from the other four. The first two are what one might be broadly called referential methodologies, the latter two nonreferential. The semiotic approach conceives its object of study as the sign whose dynamic behavior consists in referring to a signified content (the sign, need it be said? is composed of a signifier and a signified). Typically this process is addressed to the social or personal consciousness, in the interests of communication or, from the interpretive point of view, of understanding how sign systems work in the production of (normally) shared meaning. The semiotic differs from the psychoanalytic chiefly in that the latter is directed to systems of concealment or repression, though a good deal has been said about repression in semiotic systems: hence the symbol or symptom as opposed to sign as the unit of psychoanalytic study. Whereas in semiotic systems there is normally no hidden order of meaning—no censor—in psychoanalytic theory there is always a gap between manifest and latent content, and it is in this gap that psychoanalysis cuts out its work. Otherwise, the interpretive operations are virtually identical and this is the rationale for Peter Brooks referring to Freud as "a semiotician . . . attentive to all behavior as semiotic, as coded text that can be deciphered, as ultimately charged with meaning." Thus, Freud "(and the follower who best has understood his semiotic message, Lacan) points us toward a convergence of semiotics and psychoanalysis which can open up important perspectives to the literary critic who is concerned to connect literary texts to human experience" (1985: 322). In actual practice, however, a dream psychologist who is closer to a semiotic perspective is Calvin Hall. I doubt if the word *semiotic* ever passed Hall's lips, but his theory of expressiveness in dream symbolism, though an inversion of Freud's assumptions about censorship, follows Freud's semiotic method perfectly. For Hall, "[there] is no such thing as the latent content of a dream. A dream is a manifest experience, and what is latent lies outside the dream and in the verbal material that the dreamer reports when he is asked to free associate to features in the reported dream" (1966: xviii–xix). Hall compares the dream to a language "consist[ing] of pictures which are the concrete perceptible representations of the mind's ideas" (p. 10). Finally, Hall believes that dreams must be interpreted in a series, rather than individually, because only in a series can one establish how a thought gets constituted as a sign, as opposed to a one-time image, in the dreamer's personal language.

I classify the phenomenological and the structural as nonreferential only in relative comparison to the semiotic and psychoanalytic approaches. It goes without saying that an interpretive methodology cannot not refer to something beyond it (though Boss comes close) and that the idea that the phenomenologist looks only at "the things themselves" or the structuralist at pure structure must be credited as naive. In any case, what the semiotician would call a sign and the psychoanalyst a symbol the phenomenologist is apt to call an image or a thing that "gives off" a self-expressiveness beyond which the phenomenologist chooses not to look. If a lifetime of meanings is semiotically bound up in the thing, so be it; the important point is to examine what essentially meets the eye, or the image's way of being present to perception, as we have already seen in Boss's explanation of the bearded analyst. The structuralist method examines the functionality of the image (or structural unit), how the part fits into the whole (as in Proppian analysis). If there is anything referential in the structuralist's method, it has to do with the relation of the structure under examination to analogous structures outside it (such as the structure of tragedy, of scripts, of plots). In most respects, Foulkes's work (by his own admission) might be considered an example of structuralism in dream theory, but then Foulkes has also made a case for considering Freud a prestructuralist (or "transitional") structuralist (1978: 121).

Finally, the deconstructive approach, which I entertain here mainly because of the light it throws on the others, would be a study of traces rather than images, symbols, or the others. Every image carries traces of other images. To put it another way, all meanings are made of other absent meanings; hence deconstruction involves the relation of signifiers to other signifiers, there being no such thing as a transcendental signified. Here, in one sense anyway, we are at the extreme opposite of the phenomenological approach, which is concerned only with presence and essence. Still, despite its radical critique of phenomenal presence, deconstruction shares at least one procedure with phenomenology: if it is the referential methodology par excellence, even as it undermines referentiality, its eye is squarely on the oppositions it uncovers rather than on a translation of signifiers to signifieds. Thus, it is what we might call a phenomenology of disappearance. Or one might think of it as rampant psychoanalysis, and it is no accident that deconstruction-ists have an ongoing lover's quarrel with Freud, who, along with Nietzsche, taught them most of their basic principles, among which were strategic contradiction, latency, deferral, regression, and the memory trace. By the same token, if deconstruction is rampant psychoanalysis, psychoanalysis is contained deconstruc-tion, for, as Freud puts it, the trick in psychoanalysis is knowing when to stop interpreting.

But imagine taking your dream to a phenomenologist and being told it was a presence given to you by your Being, then going across the street to a deconstructionist and being told it was an infinite regression of polysemic absences filled with irreconcilable aporias—even worse: it wasn't simply a dream but a misdream as well (this would surely send you down the street to an analyst!). But, even so, there is something in all this that a treatment of meaning in dreams should not pass off lightly. What our spectrum demonstrates is not simply a range of interpretive approaches to the dream (to put aside literary texts for the moment) but something of the modes in which dreams may be perceived: as image, symbol, sign, structure, or trace, all of which present very different faces to the perceiver and imply very different theoretical expectations re-specting what dreams are and what they do for us. For a dream is, as we say, "all of the above," or at least each of these approaches brings out an aspect of the dream that is typically ignored by the others. Globus argues with Foulkes and Boss, States argues with Foulkes and Globus (for arguing with Foulkes and Boss), and all four of them may be proving the principle that deconstruction takes for granted: nobody has it right. To say, for example, that a dream is both a presence and an absence is not a contradiction but a com-plementarity. What is present only seems to be what is "there," or "all that is I see," as Gertrude says to Hamlet of the ghost's pres-

ence/absence. But a present can only be so, the deconstructionist
would say, by virtue of what it stands out from, as figure to
ground, motion to stillness, or sound to silence. What Jacques Derrida says of the text could as easily be said of the dream: "No
element can function as a sign [image, symbol, structural unit]
without relating to another element which itself is not simply present. . . . This linkage, this weaving is the *text*, which is produced
only through the transformation of another text [the "text" of the
dreamer's waking life perhaps]. Nothing, either in the elements or
in the system, is anywhere simply present or absent. There are
only, everywhere differences and traces of traces" (1981: 26). No
literary image can illustrate this point more graphically than the
dream image; for the dream image is a pastiche of memory traces,
even to the point that they oscillate before your eyes.[23] In this
connection, too, we may recall Freud's insistence that anything
mentioned by the patient that might have appeared in the dream
should be treated as being present. In other words, from the diagnostic standpoint it is the absences that count and the presence is
what merely summons them, like a horn sounding in the forest.
Thus, we may say that the semiotic and psychoanalytic approaches
are primarily concerned with absence, the phenomenological and
structural with presence, and between these two extremes we erect
our theories of dreaming. Finally, to say that a dream is a misdream
is not as silly as it sounds either—if you take a certain point of view.
The joke is based on the deconstructive notion that all readings are
misreadings, not only because any reading is necessarily partial,
leaving behind some of the text that may even contradict it, but

---

[23] Henri Bergson makes this very point in his 1901 lecture on dreams: remembrances "drawn from the darkest depths of our past" crowd into dreams,
Bergson says. "They may be (and often are) memory images of which we are but
vaguely, almost unconsciously aware during the waking state. Or again, they may
be fragments of shattered remembrances which we have collected piecemeal and
woven haphazardly into an unrecognizable and incoherent fabric. Confronted with
these odd collections of images with no plausible meaning, our intelligence . . . fills
[the gaps] by calling up other remembrances which, because they have the same
deformations and the same inconsistencies as the former, evoke in their turn still
other remembrances—and so on indefinitely" (1958: 35–36).

because every reading is contextually biased and subject to revision in any other context. If one considers the dream in Freudian terms one might say that the "dream-as-dreamt," being rife with displacements, oppositions, and disguise, is a misreading based on a psychic effort to protect the dreamer against damaging cathexes. The real dream is elsewhere. Indeed, the entire text of Freud's *Interpretation of Dreams,* as Derrida amply illustrates in "Freud and the Scene of Writing" (1978: 196–231), might from this angle be considered a study of how we misdream, that is, how dreams, shuttling between presence and absence, offer the dreamer only a surface haunted by traces of ghosts.[24]

[24] Indeed, there is something very deconstructive about dreaming as a psychic activity. Where, among the productions of the brain, could one find an experience that relies more centrally on the instability of images and the pursuit of the trace? In his well-known "Postmodernism and Consumer Society," Fredric Jameson has suggested that one of the central characteristics of postmodernism is schizophrenia. Without absorbing the usual unhealthy implications of the term, we might see dreaming as a normal form of schizophrenia, or, if you like, a permanent postmodernism of the psyche. For instance: in the waking life, "our own present is always part of some larger set of projects which force us selectively to focus our perceptions." Still, the schizophrenic/dreamer "is not only 'no one' in the sense of having no personal identity [or of assuming many different identities under the guise of dream characters]; he or she also does nothing, since to have a project means to be able to commit oneself to a certain continuity over time. The schizophrenic is thus given over to an undifferentiated vision of the world in the present . . . [in which] temporal continuities break down." As a consequence, "the experience of the present becomes powerfully, overwhelmingly vivid and 'material': the world comes before the schizophrenic with heightened intensity, bearing a mysterious and oppressive charge of affect, glowing with hallucinatory energy." Finally, schizophrenia is a "breakdown of the [normative] relationship between signifiers, . . . [offering] an experience of isolated, disconnected, discontinuous material signifiers which fail [by normal standards] to link up into a coherent sequence; . . . [and] a signifier that has lost its signified has thereby been transformed into an image" (1987: 119–20). I intend this only as an analogy whose deepest implication may simply be this: all art forms that are devised for consumer society—and surely dreams are derived *from* consumer society—have necessarily been anticipated and prepared in the mechanisms of thought itself. The dream is antecedent to postmodernism, which goes all the way back, in a manner of speaking, to the pharoah's dream of the seven fat kine and seven lean kine that ate them. Joseph, who was working with early semiotic principles, thought it was a prophecy of things to come; today we view it as a collapse of signifiers.

	Phenomenological	Psychoanalytic	Semiotic	Structural	Deconstructive
Object of study	image or thing	symbol[a]	sign	structural unit	trace[b]
Quality studied	expressiveness (givenness)	concealment (repression)	signification (semiosis)	functionality	deferral
Behavioral dynamic	appearance/essence	manifest/latent	signifier/signified	part/whole	signifier/signifier or presence/absence
Site of reception	personal or collective conscious	personal or collective unconscious	social conscious	empirical conscious	conscious or unconscious
Goal of study	*description* of image's way of being present to perception	*interpretation* of symbol's cathectic charge in field of (sexual) desire	*analysis* of sign's place in sign system and production of shared meaning	*analysis* of the strategic organization of the work as an example of literary form	*dismantling* of the "radical alterity" in all interpretation and presence

[a] or *symptom*.
[b] often *sign* as well; but *trace* denotes dynamic character better and differentiates the deconstructive from the semiotic usage.

Conclusion

As it turns out, this book is an unintentional gloss on its epigraph, which I did not discover until the first draft was completed. Only after reading Joanna Field's remarkable diary of the frustrations of not being able to paint did I understand fully how dreaming, like art, endows us with the power to perceive nature from a perspective that is not available to us in the logical attitude. This is not a belief arising from a wistful notion that reality is mundane and that therefore humans dream another, more fanciful (more beautiful or more terrifying) one into existence. I believe that dreaming and art making are biological events and that they must perform some function that benefits the individual beyond providing pleasing imaginary interludes. Or, to put it another way, pleasing imaginary interludes may be pleasing in a far more substantial way than we have suspected—closer perhaps to the pleasure of oxygen than to that of diversion.[1] It is not so much a matter of enabling us to see something that is not there as of seeing what of the world is effaced by the pragmatic point of view. We require

[1] In this vein, there is also Roland Barthes's notion that "the pleasure of the text is irreducible to physiological need. The pleasure of the text is that moment when my body pursues its own ideas—for my body does not have the same ideas I do" (Barthes, 1975: 17).

dreams and art, then, as we need the microscope and the X-ray to see the substructure of reality around us and the telescope to see its elsewheres. In the case of dreams and art, the something seen is not for the most part seeable in any physical sense, notwithstanding, for example, the new look given to orchards by Van Gogh's paintings in the 1880s. It is rather something that occurs in the field of relationships, and one could argue that Van Gogh was really painting relationships rather than landscapes and that his work simply enabled us to see new ways the things of nature go together (for example, roots, soil, and sky). This amounts to saying that he was painting meanings.

If I have a strong opinion about anything relating to dreams and stories, it is that their business is not to produce meanings (one, many, or opposed) of the sort I have questioned here. I am not denying that meanings (of that sort) can be usefully derived from dreams and fictions, as in the psychoanalytic operation, only that they have anything to do with *why* we dream or write stories, or with what either may be up to. Perhaps I can define my position as follows. If by *meaning* we refer to something that may be derived from the dream about the dreamer (or about dreaming itself), then we may say that dreams have meaning. If we refer to felt or experienced coherences in the dream material, of the sort I examine in Chapter 5, we may also say that dreams have meaning *for the dreamer*, even though the dreamer may be completely unable to conceptualize such meaning. If, however, by *meaning* we refer to any form of intentional, encoded, or symbolic message, then (as Foulkes would say) we are in the angel-counting business. Encodement necessarily implies an encoder and a decoder, a receiver/audience, or some form of transmission to and from, and inevitably our little friend is back with us, and behind the little friend there must be a still littler friend doing the planning, and so forth, ventriloquistically ad infinitum. What could be the use of having a meaning of that sort, anyway? What good is a meaning that isn't understood by the brain that makes it? But if we think of meaning as a kind of *containment*, or felt significance, then we are in a position to see how dreams and fictions are meaningful in a way that calls for no inter-

pretation by a waking intelligence. To have dreamed is to have
experienced meaning; to have created or responded to fiction is to
have experienced meaning.

By way of summing up this idea, let me return to Gadamer's
discussion of the unity of human experience. The basic question
might be, what constitutes this thing experience we have been talking about?

> If something is called or considered an experience its meaning
> rounds it into the unity of a significant whole. An experience is as
> much distinguished from other experiences—in which other
> things are experienced—as from the rest of life in which 'nothing'
> is experienced. An experience is no longer just something that
> flows past quickly in the stream of the life of consciousness—it is
> meant as a unity and thus attains a new mode of being one. . . .
> On the other hand, however, in the notion of experience there is
> also a contrast of life with mere concept. The experience has a
> definite immediacy which eludes every opinion about its mean-
> ing. Everything that is experienced is experienced by oneself, and
> it is part of its meaning that it belongs to the unity of this self and
> thus contains an inalienable and irreplaceable relation to the whole
> of this one life. Thus its being is not exhausted in what can be said
> of it and in what can be grasped as its meaning. (1985: 60)

It is my belief that one cannot fully encompass the meaningfulness
of dreams without considering them as experiences in just this
sense, though there are many ways to express the same idea (among
which we can include Gendlin's notion of felt meanings). In dreams
we experience a sense of self-unity, the relation of the part to the
whole of this one life. It is not something you take from the dream
on waking, like the theme of a book. Dreams do not add to or give
meaning to our lives; they instantiate meaning that is already there,
if only implicitly. This may seem to contradict the point I was
making in Chapter 5 that the phenomenological approach to
dreaming (Boss's, at least) claims that a dream might discover new
meanings that had not occurred to the dreamer in waking life (for

example, the woman's dream about her analyst's beard). What I mean in the present context is simply that the dreaming brain is as capable of discovering new possibilities in, say, relationships between friends, family, or coworkers, as is the waking brain. In this sense, the dream might add something to what we already know about our self or confirm something we hadn't suspected. I am claiming, however, that the dream is not a thematizing agency authored, as Daniel Dennett puts it, by "an internal dream playwright [who composes] therapeutic dream-plays for the benefit of the ego" (1991: 14). What discoveries occur in dreams are made by the dreamer as responses to the dream events, not by any homuncular author or unconscious that has put the events there (as Hamlet, in Dennett's analogy, stages *The Murder of Gonzago* for Claudius's benefit), and they are no different from those that occur in waking life when we suddenly realize, during an event, that we are being selfish or hateful or have fallen in love. It is quite possible, of course, that such discoveries may not survive the dream as useful guides to empirical living. I am personally thankful this is the case, especially where falling in love in a dream is concerned. Imagine carrying a burning passion for last night's dreamgirl much beyond 10 A.M. Here again, however, as I argue in what follows, the significant thing is that one has had the experience of falling in love every bit as intensely and genuinely as one does in waking life. The experience has been real, though the object of one's love is a chimera. Indeed, in the dream, we may, like Shakespeare's Titania, fall in love with anyone, or anything, that is nearby, but for the nonce it is real love. This emotional authenticity is what binds dream experience to waking experience and makes one a qualitative continuation of the other.

Overall, one of my main themes in this book has been that as dreamers we stand in the same relation to the dreamworld as we do to the waking world (putting aside the matter of physical contingencies and so on). Both occur to us as a function of consciousness, not as something that is, in one case, completely subjective and, in the other, completely objective. "In both cases," Robert Ornstein says, "the world we inhabit is assembled from pieces of experience produced by the various modules of the mind. It is not easy to tell a dream from waking, which should alert us to how distant we are from direct knowledge of the world around us" (1991: 198). What we have, one might add, is emotional knowledge, and it is this knowledge that we carry from one world to the other on the shuttle of a common consciousness.

This does not mean that dreams redundantly repeat waking experience, only that the perception of felt meaning requires certain lapses in practical orientation that are most thoroughly put into play in the dream state or in the waking state when we achieve, among other things, works of art, philosophy, religion, and science. There is a wonderful remark by Maurice Merleau-Ponty to the effect that the eye of the painter "sees the world, sees what inadequacies [*manques*] keep the world from being a painting, sees what keeps the painting from being itself, sees—on the palette—the colors awaited by the painting, and sees, once it is done, the painting that answers to all these inadequacies just as it sees the paintings of others as other answers to other inadequacies" (1964: 165). One may say, too, that in dreams the eye sees what inadequacies keep the waking world from being a dream and proceeds to dream these inadequacies away, leaving behind something like a living painting—or, if you will, an experience. More specifically, the inadequacies consist of the boundaries waking perception typically puts around things, enclosing them within dependable limits called wives, husbands, children, refrigerators, rivers, mountains, Tuesdays, roses, and winter. These entities have no meaning in themselves; they become meaningful only as they flow and blend in the current of experience, like the words of a sentence or a poem. What I have tried to express here is that when one sees how they blend—thus becoming meaningful—one is always in a state at least slightly outside the world, much like that state of dreaminess Field finds indispensable for truly expressive drawing. The crucial difference between waking and dream experience, as regards content, is that the dream is an imaginative condensation of experience. The dream is not better, more (or less) coherently plotted than life, it simply is not constrained by the inadequacies of the empirical world. The dream, one might say, raises the objective world to the power of the self. In this, the dream is like the experience of art which does not add meaning to experience: it simply frames the meaning that is in danger of being overlooked, the meaning that tends to disappear in the urgencies of survival. Sight, Bachelard has said, "says too many things at one time. Being does not see itself" (1969: 215). Hence the need for the painter, whose business is to remove inadequacies from the world; or for the maker of metaphors, whose business, in certain theories at least, is that of cancelling features of the object rather than multiplying them (Cohen, 1986).

Gadamer goes on to say that aesthetic experience is not simply "one kind of experience among others" but "the essence of experience itself." The work of art "suddenly takes the person experiencing it out of the context of his life . . . , and yet relates him back to the whole of his existence" (1985: 63). Though dreams can scarcely be called works of art (either in form or in affect), it could be said that like works of art they offer the essence of experience as opposed to the lived content of experience. Whether one calls that meaning or correlation or articulation or description, it is something, as Gadamer says, that "is not exhausted in what can be said of it and in what can be grasped as its meaning" (p. 60). In other words, there is, on one hand, what we might call local meaning, which is expressible in terms of concepts, something that can be formulated from experience and put to some practical use, and, on the other, the condition of meaningfulness that pervades experience in the form of a felt unity. This is clearly difficult to talk about, but then dreaming is difficult to talk about precisely because it consists of *having* such experiences, and talking about them in almost any manner tends to draw one into a conceptual mode of thought in which, as Field says in my epigraph, the process stops being a process.

Let us look at some cases that illustrate the difference between experienced meaning and the kind we derive from interpretation. Just before he dies, Hamlet asks Horatio to forego the "felicity" of suicide and live on to justify Hamlet's wounded name ("And in this harsh world draw thy breath in pain / To tell my story"). And at the end of the play, Horatio dutifully begins Hamlet's story thus:

> So shall you hear
> Of carnal, bloody, and unnatural acts,
> Of accidental judgments, casual slaughters,
> Of deaths put on by cunning and forc'd cause,
> And, in this upshot, purposes mistook
> Fall'n on th' inventors' heads. All this can I
> Truly deliver.

This is all very moving and I wouldn't want to change a syllable of it or hear a word more of the story. But the passage inadvertently bespeaks the inexpressibility of certain dimensions of meaning (and I suspect Horatio knows this). Something must inevitably be left out of this account, no matter what sort of detail might follow— short of a complete repetition of *Hamlet*. And this is the full depth of Hamlet's dying words, "The rest is silence." Indeed Horatio can relate "all this" competently, meaning the details of Hamlet's dilemma. But it has so little to do with Hamlet's "story," with the meaning of Hamlet, that one can almost imagine Hamlet speaking from the grave of Horatio's interpretation: "That is not what it meant at all. That is not it, at all."

What Horatio is in a position to tell has about as much to do with Hamlet's story as the report of a dream has to do with what was actually dreamed and with what it may mean as a psychic phenomenon. Hamlet's meaning is what we experience in Hamlet's company, word by word, gesture by gesture, scene by scene. It is durational rather than conceptual. What the experience may mean conceptually to Horatio or to you is quite different from what it may mean to me. Moreover, what it may have meant conceptually to Shakespeare, if anything, is something entirely different and not necessarily more accurate than your meaning or mine. Yet this infinite potential for new and other meanings arises from something beneath all the possible things one can say about *Hamlet*. It is never exhausted by conceptual meanings for the simple reason that it did not spring from a concept but from an adherence to a certain rhythm in human experience, and this may very well be the thing about literature, and dreaming, that is most valuable. Imagine that in his story Horatio gets to Hamlet's private thoughts about suicide (assuming that he had somehow overheard Hamlet's soliloquies) and says to his wonder-wounded hearers, "Hamlet thought about taking his own life but decided against it for several reasons," and then goes on to name these reasons (as hundreds of critics have done since). This is what we might call his interpretation of the soliloquies, of Hamlet's story, and of what it is that gave Hamlet his bad dreams—this is the *information* contained in the soliloquies. What the hearers would be missing, obviously, is precisely what Shakespeare *meant* by the speeches: that Hamlet is a man trapped between alternative courses and this is the way the mind tosses about in its restless ecstasy. This is the felt meaning of Hamlet: a man so tossed, though in saying this I should want the deepest possible implication of tossedness to be inferred. There is every likelihood that Shakespeare may have had his own intentions about the local meaning of *Hamlet*, and they may have been quite specific, or at least based, as E. D. Hirsch would say, on a specific intrinsic genre.[2] But as an interpreter of his own play, or his hero's motives, Shakespeare is finally only as reliable as Horatio. That is because the poet's intention, as Northrop Frye suggested long ago, "is centripetally directed . . . toward putting words together, not towards aligning words with meanings. . . . What the poet meant to say, then, is the poem itself" (1957: 86–87). And, he adds, the poet is in the same position as a scientist who can "state a law illustrated by more phenomena than he could ever hope to observe or count" (p. 88). This is one reason, among many, that we still read *Hamlet*. It continually means something else to us because Shakespeare didn't try to mean anything by Hamlet except what Hamlet does. And if what he does "be ta'en away" from Hamlet's story, to use his own words, then it is no longer Hamlet's story.

Let us apply this idea to a dream. Partly for its brevity and partly because I referred to it at the beginning of the book, I choose the dream of the six-year-old boy cited by Jean Piaget: "In the basin I

---

[2] An intrinsic genre is a "particular type of meaning" as opposed to a specific determinant meaning: "It is that sense of the whole by means of which an interpreter [or a speaker/poet] can correctly understand any part [of an utterance] in its determinacy" (Hirsch, 1967: 86).

saw a bean that was so big that it quite filled it. It got bigger and bigger all the time. I was standing by the door. I was frightened. I wanted to scream and run away, but I couldn't. I got more and more frightened, and it went on until I woke up" (1951: 179). This dream appears in a series in which Piaget is dealing with the question of whether there is any development in symbolism in the dreams of children which parallels their experience in play. Most analysts would have no hesitation in assigning the growing bean to the realm of sexual symbolism (for Piaget it is a symbol of erection). In short, it is not hard to find a unifying concept for the dream, and if we knew more about the boy we could be even more specific about the dream's determinants and what it meant in the boy's life: we might find, for instance, that he had a frightening response to his mother's pregnancy and his sister's appearance from her stomach. Surely even the most intrepid new dream scientist could not dispute the dream's meaningfulness by claiming that it was only a bizarre dream about a bean (especially since the boy had been having similar dreams for several months).

But let us apply Gadamer's idea to the dream. An experience, he says, "has a definite immediacy which eludes every opinion about its meaning." It is experienced by one person to whom it belongs exclusively and "thus [it] contains an inalienable and irreplaceable relation to the whole of this one life (1985: 60)." This leads us far from the pragmatic course of dream analysis and diagnosis as it is normally practiced. But where *does* it lead us? What is it in the dream that is not exhausted by the concepts we can, with good justification, attach to it? As with the meaningfulness of Hamlet, we are virtually speechless at this level—which is to say, conceptless. The experience belongs to the boy who dreamed it, and all we can do by way of appreciating what it may have meant to him is to put our own experience, as fellow-dreamers, in its stead. For me, the most profound point of sympathy with the dream would be the emotion of fright itself—not fright at a monstrous bean that stood for something *outside* the dream (erection, pregnancy, planting, bearing), but the immediacy of fright as an experience in itself, fright as a base-level emotion, fright as an indispensable biological signal, fright as part of a lifetime education in wariness, and, specifically in this instance, fright at the terrible power of transformation inherent in nature. Why should the boy be frightened of his erection or his mother's pregnancy if not out of an inadequate preparation for what such transformations mean in a world where things—to a boy of six—are expected to remain substantially what they are? We can safely predict that this is one of many fright dreams the boy will experience in his lifetime, and each dream, though concerned with a different object of fright, will have the same consequence. Fright is fright: it has its own narrative structure and its own feeling. I am not suggesting that fright, or any other emotion, has a single or universal significance, only that it is an elemental experience, irreducible (like Hamlet's tossedness) to anything else—and it matters little whether it is aroused by a plausibly vicious dog or a bizarre bean with a mind of its own.[3]

I realize that all this is rather like saying that a rose is a rose is a rose; but what Gertrude Stein was trying to express in this famous tautology is the nonreferentiality of roseness. Hers is an immanently phenomenological piece of poetry designed to prevent our seeing a rose semiotically, as a sign—as having a meaning outside itself. Likewise, to trace a dream emotion to its possible causes in immediate psychic life is to treat the dream as a signifier, as a kind of box in which something more meaningful has been shipped to you. It is also tantamount to considering *Hamlet* the carrier of a concept (take your choice) as opposed to an experience in which you live the Hamletic part of your life through Hamlet. As for the signifying value of the bean, one might argue not that it is a symbol

[3] Mikkel Borch-Jacobsen, in his stunning revision of Freud's theory of sexuality in relation to dreams, goes a step further in this direction: "What we should expect to find, inexhaustibly, at the root of fantasies, dreams, and symptoms," he says, is not sexuality but something quite different: jealousy, for example, or envy, or rivalry, or ambition, all of which are passions aroused by the mimesis of another whom one wishes to equal, to replace, to *be* (1988: 28). I am sure Borch-Jacobsen would have more to say about my rather innocent notion of fright, which certainly must have deep psychic roots in the boy's life as a child of six. All I wish to say is that there are emotions shared by everyone and fright is one of them, irrespective of its first arousal in infantile sexual life.

of erection (if that is the right referent) but that it stands in a metaphorical relationship to erection in which two life experiences are seen to share a certain likeness, not one as a substitute, or concealment of the other, but one as being like the other. We may emphasize the likeness or we may emphasize the causal priority; the latter takes us to the realm of concepts, the former to the realm of essence. Of course, we do not know where the bean came from, and Piaget does not tell us how the idea of erection comes into the picture. But I am willing to accept the strong probability that they come together in the bean image, together with a great deal more that Piaget could not possibly have known. The point is that it is not a mystery, a symptom of randomness, or a disguise that a dream should put *bean* and *erection* into a common category, or that it should graphically represent the bean instead of the erection (to-morrow night, as Calvin Hall would say, it may be the other way around). To take another page from Piaget: "Since affective life is adaptation, it . . . implies continual assimilation of present situa-tions to earlier ones—assimilation which gives rise to affective schemas or relatively stable modes of feeling or reacting—and con-tinual accommodation of these schemas to the present situation" (1951: 205–6). My suggestion is that such assimilation is one of the sources of unity in experience, and two of the consequences of the process are dreams and art.[4]

---

[4] Gerald Edelman puts this whole idea in a nutshell in his description of categori-zation in *Bright Air, Brilliant Fire: On the Matter of Mind:* "The flux of categorizations in a selective system leading to memory and consciousness alters the ordinary rela-tions of causation as described by physicists. A person, like a thing, exists on a world line in four-dimensional spacetime. But because individual human beings have in-tentionality, memory, and consciousness, they can sample patterns at one point on that line and on the basis of their personal histories subject them to plans at other points on that world line. They can then enact these plans, altering the causal relations of objects in a definite way according to the structures of their memories. It is as if one piece of spacetime could slip and map onto another piece. The difference, of course, is that the entire transaction does not involve any unusual piece of physics, but simply the ability to categorize, memorize, and form plans according to a conceptual model. Such an historical alteration of causal chains could not occur in so rich a way in any combination of inanimate nonintentional objects, for they lack the appropriate kind of memory" (1992: 169).

What I have said here about the emotion of fright may be traced to the basic conditions of world continuity in which emotions and feelings are aroused in dreams. One of the most intriguing aspects of dreams is that in the dream state we always accept the people, environments, and conditions cast up by the dream as being indubitable. In a dream my friend Mark may appear as a complete stranger and I will look straight through my familiarity without noticing the contradiction; or, the apparent old friends I am with at a dream party are taken to be old friends though I have never seen their like in real life. Thus, the experience of strangeness or old friendness is at once independent of my specific history in these matters yet based on it in the same way the emotion of fright is based on an assimilation of frightening situations. This is to say, simply, that dreams recover our manner of experiencing the familiarity, or the nonfamiliarity, of the waking world without any necessary reference to the things that are familiar or unfamiliar in it. All that is required is that a history of experience has taken place; and this, I take it, is what makes possible the astonishing mutability of the dream. Dreams *imitate* experiencing, not experience. I hasten to add that I put the verb "imitate" in quotes because I don't believe that dreams are imitations, any more than memories or reflections are. Rather, they are real experiences, there being no qualitative difference between, say, fright or embarrassment or joy in a dream and these same feelings as they occur in waking life.[5] The fact that

---

[5] Dreams may be considered imitations in still another sense: they do transmit, as I have suggested, patterns of behavior and cultural usage (scripts and archetypes), so they could be said to *represent* the ways of the world in roughly Aristotle's sense of "imitation of an action." But in this respect waking behavior itself, at least at times, is mimetic in the sense that we imitate ourselves. The point is that dreams, however they might replicate the actions of the waking world—"the kinds of things that can happen," as Aristotle says—are not deliberate or intentional constructions aimed, as poems, dramas, and paintings are, at producing pleasure and instruction.

Another possibility of mimesis is brought to my attention by Daniel Dennett in his discussion of Richard Dawkins's concept of the meme. A meme, according to Dawkins, is "a unit of cultural transmission, or a unit of imitation"—such things as "tunes, ideas, catch-phrases, clothes fashions," ways of "making pots or of building arches" (quoted by Dennett, 1991: 202) and such concepts as faith, tolerance, conspiracy, or freedom of speech (p. 206). One could say that scripts and archetypes are

one can't buy things in the empirical world with the buried treasure discovered in a dream doesn't in the least extend to the expenditure of emotions and feelings, which are the common coin of both realms. And it seems to me that we can say much the same thing about art, even though art is quite clearly a form of mimesis. For this continuing indubitability of the reality of dream objects, and their capacity for arousing real emotions, bears directly on the dreamy mood of reciprocity in which the painter, as Field says, accepts what appears on the canvas as a part of the world of the painting rather than as something *done to* a world that presumably exists beyond the painting, of which the painting is simply a rendering. This readiness to accept the "imitation" as real—as having no alternative existence elsewhere—to inhabit the reality of the imitation (like the man in *Akira Kurosawa's Dreams* who walks into the painting), is passed on to the reader or auditor as well. In short, reciprocity is not the exclusive province of the artist.

Perhaps I can make the point more graphically with a final example. Having begun my book with a story about a wheelbarrow, it seems appropriate to end with a variation on the same topic. And it so happens there is a perfect vehicle at my disposal in a poem by William Carlos Williams titled "The Red Wheelbarrow," which, it turns out, is hauling much the same thematic load as the wheelbar-

---

based on memes, though in many cases it might be difficult to tell one from the others. I suppose that *Antigone* may be thought of as a mimesis based on the collision of memes or a collision of scripts based on the memes of state authority and family burial rights. The relevance of memes to my discussion is that they allow us still another view of how dream construction is derived from the patterns of social behavior. Dawkins says, "Just as genes propagate themselves in the gene pool by leaping from body to body via sperm or eggs, so memes propagate themselves in the meme pool by leaping from brain to brain via a process which, in the broad sense, can be called imitation. If a scientist hears, or reads about, a good idea, he passes it on to his colleagues and students. He mentions it in his articles and his lectures. If the idea catches on, it can be said to propagate itself, spreading from brain to brain" (quoted by Dennett, 1991: 202). So too memes leap from waking brain to dreaming brain and thus the dream becomes a meme vehicle, in Dennett's term, which further propagates the ideas, slogans, and habits of thought and action that make the world go round—not so much a mimesis as a memesis (see also Douglas Hofstadter's discussion of Dawkins's memes; 1986: 50–58).

row in my tale of the factory worker. In its entirety, the poem goes
like this:

> so much depends
> upon
> a red wheel
> barrow
> glazed with rain
> water
> beside the white
> chickens.

My specific concern with this deceptive little poem—the closest
thing to a painting I know in Western poetry—is with the affective
experience it offers the reader who is willing to abide with it for
more than a casual reading. I suggest that, like a dream, it ceases to
be an imitation, a mimesis of a barnyard scene, when you consider
it as something occurring in your head or, as Field says, as a fusion
or con-fusion of seer and seen. From this standpoint, we may legit-
imately claim that it creates nature rather than simply representing
it, because it is creating the power to perceive nature, and where
would nature be (as J. T. Fraser or Paul Valéry would say) without
our perception of it? Thus it is beside the point that the real scene is
absent and that all you are literally seeing here is black scratchings
on a white page rather than a real red wheelbarrow surrounded by
real white chickens. Moreover, what we are seeing here is more
than the combination of these presences and absences which go into
the phenomenology of the object. The thing itself in this case is not
a scene in the empirical world but an experience in Gadamer's full
meaning of the term. Indeed, the real scene would bring you no
closer to the experience unless, like Williams, you could perform a
certain trick of vision on which so very much of poetry depends;
and one of the points Williams is quietly making is that you probably hadn't *seen* such a scene while standing before one and that the
poem is referring you to something stored in your memory of the
world rather than to something you can see, if you're lucky, by

walking into a backyard where there are chickens and a wheelbarrow. In short, there would be no need to make a poem if everybody saw what Williams saw and *knew* that they had seen it; one makes a poem about such things only as a response to certain inadequacies (*manques*) in the world that tend to inhibit perception. As in my story of the factory worker, one must think away the debris that surrounds the glazed wheelbarrow and the white chickens and prevents one from seeing them for what they are *doing* there.

What is the "so much," then, that "depends upon" these three barnyard things—barrow, chickens, and rain? There are many ways of expressing it, no doubt; but I am moved most by what Williams himself said of the scene when he wandered upon it "outside the window of an old negro's house on a back street" in the suburb where he lived: "It was pouring rain and there were white chickens walking about in it. The sight impressed me somehow as about the most important, the most integral that it had ever been my pleasure to gaze upon. And the meter though no more than a fragment succeeds in portraying this pleasure flawlessly, even it succeeds in denoting a certain unquenchable exaltation—in fact I find the poem quite perfect" (1933: 60). There is not a word here about a meaning that can be got *out of* the scene, only a recognition of something important in the way it comes together, as if one of nature's patterns of being had momentarily divulged itself. Clearly Williams has no interest in what the poem means otherwise, in the sense of what might easily be derived from the cultural, historical, or economic connections between chickens, wheelbarrows and rain in suburban America. The intense pleasure and unquenchable exultation he felt in gazing on this scene derives, one might say, from the scene's own meter, rather than from its elements. Meter is not a thing but the dance of images, the law of gravity, or (if you will) the Platonic Idea that makes them integral to each other. What is transmitted from scene to poem and from poem to reader, then, is a rhythm in nature that somehow establishes itself in the commotions of one's own body, somewhat as God is said to be within you and outside you at the same time. Indeed, Donald Pearce (who introduced me to "The Red Wheelbarrow") suggests that it is finally a religious poem, "having to do with redemptive vision and the radical alteration of one's point of view: doesn't it, after all, propose that things, any things, can be seen again in their immaculate character, the way they always really are wherever instrumental vision, for lack of a better term, is, if only for a moment, lifted?" (1989: 257). This, I must quickly point it, is not an interpretation of the poem but a description of what happens when one kind of vision is temporarily lifted to reveal another that falls redemptively on an otherwise invisible world.

Like Williams, artists characteristically have little interest in what their work means and they often wear a different kind of glazed look when someone tries to attach specific meanings to it. Collaterally, most readers (perhaps all readers except literary critics and their students) are perfectly content to be engrossed in fictional works, to think about them thereafter, and perhaps even to reread them without the least interest in translating them into a conceptual language. It seems to me, in the first instance, that the artist's discontent rests primarily on an instinctive understanding of the nonequivalence of interpretation and meaning and of how interpretation diminishes the openness of the work and the manner in which truth discloses itself in it, to use Heidegger's phrase (1975: 75). And the gratification of reading as an end in itself seems to be a corroboration of the artist's unease with interpreters who not only read their work but convert it into conceptual propositions, which is to say back into the realm of the world's inadequacies. For it cannot be that what we get out of art (or dreaming) is a consequence of our interpreting it; it seems rather to be a result of having assimilated something that has no conceptual name. To understand a work (or a dream) is simply to perceive wherein it is a true version of world experience, for there is no understanding to be had from a work that sets forth a false version of experience, and it doesn't take a literary critic to detect the difference. Understanding, as Mark Johnson has put it, is "our mode of 'being in the world.' It is the way we are meaningfully situated in our world through our bodily interactions, our cultural institutions, our linguistic tradition, and our historical context" (1987: 102). Understanding, one might say, is recognition, which is to say a repetition of what we already know, but perhaps did not know we knew or forgot we knew, about the world—a point Plato elaborates at some length in *The Meno*. The most bizarre dream is a repetition in the sense that an old emotion is attaching itself, as it invariably does in waking life as well, to a new narrative.

My own understanding of the dream is unavoidably that of a Westerner; however, it is not meant to exclude or discredit other beliefs but in some measure to offer an adjustment of our prevailing Western tendency to equate the meaning and importance of dreams with what can be got out of them conceptually. The kind of meaning I have been elaborating here is untranslatable: it is virtually identical with being, and if one moment or experience seems more meaningful than another it is because there is more of being in it, as in the adventure, the discovery, or Williams's backyard epiphany— all moments in which (as Walker Percy once said of the metaphor) a big thing is happening in a small place. There is a colossal difference between saying "My love is fresh, delicate, soft, beautiful, fragrant" and "My love is like a red red rose," and the difference is that one is a string of qualities (much like a letter of recommendation) and the other is a sensory experience that calls up the endless interdependencies in the world but somehow manages to localize them in a small red place. It is very much like Freud's Oceanic feeling. Dreams and fictions have in common the ability to condense being into narratives of felt meaning. Finding other, more specific meanings beyond such understanding surely serves certain purposes relevant to social life, politics, psychoanalysis, criticism, the study of authors and literary periods, and so on; so the point is not to deny that there are other kinds of meaning or to lament that they get attached to dreams and fictions. But all of them are at best incidental to the real purposes of storytelling and dreaming and to why they persist as involuntary exercises of the imagination. Like almost everyone else, I am at a loss to say what those purposes may be, and every theory I encounter or have myself conceived leaves me with the same sense of unease and oversimplification I experience in the presence of any interpretation of a dream or fiction. Whatever the purposes of dreams may be, however, I am somehow confident that they have nothing to do with such things as message sending, trashing excess memory, symbolic disguise, suppression, random nonsense, or recommendations for better living. All these things may be got out of them, or read into them, but what is always left behind is the dimension of meaning that cannot survive translation out of the storytelling mode—that is, the mode in which experience itself unfolds.

References

Abbott, Edwin A. (1983). *Flatland: A Romance of Many Dimensions*. New York: Harper and Row.

Antrobus, John S. (1977). "The Dream as Metaphor: An Information-Processing and Learning Model." *Journal of Mental Imagery* 2:327–38.

Aristotle (1981). *Poetics*. Trans. Leon Golden, commentary O. B. Hardison, Jr. Tallahassee: Florida State University Press.

Armstrong, Paul B. (1990). *Conflicting Readings: Variety and Validity in Interpretation*. Chapel Hill: University of North Carolina Press.

Arnheim, Rudolf (1974). *Entropy and Art: An Essay on Disorder and Order*. Berkeley: University of California Press.

Austin, J. L. (1975). *How to Do Things with Words*, 2d ed. Cambridge, Mass.: Harvard University Press.

Bachelard, Gaston (1969). *The Poetics of Space*. Trans. Maria Jolas. Boston: Beacon Press.

Bachelard, Gaston (1986). *Lautréamont*. Trans. Robert S. Dupree. Dallas: Dallas Institute Publications.

Bakhtin, M. M. (1987). *Speech Genres and Other Late Essays*. Trans. Vern W. McGee. Austin: University of Texas Press.

Barthes, Roland (1974). *S/Z*. Trans. Richard Miller. New York: Hill and Wang.

Barthes, Roland (1975). *The Pleasure of the Text*. Trans. Richard Miller. New York: Hill and Wang.

Benjamin, Walter (1977). "The Work of Art in the Age of Mechanical Reproduction." In *Illuminations*. Trans. Harry Zohn. New York: Schocken Books.

Bergson, H. (1958) [1901]. *The World of Dreams*. Trans. Wade Baskin. New York: Philosophical Library.

Black, Max. (1954–55). "Metaphor." *Proceedings of the Aristotelian Society* 55:273–94.

Blagrove, Mark (1992). "Scripts and the Structuralist Analysis of Dreams." *Dreaming* 2 (March): 23–37.

Bohannan, Laura (1966). "Shakespeare in the Bush." *Natural History* 75 (Aug./Sept.): 28–33.

Bonato, Richard A., Alan R. Moffitt, Robert F. Hoffmann, Marion A. Cuddy, and Frank L. Wimmer (1991). "Bizarreness in Dreams and Nightmares." *Dreaming* 1 (March): 53–61.

Borch-Jacobsen, Mikkel (1988). *The Freudian Subject*. Trans. Catherine Porter. Stanford: Stanford University Press.

Boss, Medard (1958). *The Analysis of Dreams*. Trans. Arnold J. Pomerans. New York: Philosophical Library.

Boss, Medard (1977). *I Dreamt Last Night*. Trans. Stephen Conway. New York: Gardner Press.

Bregman, Albert S. (1977). "Perception and Behavior as Compositions of Ideals," *Cognitive Psychology* 9:250–92.

Brooks, Peter (1985). *Reading for the Plot: Design and Intention in Narrative*. New York: Vintage.

Burke, Kenneth (1953). *Counter-Statement*. Los Altos, Calif.: Hermes.

Burke, Kenneth (1957). *The Philosophy of Literary Form: Studies in Symbolic Action*. Rev. ed. New York: Random House.

Burke, Kenneth (1962). *A Grammar of Motives and a Rhetoric of Motives*. Cleveland: World.

Casey, Edward (1979). *Imagining: A Phenomenological Study*. Bloomington: Indiana University Press.

Cohen, L. Jonathan (1986). "The Semantics of Metaphor." In *Metaphor and Thought*, ed. Andrew Ortony. Cambridge: Cambridge University Press, pp. 64–77.

Cohen, Ted (1975). "Figurative Speech and Figurative Acts," *Journal of Philosophy* 72 (November 6): 669–84.

Crick, Francis, and Graeme Mitchison (1986). "REM Sleep and Neural Nets." *Journal of Mind and Behavior* 7 (Spring/Summer): 229–49.

Culler, Jonathan (1981). *The Pursuit of Signs: Semiotics, Literature, Deconstruction*. Ithaca: Cornell University Press.

Culler, Jonathan (1985). *On Deconstruction: Theory and Criticism after Structuralism*. Ithaca: Cornell University Press.

Davidson, Donald (1978). "What Metaphors Mean," *Critical Inquiry* 5, no. 1: 31–47.

Dennett, Daniel C. (1976). "Are Dreams Experiences?" *Philosophical Review* 85:151–71. Reprinted in *Philosophical Essays on Dreaming*, ed.

Charles E. M. Dunlop. Ithaca: Cornell University Press, 1977, pp. 227–50.

Dennett, Daniel C. (1991). *Consciousness Explained*. Boston: Little, Brown.

Derrida, Jacques (1978). *Writing and Difference*. Trans. Alan Bass. Chicago: University of Chicago Press.

Derrida, Jacques (1981). *Positions*. Trans. Alan Bass. Chicago: University of Chicago Press.

Dufrenne, Mikel (1973). *The Phenomenology of Aesthetic Experience*. Trans. Edward Casey, Albert A. Anderson, Willis Domingo, and Leon Jacobson. Evanston, Ill.: Northwestern University Press.

Edelman, Gerald M. (1987). *Neural Darwinism: The Theory of Neuronal Group Selection*. New York: Basic Books.

Edelman, Gerald M. (1989). *The Remembered Present: A Biological Theory of Consciousness*. New York: Basic Books.

Edelman, Gerald M. (1992). *Bright Air, Brilliant Fire: On the Matter of Mind*. New York: Basic Books.

Evans, Christopher (1983). *Landscapes of the Night: How and Why We Dream*. New York: Viking Press.

Field, Joanna (1983). *On Not Being Able to Paint*. Los Angeles: Tarcher.

Fish, Stanley E. (1980). "Literature in the Reader: Affective Stylistics." in *Reader-Response Criticism from Formalism to Post-Structuralism*, ed. Jane P. Tompkins. Baltimore: Johns Hopkins University Press, 1980, pp. 70–100. The essay appeared originally in *New Literary History* 2, no. 1 (Autumn): 123–62.

Fogelin, Robert J. (1988). *Figuratively Speaking*. New Haven: Yale University Press.

Foulkes, David (1978). *A Grammar of Dreams*. New York: Basic Books.

Foulkes, David (1985). *Dreaming: A Cognitive-Psychological Analysis*. Hillsdale, N.J.: Erlbaum.

Fraiberg, Selma (1956). "Kafka and the Dream." *Partisan Review* 23 (Winter): 47–69.

Fraser, J. T. (1980). "Out of Plato's Cave: The Natural History of Time." *Kenyon Review*, New Series 7 (Winter): 142–62.

Fraser, J. T. (1990). *Of Time, Passion, and Knowledge: Reflections on the Strategy of Existence*. Princeton: Princeton University Press.

Freud, Sigmund (1973 [1900]). *The Interpretation of Dreams*. Standard Edition, vols. 4 and 5. Ed. James Strachey. London: Hogarth, 1973.

Freud, Sigmund (1973 [1905]). *Jokes and Their Relationship to the Unconscious*. Standard Edition, vol. 8. Ed. James Strachey. London: Hogarth.

Freud, Sigmund (1973 [1908]). "The Relation of the Poet to Daydreaming." Standard Edition, vol. 9. Ed. James Strachey, London: Hogarth.

208   *References*

Freud, Sigmund (1973 [1919]). "The Uncanny." Standard Edition, vol. 17. Ed. James Strachey. London: Hogarth.

Frye, Northrop (1957). *The Anatomy of Criticism: Four Essays.* Princeton: Princeton University Press.

Gackenbach, Jayne (1991). "Frameworks for Understanding Lucid Dreaming: A Review." *Dreaming* 1 (Spring): 109–28.

Gadamer, Hans-Georg (1985). *Truth and Method.* New York: Crossroad.

Gendlin, Eugene T. (1962). *Experiencing and the Creation of Meaning: A Philosophical and Psychological Approach to the Subjective.* New York: Free Press of Glencoe.

Gendlin, Eugene T. (1977). "Phenomenological Concept vs. Phenomenological Method: A Critique of Medard Boss on Dreams." In *On Dreaming: An Encounter with Medard Boss,* ed. Charles E. Scott. Chico, Calif.: Scholars Press, pp. 57–72.

Genette, Gérard (1980). *Narrative Discourse: An Essay on Method.* Trans. Jane E. Lewin. Ithaca: Cornell University Press.

Globus, Gordon (1987). *Dream Life, Wake Life: The Human Condition through Dreams.* Albany: State University of New York Press.

Globus, Gordon (1991). "Dream Content: Random or Meaningful." *Dreaming* 1 (March): 27–40.

Gombrich, E. H. (1965). *Art and Illusion: A Study in the Psychology of Pictorial Representation.* New York: Pantheon.

Goodman, Nelson (1978). *Ways of Worldmaking.* Indianapolis: Hackett.

Goodman, Nelson (1984). *Of Mind and Other Matters.* Cambridge: Harvard University Press.

Hall, Calvin (1966). *The Meaning of Dreams.* New York: McGraw Hill.

Hayles, N. Katherine (1990). *Chaos Bound: Orderly Disorder in Contemporary Literature and Science.* Ithaca: Cornell University Press.

Heidegger, Martin (1975). *Poetry, Language, Thought.* Trans. Albert Hofstadter. New York: Harper and Row.

Herr, Barbara (1981). "The Expressive Character of Fijian Dream and Nightmare Experience." *Ethos* 9 (Winter): 331–52.

Hillman, James (1977). "An Inquiry into Image." *Spring,* 1977: 62–88.

Hirsch, E. D. (1967). *Validity in Interpretation.* New Haven: Yale University Press.

Hobson, Allan J. (1988). *The Dreaming Brain.* New York: Basic Books.

Hofstadter, Douglas R. (1980). *Gödel, Escher, Bach: An Eternal Golden Braid.* New York: Vintage Books.

Hofstadter, Douglas R. (1986). *Metamagical Themas: Questing for the Essence of Mind and Pattern.* New York: Bantam Books.

Hrushovski, Benjamin (1979). "The Structure of Semiotic Objects: A Three-Dimensional Model." *Poetics Today* 1, nos. 1–2: 363–76.

Hunt, Harry T. (1986). "Some Relations between the Cognitive Psychology of Dreams and Dream Phenomenology." *Journal of Mind and Behavior* 7 (Spring/Summer): 213–28.

Hunt, Harry T. (1989). *The Multiplicity of Dreams: Memory, Imagination, and Consciousness*. New Haven: Yale University Press.

Hunt, Harry T. (1990). "The Multiplicity of Dreams." *ASD Newsletter* 7 (Sept.-Oct.): 9–11.

Jameson, Fredric (1987). "Postmodernism and Consumer Society." In *The Anti-Aesthetic: Essays on Postmodern Culture,* ed. Hal Foster. Port Townsend,. Wash.: Bay Press, pp. 111–25.

Johnson, Mark (1987). *The Body in the Mind: The Bodily Basis of Meaning, Imagination, and Reason*. Chicago: University of Chicago Press.

Jung, Carl G. (1973). *Memories, Dreams, Reflections*. Ed. Aniela Jaffe, trans. Richard and Clara Winston. New York: Random House.

Kermode, Frank (1970). *The Sense of an Ending: Studies in the Theory of Fiction*. London: Oxford University Press.

Koestler, Arthur (1969). *The Act of Creation*. New York: Macmillan.

Kramer, Milton (1991a). "Hall! Like Gaul, Dreamers Are Divided into Three Provinces (Commentary on Hall's Paper)." *Dreaming* 1, no 1: 103–05.

Kramer, Milton (1991b). "Dream Translation: A Nonassociative Method for Understanding the Dream." *Dreaming* 1, no. 2: 147–59.

Krippner, Stanley (1986). "Dreams and the Development of Personal Mythology." *Journal of Mind and Behavior* 7, nos. 1 –2: 319–32.

Kubie, Lawrence S. (1970). *Neurotic Distortion of the Creative Process*. New York: Farrar, Straus, and Giroux.

Kuiken, Don (1991). "Systematic Phenomenological Dream Interpretation." Paper presented at the Annual Conference of the Association for the Study of Dreams, Charlottesville, Va., June 1991.

Kuiken, Don, and David Miall (1991). "Correspondences between Dream Formation and Literary Understanding." Paper presented at the Annual Conference of the Association for the Study of Dreams, Charlottesville, Va., June 1991.

Kuper, Adam (1983). "The Structure of Dream Sequences," *Culture, Medicine and Psychiatry* 7:153–75.

Lakoff, George (1987). *Women, Fire, and Dangerous Things: What Categories Reveal about the Mind*. Chicago: University of Chicago Press.

Lakoff, George, and Mark Johnson (1980). *Metaphors We Live By*. Chicago: University of Chicago Press.

Leiris, Michel (1987). *Nights as Day, Days as Night*. Trans. Richard Sieburth. Hygiene, Colorado: Eridanos Press.

Lessa, William A. (1972). "Discoverer-of-the Sun: Mythology as a Reflection of Culture." In *Mythology: Selected Readings*, ed. Pierre Maranda. Harmondsworth: Penguin, pp. 71–110.

Levin, Ross, Jodi Galin, and Bill Zywiak (1991). "Nightmares, Boundaries, and Creativity." *Dreaming* 1 (March): 63–74.

Lévi-Strauss, Claude (1966). *The Savage Mind*. Chicago: University of Chicago Press.

Llinás, R. R., and D. Paré (1991). "Of Dreaming and Wakefulness." *Neuroscience* 44, no. 3: 521–35.

Lodge, David (1977). *The Modes of Modern Writing: Metaphor, Metonymy, and the Typology of Modern Literature*. Ithaca: Cornell University Press.

Lukács, Georg (1974). *Soul and Form*. Trans. Anna Bostock. Cambridge, Mass.: MIT Press.

Macherey, Pierre (1978). *A Theory of Literary Production*. Trans. Geoffrey Wall. London: Routledge and Kegan Paul.

Mandler, George (1975). *Mind and Emotion*. New York: Wiley.

Marshall, John C. (1983). "*Commentary/* Wilensky: Story Grammars versus Story Points." *Behavioral and Brain Sciences* 6:604.

Matisse, Henri (1965). "Notes of a Painter." In *The Problems of Aesthetics: A Book of Readings,* ed. Eliseo Vivas and Murray Krieger. New York: Holt, Rinehart and Winston, pp. 255–61.

Matte Blanco, Ignacio (1975). *The Unconscious as Infinite Sets: An Essay in Bi-Logic*. London: Duckworth.

Merleau-Ponty, Maurice (1964). *The Primacy of Perception and Other Essays on Phenomenological Psychology, the Philosophy of Art, History, and Politics*. Ed. James M. Edie. Evanston, Ill.: Northwestern University Press.

Minsky, Marvin (1988). *The Society of Mind*. New York: Simon and Schuster.

Ogden, C. K., and I. A. Richards (1923). *The Meaning of Meaning*. New York: Harcourt, Brace, and World.

Olson, Elder (1966). *Tragedy and the Theory of Drama*. Detroit: Wayne State University Press.

Ornstein, Robert (1991). *The Evolution of Consciousness: Of Darwin, Freud, and Cranial Fire—The Origins of the Way We Think*. New York: Prentice Hall.

Palombo, S. R. (1978). *Dreaming and Memory*. New York: Basic Books.

Pearce, Donald (1990). *Para Worlds: Entanglements of Art and History*. University Park: Pennsylvania University Press.

Piaget, Jean (1951). *Play, Dreams, and Imitation in Childhood*. Trans. C. Gattegno and F. M. Hodgson. London: William Heinemann.

Poulet, Georges (1966). *The Metamorphoses of the Circle*. Trans. Carley Dawson and Elliott Coleman. Baltimore: Johns Hopkins University Press.

Poulet, Georges (1981). "Criticism and the Experience of Interiority." In *Reader-Response Criticism from Formalism to Post-Structuralism*, ed. Jane P. Tompkins. Baltimore: Johns Hopkins University Press, pp. 41–49.

Propp, V. (1970). *Morphology of the Folktale*. Trans. Laurence Scott. Austin: University of Texas Press.

Ray, William (1984). *Literary Meaning from Phenomenology to Deconstruction*. Oxford: Basil Blackwell.

Rechtschaffen, Allan (1978). "The Single-Mindedness and Isolation of Dreams." *Sleep* 1:97–109.

Remshardt, Ralf (1991). *Stages of Deformation: A Study of the Grotesque in Aesthetics Theory and Theatre*. Ph.D. diss., University of California at Santa Barbara, Department of Dramatic Art.

Ricoeur, Paul (1980). "Narrative Time." *Critical Inquiry* 7, no. 1: 183.

Ricoeur, Paul (1984). *Time and Narrative*. Trans. Kathleen McLaughlin and David Pellauer. Chicago: University of Chicago Press, 2 vols.

Ricoeur, Paul (1988). *Time and Narrative*, vol. 3. Trans. Kathleen Blamey and David Pellauer. Chicago: University of Chicago Press.

Robinson, William S. (1988). *Brains and People: An Essay on Mentality and Its Causal Conditions*. Philadelphia: Temple University Press.

Sartre, Jean-Paul (1966). *Being and Nothingness: A Phenomenological Essay on Ontology*. Trans. Hazel E. Barnes. New York: Washington Square Press.

Schank, Roger C. (1986). *Dynamic Memory: A Theory of Reminding and Learning in Computers and People*. Cambridge: Cambridge University Press.

Schank, Roger C., and Robert P. Abelson (1977). *Scripts, Plans, Goals, and Understanding: An Inquiry into Human Knowledge Structures*. Hillsdale, N.J.: Erlbaum.

Schank, Roger C., and Colleen M. Seifert (1985). "Modeling Memory and Learning." In *How We Know*, ed. Michael Shafto. San Francisco: Harper and Row, pp. 60–88.

Segal, Dmitry M. (1972). "The Connection between the Semantics and the Formal Structure of a Text." In *Mythology: Selected Readings*, ed. Pierre Maranda. Harmondsworth: Penguin, pp. 215–49.

Shklovsky, Victor (1965). "Art as Technique." In *Russian Formalist Criticism: Four Essays*. Trans. Lee T. Lemon and Marion J. Reis. Lincoln: University of Nebraska Press, pp. 3–24.

Singer, Jerome L. (1966). *Daydreaming: An Introduction to the Experimental Study of Inner Experience*. New York: Random House.

Skura, Meredith Anne (1980). "Revisions and Rereadings in Dreams and Allegories." In *The Literary Freud: Mechanisms of Defense and Poetic Will. Psychiatry and the Humanities*, vol. 4, ed. Joseph H. Smith. New Haven: Yale University Press, pp. 345–79.

Snyder, Frederick (1966). "Toward an Evolutionary Theory of Dreaming." *American Journal of Psychiatry* 123:121–36.

Snyder, Frederick (1970). "The Phenomenology of Dreaming." In *The Psychodynamic Implications of the Physiological Studies on Dreams*, ed. L. Madow and L. Snow. Springfield, Ill.: Thomas, pp. 124–51.

Sokel, Walter H. (1959). *The Writer in Extremis: Expressionism in Twentieth-Century German Literature*. Stanford: Stanford University Press.

Stacy, R. H. (1977). *Defamiliarization in Language and Literature*. Syracuse, N.Y.: Syracuse University Press.

States, Bert O. (1978). "The Art of Dreaming." *Hudson Review* 31, no. 4: 571–86.

States, Bert O. (1988). *The Rhetoric of Dreams*. Ithaca: Cornell University Press.

States, Bert O. (1990). "Dreaming and Storytelling," *Hudson Review* 43, no. 1: 21–37.

States, Bert O. (1992a). "Bizarreness in Dreams and Other Fictions." In *The Dream and the Text: Essays in Language and Literature,* ed. Carol S Rupprecht. Albany State University of New York Press, pp. 13–31.

States, Bert O. (1992b). "The Meaning of Dreams." *Dreaming* 2 (December): 249–63.

Strindberg, August (1986). "Note from the Author" [for *The Dream Play*]. In *Selected Plays,* vol. 2.: The Post-Inferno Period. Trans. Evert Sprinchorn. Minneapolis: University of Minnesota Press.

Todorov, Tzvetan (1980). *The Fantastic: A Structural Approach to a Literary Genre*. Ithaca: Cornell University Press.

Tolaas, Jon (1978). "REM Sleep and the Concept of Vigilance," *Biological Psychiatry* 13:135–48.

Ullman, Montague (1961). "Dreaming, Altered States of Consciousness, and the Problem of Vigilance." *Journal of Nervous and Mental Disorders* 133:529–35.

Ullman, Montague (1969). "Dreaming as Metaphor in Motion." *Archives of General Psychiatry* 21 (December): 696–703.

Ullman, Montague, and Edward F. Storm (1986). "Dreaming and the Dream: Social and Personal Perspectives." *Journal of Mind and Behavior* 7, nos. 1–2: 299–318.

Van Dusen, Wilson (1972). *The Natural Depth in Man*. New York: Harper and Row.

Warnock, Mary (1978). *Imagination*. Berkeley: University of California Press.

Warshaw, Howard (1980). "Vision Made Visible." *Spectrum Anthology, 1957 to 1978.* University of California, Santa Barbara.

White, Hayden (1980). "The Value of Narrativity in the Representation of Reality." *Critical Inquiry* 7 (Autumn): 5–27.

Wilensky, Robert (1983). "Story Grammars versus Story Points." *Behavioral and Brain Sciences* 6:579–623.

Williams, William Carlos (1933). In *Fifty Poets: An American Auto-Anthology,* ed. William Rose Benét. New York: Duffield and Green, pp. 60–61.

Winson, Jonathan (1990). "The Meaning of Dreams." *Scientific American* 263 (November): 86–96.

Index

213

Shklovsky, Victor, on defamiliarization, 43–44
Similie, 162–65; in dreams, 22–25
Simulus, Minsky on, 22
Singer, Jerome L., on hypnogogic state, 71n
Single-mindedness: in fiction, 36; in Kafka, 33; Koestler on, 18–20; Rechtschaffen on, 14, 17–19, 20
Skura, Meredith, on botanical-monograph dream, 49; on meaning in dreams and allegories, 144–50
Snyder, Frederick, 17; on bizarreness, 27–28
Soap operas and dreams, 91
Sokel, Walter H., on Expressionism, 29n–30n
Sophocles: *Antigone*, 123; *Oedipus Rex*, 60, 118; *Philoctetes*, 115–17
Stacy, R. H., 43n
Stein, Gertrude, 196
Stoppard, Tom, 59
Stories: bedtime, 96–97, 100–101; Cinderella, 116n; and dreams, 111–39; logic of, 132
Storytelling: in dreams and fiction, 76–77, 111–39; meaning and, 188; purpose of (Foulkes), 111; Ricoeur on, 74–75. *See also* Narrative; Plot; Scripts
Strindberg, August, the dream play and, 33–34
Structuralism. *See* Interpretation

Thomas, Dylan, 134
Thrownness, in dream state, 29, 61, 95
Todorov, Tzvetan, on the uncanny, 35–36
Tolstoy, Leo: *Anna Karenina*, 124–26; *War and Peace*, 64, 79

Ullman, Montague, on metaphor, 30, 138, 174n
Umwelten. See Fraser, J. T.
Uncanny: Freud on, 44; in Poe, 34n; Todorov on, 35–36

Van Dusen, Wilson, on hypnogogic state, 70n–71n
Van Gogh, Vincent, 188
Vigilance, concept of, 136n–37n

Waking experience. *See* Dreams; Experience(s)
Warnock, Mary, on the image, 30, 70
Warshaw, Howard, 157n
White, Hayden, on narrative, 112
Wilensky, Robert, on action sequence, 65
Williams, William Carlos, "The Red Wheelbarrow," 199–202
Wilson, Edmund, 115–16
Winson, Jonathan, 120
Wordsworth, William, "My Heart Leaps Up," 89